Policy and Politics in Contemporary Poland

Reform, Failure, Crisis

Edited by

Jean Woodall

St. Martin's Press, New York

ISBN 0-312-61999-5

Library of Congress Cataloging in Publication Data
Main entry under title:

Policy and politics in contemporary Poland.

   Includes index.
   Contents: Introduction / Jean Woodall—Poland and
Eastern Europe / George Schöpflin—The response of
the Polish Communist leadership to the continuing crisis
(summer 1980 to the Ninth Congress, July 1981) / George
Sandford— [etc.]
   1. Poland—Politics and government—1945-
I. Woodall, Jean, 1950-
DK4440.P62   1982   320.9438   81-47980
ISBN 0-312-61999-5   AACR2

This book is dedicated by the authors to the spirit of August 1980.

CONTENTS

LIST OF CONTRIBUTORS

George Blazyca   Lecturer in Economics at Thames Polytechnic

George Kolankiewicz Lecturer in Sociology at the University of Essex

Paul G. Lewis   Lecturer in Government at the Faculty of Social Sciences at the Open University

Chris Russell-Hodgson Post-graduate research student at the Centre for Russian and East European Studies at the University of Birmingham

George Sanford   Lecturer in Politics at the University of Bristol

George Schöpflin   Lecturer in Communist Politics at the London School of Economics

Janusz Tomiak   Lecturer at the Institute of Education and the School of Slavonic and East European Studies, University of London

Jean Woodall   Lecturer in Politics at Kingston Polytechnic

LIST OF DIAGRAMS AND TABLES

LIST OF MAJOR ABBREVIATIONS USED IN THE TEXT

CPSU	Communist Party of the Soviet Union
CKKP	Central Party Control Commission (Centralna Komisja Kontrola Partyjna)
CRZZ	Central Trade Union Council (Centralna Rada Związków Zawodowych)
FJN	National Unity Front (Front Jednośći Narodowy)
FZSZMP	Socialist Federation of Unions of Polish Youth (Federacja Socjalistycznych Związków Mlodzieży Polskiej)
GOZ	Rural Health Centre (Gminny Osrodek Zdrowia)
GUS	Central Statistical Office (Główny Urząd Statystyczny)
IPPMC	Institute of Basic Problems of Marxism–Leninism (Instytut Podstawowej Problemy Marksism–Leninism)
KC	Central Committee (Komitet Centralny)
KD	District Committee (Komitet Dziełnicowy)
KM	Town Committee (Komitet Miejscowy)
KOR	Workers' Defence Committee (Komitet Obrony Robotników)
KSR	Conference of Workers' Self Management (Konferencja Samorząd Robotniczego)
KKPOP	Primary Party Organization Consultative-Co-ordinating Committee (Komisja Konsultacyjno-Porozumiewawcza Podstawowego Organizacji Partyjnego)
KZ	Factory Committee (Komitet Zakładowy)
MKZ	Inter-Factory Strike Committee (Między-Zakładowy Komitet Strajkowy)
NIK	State Control Chamber (Naczelna Iżba Kontroli)
NFOZ	National Health Care Fund (Narodowy Fundusz Ochrony Zdrowia)
NSZZ	Independent, Self-Governing Trade Union (Niezależne i Samorządne Związki Zawodowe)
NZS	Independent Students' Association (Niezalezne Związek Studentów)
POP	Primary Party Organization (Podstawowa Organizacja Partyjna)
PRL	People's Republic of Poland (Polska Rzeczypospolita Ludowej)

PZPR	Polish United Workers' Party (Polska Zjednoczona Partia Robotnicza)
RR	Workers' Council (Rada Robotnicza)
SED	Socialist Unity Party
STR	Scientific-Technological Revolution
WOG	Large Production Unit (Wiełka Organizacja Gospodarcza)
WSNS	Higher Party School (Wyższa Szkoła Nauk Społecznych)
ZOZ	Area Health Authority (Zespół Opieki Zdrowotniej)
ZSL	United Peasants' Party (Zjednoczone Stronnićtwo Ludowej)
ZSMP	Sociliast Union of Polish Youth (Związek Socjalistyczny Młodżieźy Polskiej)

EDITORIAL NOTE AND PREFACE

The Possibility of Socialist Renewal

When this book was conceived in April 1981, all the contributors had been involved in specialized studies of Polish political, social and economic life for a number of years, and were following the events since August 1980 with avid interest. The temptation to avoid expressions of surprise at the rapid pace of change in Poland since that time proved too great for many of the present authors: several of us were to insist that we had 'seen it all coming'. Blessed though we might all be with such prophetic vision, academic reputation has to rest on a more solid foundation. The West has been fascinated by the emergence of the independent self-governing trade-union movement: Solidarity. Yet, the present authors felt that journalistic analyses that abstract the train of events since August 1980 from their historical context can only provide a distorted explanation. It was at this juncture that the present volume acquired its *raison d'être*.

The central theme of *Policy and Politics in Contemporary Poland* is to provide the reader with some logical explanation of the turbulent sequence of events since the summer of 1980, and to evaluate their significance in the context of the political reform and policy innovation that took place in Poland after December 1970 when Edward Gierek became First Secretary of the Polish United Workers' Party (PZPR). All too often the origins of political protest can be ascribed to the existence of an unresponsive and reactionary regime. Such a simplistic assertion is certainly not the case with Poland, as the following chapters demonstrate. While the price of food has been taken as a barometer of political protest, it would also be naïve to dismiss the events of December 1970, June 1976 and August 1980 as caused by this alone. Although there is by no means complete agreement between the present authors on the causes of the events in Poland, they do all concede the complexity of a situation which is due not simply to the insensitivity and lack of vision on the part of the PZPR and the government, but rather to an over-ambitious blueprint for reform designed to embrace all aspects of social and economic life – a reform which became increasingly out of step with material reality.

The book is divided into two sections: politics and policy. On closer examination it can be seen that the content of both cannot be kept in complete analytic isolation. Obviously considerations of time and length have meant that many aspects of Polish social life have been excluded. Perhaps the most glaring omission is a chapter devoted to the problems of agriculture and the peasantry. Similarly, Church-State relations and the emergence of the underground Democratic Opposition in the 1970s do not receive full attention. There is some effort to refer to these three subjects in individual chapters and they have already been examined elsewhere.[1]

The first section on politics commences with an examination of the Marxist-Leninist doctrine that provided the window-dressing during Gierek's ten-year period of office. By 1975 this had become encapsulated in the concept of preparing the transition to a 'Developed Socialist Society'. The contrast between this vision and the realities of life for the majority of Polish people became more acute in the second half of the decade. This is why any theoretical innovation taken on board by the considerably weakened and bewildered PZPR after August 1980, could not in any way be a continuation of the past doctrinal 'line'. Hence the fundamentalist conception of 'Socialist Renewal', forced upon the party leadership at the Sixth Plenum of the Central Committee in October 1980, became a conceptual battlefield both between factions within the party and between the party and Solidarity. It has to be seen as a reaction to the pompous heraldry of Poland's entry into the phase of 'Developed Socialism'. The first chapter attempts to trace the pedigree of 'Developed Socialism' and the attendant concept of the 'Scientific Technological Revolution'. The aim is to indicate the way in which this inherently blinkered view of social development underpinned various policies and eventually backfired. While this is intended to provide the theoretical 'backdrop' for subsequent chapters, George Schöpflin is somewhat more sceptical about the ability of Marxist-Leninist doctrine to generate a vision of social development: the formal values of Marxism-Leninism have acted as a legitimating formula, but the source of new values is wider. He also notes the anxiety of East European leaderships over the course taken by events in Poland as expressed in official statements. At the same time he reflects on the likely impact of the events upon the relation between domestic political structures and society elsewhere in Eastern Europe. He comes to the conclusion that Poland as yet has no short-term impact, but suggests that should the situation stabilize, then evidence of a system in operation that is so radically different from that conventionally ascribed to the 'leading role of the party' will act to influence other East European countries.

This raises the question of the strategy of the Polish leadership in responding to the crisis. George Sanford examines the relationship between leadership turnover and policy change in the eleven months between August 1980 and July 1981. His argument is that far from just muddling through in response to social initiatives, Kania's leadership developed a sophisticated strategy for dealing with the delicate balance of power between shifting factions in the PZPR, whose protagonists rose and fell intermittently in the 'carousel' of power. Thus the PZPR chose to cope with the crisis by means of a policy of elite turnover, rather than mass expulsion. Despite his vulnerability and isolation in the Politburo, Kania was able to make scapegoats of the old leadership in order to legitimate himself and to stabilize the crisis.

While George Sanford demonstrates Kania's success in stabilizing the balance of power between factions of the PZPR elite, and in routing the old Gierek elite, George Kolankiewicz is concerned more with the fate of party democracy within the PZPR. In Chapter 4 he notes that a selective incorporation of members for statistical balance, de-ideologization and a consolidation of the power of the party apparatus had occurred in the period between 1970 and 1980. The outcome was a form of 'bureaucratic centralism' in which grass-roots party organizations were structurally isolated. It is for this reason that the demands for reform after the Sixth Central Committee Plenum in October 1981 recognized that the mere replacement of individuals would not be satisfactory. Structural change was imperative to ensure the full accountability of officials to the grass roots, and George Kolankiewicz demonstrates the significance of the campaign for democratic elections in the achievement of this. He also explains how an extremely radical interpretation of inner party democracy encapsulated in the 'horizontalist' movement was eventually thwarted in the delegate selection process for the Ninth PZPR Congress. The legacy of negative selection and de-ideologization left over from the 1970s had left its mark.

The final chapter in the section on 'Politics' indicates how impossible it is to consider the political shortcomings of the Gierek regime in isolation from policy outputs. Paul Lewis reveals the fervour with which the Gierek regime pursued institutional reform of the state apparatus (especially in local government) intending it to facilitate administrative efficiency, regional planning, and the equalization of opportunity between rural and urban areas. He explains how these reforms were misconceived because of the conflict between the PZPR's capacity to control and supervise, and the need for responsiveness to local needs. Also the desire to increasingly concentrate industrial production and improve administrative efficiency for the purpose of increasing effectiveness, especially in resource allocation, conflicted with the encouragement of particularistic sectional demands.

Turning to the second section of this book, four areas of policy have been chosen for their causal significance in the crisis in Poland since August 1980. No account of the crisis would be complete without some reference to economic policy. In Chapter 6, George Blazyca is at great pains to show how the misconceived (and only partially implemented) 'New Economic Financial System' introduced in 1972 ran into problems. Despite a change of course in the Economic Manoeuvre of 1975, a vicious spiral of deteriorating industrial economic performance caused planners and managers to resort increasingly to the use of central commands: the very procedure which the reforms had been intended to abolish. It also had deleterious effects upon agriculture. The 'Modified Economic Financial System' introduced in 1977 was but a desperate attempt to halt the slide into crisis. Blazyca concludes that the weakness of the government and its inability to resist sectional demands, the power-mania of the large industrial branch ministries, and continuous and persistent wage demands interacted with one another to prevent a reversal of economic decline. Looking to the future, Blazyca feels that perhaps the only course for optimism in the current debate on economic reform is the more open, less technocratic, discussion and shift of focus from the management mechanism to questions of industrial democracy.

Industrial democracy is the theme of Chapter 7, and the rise of the workers' councils during the Polish October of 1956 is well known. The formalistic 'incorporation' of these institutions and their subsequent fate after 1958 is also a commonplace. However, George Kolankiewicz shows that the ideal of workers' self-management has a long pedigree stretching back to the 1940s. The revival of debate on this issue since August 1980 cannot be reduced to the simple matter of management versus blue-collar interests, but questions concerning the relationship between industrial enterprise, the State and society, have also been raised. Government proposals on the subject have stressed only the right of workers to be consulted, while the demands of Solidarity go further in calling for veto powers and in challenging the Polish constitution by opening up a debate on the status of property. The notion of the 'social enterprise' is at the heart of the dispute over workers' self-management, and goes far beyond the issue of mere workers' control. The appointment and dismissal of senior enterprise directors is not just a source of conflict between party and workers, but also involves a tussle between the respective vested interests of the party *nomenklatura* over industrial appointments, and central State bureaucracy.

Industrial democracy has always been a very glamorous area for research on Eastern Europe, but the slightly more neglected areas of educational and social welfare policy have a tremendous importance in any understanding of the course taken by events since August 1980. In Chapter 8, Janusz Tomiak argues that if education is to be a positive force in society, it must contribute to social harmony, genuine political participation, and economic progress; and also it must offer the opportunity for everyone to participate actively in the national cultural heritage. Sadly, the Polish experience falls wide of the mark, and the government failed to take advantage of the research results and opportunities available in the early 1970s. By the end of the decade, not only was there greater inequality in educational opportunity, but the curriculum in both higher and elementary education, the appointment of staff, and the selection of students, had become highly politicized issues.

Any comparisons of social welfare policy between East and West come up against the obstacle of different definitions of the policy area. In Eastern Europe the workplace plays a much greater role in income maintenance, health, and recreation than in the West. Moreover, social policy is usually, for historical reasons, wholly contingent upon economic policy. In Chapter 9, Chris Russell-Hodgson notes that there was a change of emphasis during Gierek's period of office, and health policy came to play a prominent role in the strategy for achieving 'Developed Socialism'. How was it then that health was still a major demand in the Gdańsk Agreement of August 1980? As in the case of education, grandiose schemes for reform were backed up with inadequate resources. However, Chris Russell-Hodgson shows that the problem was not just poor overall standards, but distributional failings (luxury care for certain government and security service employees but appalling conditions for the rest — especially in rural areas), poor regional integration of the different types of care, and an irrational use of capital equipment. At the end of the decade Polish age-specific mortality rates had actually increased! In her conclusion, Chris Russell-Hodgson feels that the failures in health policy can be attributed to three main issues. Firstly, despite lip-service paid to primary care, specialized hospital based medicine took the lion's share of the resources. Secondly, sectional interests produced inertia in the decision-making process. Finally, the health system was affected by factors in the wider economic system: declining economic growth and bottlenecks in supplies.

It is unfortunate to end this editorial summary on such a pessimistic note. At the time of writing the first national Congress of Solidarity has just held its first session in Gdańsk. This took place against a background of declining economic performance (a fall in output of around 13 per cent is anticipated for the whole of 1981 in comparison with 1980), following on from meetings between the Polish Government and Western financial institutions to re-schedule the debt of $10.5 billion that falls due to the West in 1982; and was accompanied by much sabre-rattling on the part of the Warsaw Pact forces which mounted a 100,000 man military manoeuvre close to Polish borders and coastline. Yet, it is alone amazing that such a Congress could ever take place, and the whirlwind pace of events since August 1980 has brought dramatic changes in Polish political and social life. The Western press has been attracted most by the emphasis laid upon the declaration by Solidarity of support for efforts to establish free trade unions elsewhere in Eastern Europe, but the atmosphere is more than ever one of caution and compromise. Decisions over elections to Parliament (Sejm), public control over the mass media and workers' self-management and control over management appointments in industry suggest that the immediate abandonment of the ideological baggage of Marxism–Leninism is out of the question. Socialist Renewal is taking place as a consequence of the ponderous manoeuvres between social forces and the party and governmental apparatus, but dreams of a self-managed society will not be easy to realize.

The chapters in this book have been completed at different times over the last three months and therefore do not all take account of the events between July and September 1981. Needless to say the effort of producing this work in so short a time has precluded the possibility of adequate final reflection and conclusions. The authors have, however, benefited from the comments and criticism from numerous colleagues (both specialists and non-specialists in Polish affairs) on earlier drafts. They wish to make their collective gratitude for this clear and also to thank Mrs Jane Jeffery for help with preparation of the final typescript. Finally, all opinions expressed and errors committed remain the responsibilities of the authors.

Jean Woodall

September 1981

1   On the subject of agriculture see:
    A. Korboński, *The Politics of Socialist Agriculture in Poland 1945–1960*, New York, Columbia University Press, 1965;
    P. G. Lewis, 'The Peasantry' in G. Kolankiewicz and D. Lane, *Social Groups in Polish Society*, London, Macmillan, 1974;
    G. Kolankiewicz, 'The New Awkward Class: the Peasant-Worker in Poland', *Sociologica Ruralis*, 20 (1980), 28–37.;
    Olga Narkiewicz, *The Green Flag: Polish Populist Politics 1867–1970*, London, Croom Helm, 1976.

On Church–State relations see:

Bohdan Bociurkiw and John W. Strong (eds), *Religion and Atheism in the USSR and Eastern Europe*, London, Macmillan, 1975.

On the dissident movement see:

R. L. Tokes (ed.), *Opposition in Eastern Europe*, London, Macmillan, 1979;

T. Deutscher, 'Voices of Dissent' in *Socialist Register 1978*, London, Merlin, 1979, pp. 21–43.

PART I POLITICS

1 Introduction: The Construction of a 'Developed Socialist Society' and 'Socialist Renewal'*

JEAN WOODALL

The period from the events of August 1980 right up until the Ninth Extraordinary Congress has witnessed no less than nine plenary sessions of the Polish United Workers' Party (PZPR) Central Committee. Ideological self-searching in the course of these meetings has focused on the problem of developing a programme for 'Socialist Renewal' (Odnowa Socjalistyczny). While by no means rejecting the central tenets of a Marxist–Leninist party (the leading role of the party in social life, and democratic centralism within party life), this does represent a considerable ideological leap away from the discussions in the 1970s about the effects of the 'Scientific Technological Revolution' (STR) upon Poland's entry into the phase of 'Developed Socialism'. It is easy to dismiss doctrinal debates within a Marxist–Leninist party as propaganda or an ex-post rationalization, but the view of the present author is that, to the contrary, an exploration of the prescriptions of and limitations to 'Developed Socialism', and the STR, can provide a partial reason as to why events since August 1980 have culminated in a demand for 'Socialist Renewal'.

1. The Semantics of Socialist Renewal

The speech of First Secretary Kania at the Ninth Congress (after pondering over the course taken by events since August 1980) pronounced that the PZPR would assume a guiding (*przodującej*) as opposed to directing (*kierowniczej*) role in society as embodied in the programme of socialist renewal inaugurated at the Sixth Central Committee Plenum.

> In essence it involves a return to fundamental socialist values in national life, and to Leninism in the ideological political life of the party; an inclination towards profound economic reform; the development of socialist democracy, upholding the law and the strengthening of socialist discipline. This course of development will serve to extend the leading (*przewodniej*) role of the party. It involves a return to the practice of

* An earlier draft of this chapter was presented as a paper at the Lancaster Joint Sessions of The European Consortium for Political Research, 1981.

the notion of social justice, and the maintenance of ethical principles, creating the conditions for the achievement of humanistic inter-personal relations, and respect for the rights of man as a worker and as a citizen.[1]

Those familiar with the general style of Marxist–Leninist rhetoric may wonder at the present author's reason for including such a quotation stamped with the lofty but threadbare intention of reform. On closer inspection, it can be observed that key words such as the 'guiding' role of the party, the 'upholding of the law' and 'social justice' stand out. While it is easy to see this as the fruit of sterile semantic wrangling, it masks genuine debate over policy options. Take for example the 'guiding' role of the party. Normally the Leninist principle of the 'leading role of the party' is expressed in Polish as *kierowniczy*, but this adjective also has the connotation of directing/managing. After August 1980, such active involvement of the PZPR in the direction/management of socio-economic life was construed as both meddlesome and stultifying, not only by the mass of society, but also by a sizeable proportion of the PZPR membership. That 20 per cent of the delegates to the Ninth Congress were also members of Solidarity[2] is indicative of dissatisfaction with the interpretation of this Leninist principle, to the extent that communication had broken down between different levels of the party and that the rank and file and grass-roots organizations had become structurally atomized. While a subsequent chapter will demonstrate how the resulting confusion, disorientation and dissension prompted various party organizations to act autonomously and eventually form horizontal, direct, unmediated links with one another,[3] such an anti-apparatus movement required a new interpretation of the hallmark of a Marxist–Leninist party: democratic centralism, and the leading role of the party. The reformers within the PZPR pushed for changes in the party Statutes in order to reduce the overly close correspondence of those simultaneously holding positions as functionaries in the executive apparatus of the party, and positions of responsibility in the state administration, with its consequential effect of preventing rank-and-file contact.

On closer inspection then, the semantic interpretation of the leading role of the party is vital and opened up a 'Pandora's Box' of demands voiced within the PZPR between the Seventh Plenum in December 1980 (after which the anti-apparatus movement secured considerable victories in the selection and accountability of Congress delegates), and the Ninth Congress. Secondly, the emphasis upon socialist democracy concerned the role that the party was to assume in representative institutions and the precise form of the accountability of officials. It also reflected the wrangling with Solidarity over reform projects for industrial enterprise law and workers' self-management,[4] and has wider implications for the running of other areas of social life from the universities and schools to the health service.

Thirdly, the emphasis upon social justice directs attention to a major weakness of the Polish economy: distribution. Irrespective of political evaluation, the failings of state socialist economic management in Gierek's Poland were not just to be located in inefficient resource allocation, or over-investment in Group 'A' at the expense of Group 'B' industries, or even a lack of individual incentives, but also in the *manner* by which workers received the reward for their labour. Although the principles of socialist social justice rest on the concepts of merit (to each according to his labour) and need, neither could be simply adhered to in practice. Not only did individual incomes fail to reflect the principle of merit after the mid 1970s, but notions of a social minimum were violated by the intervention of market influence into social consumption (social services) provided either by the local authority or (increasingly so) at the work-place. Party membership or tenure of a position of authority enhanced the 'property rights' of some individuals, and the party and government sanctioned inequalitites whose visible manifestation was transparently obvious. As the consumer boom of the mid 1970s tailed off towards the end of that decade, it was still possible to obtain luxury items imported from the West, and later the necessities of life produced at home — but in the hard-currency shops whose relatively well-stocked shelves contrasted sadly with those of State sector distribution outlets.

Finally, 'Socialist Renewal' involved universal observance of the law in society. For too long those in privileged positions of authority had been able to bend the law in their favour with respect to access to material goods ranging from foreign trips to holiday homes. In contrast, disciplinary proceedings under the terms of the 1974 Labour Code were readily taken against those who engaged in industrial action over their work conditions or who were persistently drunk or absent from work. Furthermore, those members of the Democratic Opposition (including groups such as KOR), who vociferously complained about this or who joined the Flying University (TKN) in an attempt to acquire an 'unbiased' view of the world, were hounded as anti-socialist and counter-revolutionary dissidents. Thus the respect of the rights of man as a worker and a citizen was an important element to be met by the PZPR after August 1980.

Returning to the text of Kania's speech at the Ninth Congress, four key phrases sum up issues of vital importance in the future direction of Polish politics:

(1) the leading role of the party;
(2) the nature of socialist democracy;
(3) the adherence to the principles of social justice;
(4) the observation of socialist legality and the respect for human rights

The potential for these issues to tear the PZPR apart seriously was checked at the Ninth Party Congress which was preceded by the receipt of the letter from the CPSU at the Eleventh Plenum in June calling upon the Polish Party to 'put its house in order'. To determine whether the 'Socialist Renewal' movement would have taken place without the presence of Solidarity or would have errupted anyway, is not however, the purpose of this chapter. Rather the aim is to trace the elements contained in the formula of 'Socialist Renewal' back to the vision of socialist development espoused by the regime of Edward Gierek from 1970 to 1980; and to ask the question of how these ideological doctrines related to the actual course of development in Polish economic, political and social life in the 1970s.

2. Developed Socialism and the USSR

To commence with the concept of 'Developed Socialism' it is necessary to turn first to Soviet discussions. The term was first employed at the International Conference of Communist and Workers' Parties held in Moscow in November 1960,[5] and gradually during the period 1967–71, it became incorporated into official Soviet policy statements. While it is popularly believed that Soviet theorists view the course of the proletarian revolution as passing through the intermediate stage of socialism until the achievement of the communist millenium, the present level of theorizing is much more complex. The writings of Karl Marx were none too specific on this matter, but in 'The Critique of the Gotha Programme', he wrote of social development passing through two periods after the revolution: the 'first phase' of communism, and the 'higher phase' of communist society. This was expanded upon by Lenin who located Soviet historical development in three periods (two of which were to be more 'advanced' than capitalism: 'socialist construction' by a workers' state in a mixed socio-economic setting; 'socialism', a higher but still transitional phase; and 'communism', the classless, stateless society.[6] Stalin, while accepting this three-fold classification was somewhat bolder about the pace of achievement, and insisted in 1936, that socialism had been achieved 'in the main'. Inspired by such heady claims, Stalin's successor, Khrushchev, rashly announced a precise timetable for the attainment of communism in the USSR. His 'programme of the CPSU' claimed, in 1961, that the USSR would surpass the USA in economic and technological matters during the period 1961–70, and that by 1980, the USSR would stand on the threshold of communism. It was after the removal of Khrushchev in 1964 that the doctrine of 'Developed Socialism' emerged. Commencing with a speech in 1967 on the occasion of the fiftieth anniversary of the October Revolution, and culminating in his report to the Twenty-Fourth Congress of the CPSU in 1971, Brezhnev placed increasing emphasis upon the fact that the USSR had entered a phase of 'Developed Socialism'. This now meant that Soviet history fell into four distinct periods: 'socialist construction', 1917–36; 'a socialist society whose foundations have been constructed' (or 'basically socialist society') after 1936; 'developed socialism' which the USSR had attained in the early 1960s; and 'communism' which was still the ultimate goal. At the Twenty-Fifth Congress of the CPSU in 1976, Brezhnev called for a change in the Soviet constitution (enacted May 1977) in recognition of this.[7]

Obviously, the question arises as to what prompted this doctrinal change. There are several reasons. They concern the embarrassment caused by Khrushchev's over-ambitious claims, the personal status of Brezhnev as CPSU leader; the international position of the USSR and its East European allies in the era of *détente*; and above all, the problems of economic growth in general and of industrial development in particular.[8] Khrushchev's assertion that the USSR would 'catch up and surpass' the West coincided with an economic growth crisis; a misconceived project for the decentralization of planning and management to Regional Economic Councils (*Sovnarkhoze*) in 1957, and the agronomical disaster subsequent to the cultivation of the 'Virgin Lands'. Not only did this contribute to his downfall, but also to the embarrassment of his successors. Hence the first purpose of the doctrine of 'Developed Socialism' was to forestall invidious comparison between the Marxist–Leninist ideal and Soviet social reality when 1980 arrived; and to provide a formula that would dispel scepticism about the current state of progress. Evans also holds that this reformulation provided the opportunity to present Brezhnev as a significant contributor to Marxist–Leninist thought in the lineage of first general secretaries of the CPSU that stretches back to Lenin, but he overlooks the changing status of East–West relations.[9] The 'Ostpolitik' adopted by West German Chancellor Willi Brandt and the period of *détente* since 1970 drew attention to the level of Soviet socioeconomic achievement. On the one hand, the closer relations with West Germany (to whom the East German Ulbricht leadership was opposed) and at the other extreme, the Helsinki Declaration of 1975 following as a result of the concessions wrung from the Soviet Union at the European Conference of

Security and Co-operation, meant that the USSR had to weather Western scrutiny and demonstrate that its economic might was impressive and received popular endorsement at home.

It was, however, on the subject of economic performance that the Soviet Union was particularly vulnerable. Indeed, the successive reformulations of the course of Soviet history belie considerable concern with economic growth in general, and with industrial performance in particular. Indeed, in a country devastated by war, encircled by hostile political powers and eventually isolated from Western markets, the issue of how to industrialize was of paramount importance in the Soviet Union of the 1920s. After the relatively open mixed economy characteristic of the New Economic Policy, the decision to embark upon an autarchic, planned ('forced') industrialization strategy complemented by agricultural collectivization meant that the Stalin leadership need to legitimate high rates of growth in industrial output, but a low standard of living by claiming the superiority of the socialist industrialization process over that within capitalism.

Economic growth became the touchstone of CPSU legitimacy but the slump in growth rates of national income from an official annual average of 14.1 per cent for 1928–40 down to 8.8 per cent for the period 1955–65,[10] caused a panic among planners that was reflected in the doctrinal statements of the CPSU. The major source of the problem was located in agriculture, but industrial growth rates were now modest, at a time when an increasing percentage of net material product was being reinvested. Proposals for industrial economic reform which had been regarded half seriously in the East European countries in the 1950s, were suddenly placed upon the political agenda after the publication of Liberman's article 'Plan, Profits, Bonuses' in *Pravda* in 1962. That similar notions had been floated in Poland in 1956 and in the GDR (where, if anything, the Liberman article provided the signal for the announcement of the New Economic System whose major elements had long since been prepared),[11] and that the Soviet Union was relatively late in introducing economic reforms incorporating the use of 'parameters' to 'optimize' production according to criteria of 'profitability',[12] indicated that far from leading the march into communism, the Soviet Union was probably dragging its feet behind some of its allies. Furthermore, by late 1967, it looked as if intellectuals in the Czechoslovak Communist Party were proposing an economic reform that would wreak havoc on the Marxist–Leninist interpretation of the law of value (as market and planning system were no longer conceived of as polar opposites, but rather as capable of synthesis). Thus another reason for the announcement that the Soviet

Union was on the threshold of 'Developed Socialism' lies in the mistrust and fear of the greater degree of economic, ideological, and socio-cultural innovation in Eastern Europe during the late 1950s and 1960s.

Finally, the obsession with economic growth is also reflected in the emphasis in economic texts upon the need to shift from an 'extensive' phase of 'socialist construction' (with the purpose of drastic and rapid industrialization and urbanization) to an 'intensive' phase where the aim was to make less radical changes but such as would nevertheless raise productivity and open up the economy to the benefits of the 'international division of labour'. However, the enhancement of contact with the West would draw attention to a comparison between the achievements of the Soviet economy, and also to the similarity in the production process. Consciousness of this is reflected in a virulent attack upon Western notions of convergence and post-industrial society, and the theory of the Scientific Technological Revolution (STR).

3. A Socialist Industrial State, But Not Through Convergence

To commence with the attack upon convergence theory, it is motivated by ideological consideration as much as by empirical reality. It was the East German Socialist Unity Party (SED) that originally took most interest in this subject. The need to distinguish the New Economic System from the West German *Wirtschaftswunder*, the obligation to demonstrate loyalty to the Soviet Union in the wake of the Soviet invasion of Czechoslovakia; and the commencing of trade agreements with the EEC, all coincided with the onslaught upon convergence theory at the SED Central Committee plenum in 1968. An examination of the Soviet and Polish debates upon 'convergence' shows a tendency to 'collapse' the various formulations of convergence towards a common form of industrial/post-industrial society into a single category. There is some acknowledgement of differences existing between Western theorists as exemplified in their blunt classification into 'optimistic', 'catastrophic' and 'intermediate' categories,[13] but this is still over-simplistic.

Although the development of the disciplines of Western social science has been intimately associated with the rise of industrial society, there was by no means a consensus to be found among the founding fathers of sociology on the causes and consequences of industrial society.[14] Latterday apostles of convergence towards a common form of industrial/post-industrial society display greater consensus and conviction about a logic of industrialization in which technological development acts as a unifying force, but their claims have not met with universal acceptance. The literature of economics and sociology abounds with methodological reservations, theoretical refutations and empirical rejection of the validity of the concept. For example, the inability to perceive *empirically* that technology passes through a cultural 'filter',[15] and that the ensuing division of labour is socially determined,[16] contributes to a crude technological determinism. Secondly, too high a level of abstraction in the concepts employed (urbanization, rationalization, bureaucratization, secularization etc.) leads on the one hand to undue focus on the similarities[17] and the belittling of differences between East and West,[18] and on the other, to some incorrect observations. Broad generalizations such as the displacement of the manufacturing base by a service economy; the expansion of office work; the growth of professionalism; and the growing legitimacy of knowledge as the basis for political decision making are shown to be at worst gross inaccuracies, or at best half-truths by Kumar.[19] He also points out that the apparent novelty of the theory of post-industrial society arises from the selection of tendencies often overlooked in the historical and sociological analyses of industrialism, but which were often present already in the late nineteenth century (the growth of the service sector, professionalization, and the need for theoretical knowledge). Above all, the woolly definition of industrial society and the lack of clarity as to which variables are its causes, and which are integrated into the process as consequences, results in tautology. Finally, this is especially evident in the treatment of the role of the State:[20] there is ambivalence over whether the state is a functional instrument of greater economic growth and technological development, or alternatively is a barrier to this; and over whether it is the prisoner of a dominant class; or is amenable to the penetration of a scientifically educated and responsible technocratic/meritocratic elite; or is bureaucratically unresponsive to social demands and feed-back.

While the murky methodology and wild observations of some theorists of convergence are a never-ending source of academic discourse in the West, the Soviet and East European reviews formally reject the possibility that this could be applicable to them.[21] With respect to the convergence of economies it is conceded that there are similarities in the organization of the labour process, yet to claim that technology is the primary determinant of this is to ignore fundamental questions of ownership and control. Secondly, although in the West there has been a remarkable growth in the number of scientifically trained specialists (signifying a greater rationalization of management processes) it is firmly argued that because they still function within capitalist property relations, they cannot be a major force for social change. As to the observed increasing concentration of economic power in the West, the Soviet critique argues that this is not the consequence of technological change, but is the exegesis of oligarchical control of finance capital. Similarly, the growing tendency for bourgeois governments and quasi-independent agencies to intervene is ultimately seen to reflect the defence of monopoly interests, and the growing presence of planning in both systems is not evidence of convergence: capitalist planning is limited to sectors and is again dominated by monopoly interests.

Turning to the refutation of convergence theory at a societal level, there is a firm dismissal of the claim that class struggle has abated in the West. Although, on the one hand there is some recognition of the emergence of a distinct group of managers/technocrats, that they constitute a new class is resolutely denied: in capitalist societies they are held to have more in common with the proletariat than with the employer. Furthermore, far from decreasing in numbers, the ranks of the Western proletariat are increasingly swollen by recruits from the white-collar petty bourgeoisie: the result is increasing differentiation within the working class rather than its decline.

Finally, on the subject of ideological and political change, the end of ideology and the rise of pragmatic belief systems is dismissed on the one hand as unduly optimistic, and on the other as an attempt to bamboozle the Western working class and to 'pollute' the ideological purity of Marxism–Leninism. Non-Marxist 'laws' of socio-economic development which disclaim the importance of political organization are rejected. On the other hand, the process of the transformation of capitalism is mapped out into stages: firstly, similarities in technological advance are associated with 'separate but parallel' development of Eastern and Western systems; and secondly, a higher stage in which the transformation of class relations will accompany the final victory of socialism.[22]

Oddly enough, the literature on convergence towards a common form of industrial/post-industrial society has received its warmest reception from dissident writers in the Soviet Union and Eastern Europe, who acknowledge the direct relation between technology and social change.[23] A common concern with the political role of technical specialists links both the neo-Marxists and those who are looking for a 'third way'.[24] In all cases the role of science and technology is central to their argument.

The role of science and technology assumes a crucial importance in the Marxist–Leninist refutation of both convergence theory and the endorsement of 'Developed Socialism'. In the first case it was conceded that the two systems of East and West rest on the same technical–economic basis, and face similar problems (the relationship between science, technology and the natural environment; the role of experts and their education and deployment; and the development of the service sector).[25]

Scientific and technical progress limit the range of choice of solutions to these problems, but it is held that ultimately the choice of solution is determined by the different political-ideological natures of the system. It is for this reason that the political neutrality of science and technology is a sensitive issue, and both the discussion of 'Developed Socialism' and the refutation of convergence theory are intimately related with a whole series of writings on the Scientific Technological Revolution.

4. The Scientific Technological Revolution

This phrase was originally used in the West by J. D. Bernal.[26] It also appeared in the CPSU Central Committee documents in 1955, but was seized upon for more advanced theoretical development by the East Germans in the late 1950s, and in 1965 a Congress on the subject was held in East Berlin.[27] For obvious reasons, Soviet ideologists have been anxious to avoid using technological advance as a criterion for distinguishing between historical eras, and the official interpretation of historical materialism during Stalin's period of office labelled science as a 'spiritual' activity to be located in the 'superstructure', thereby implying its ideological dependence upon the 'base' (such a rationalization was behind Lysenko's travesty of genetic research).[28] After Stalin's death, commencing with linguistics, there was an attempt to prove that language and scientific thought could outlive a social formation, and were therefore not part of the 'superstructure'. Gradually scientific advance was accorded an increased status in the process of transition to communism, and in 1961 there was a return to a position very similar to that held by Karl Kautsky, whereby science acquired the status of a force of production in the course of the STR: an era distinguishable from the past by the acceleration of scientific progress, and the 'scientization' of all domains of social life. By the mid 1960s the implications of the STR for individual disciplines were under exploration and in 1967 a conference of the editorial leadership of philosophical and sociological journals in socialist countries, proclaimed that the STR symbolized a gigantic leap forward in the productive forces of society.[29] However, what precisely was to be included in the category of 'productive forces' and the degree of possible social control over their development was the subject of differing interpretation.

The Soviet argument commences with an examination of the changed relation between science and production, whereby science shifts from being a passive force to being actively involved in controlling production. During the course of the industrial revolution, it is drawn into the role of analysis and explanation of the principles of machine operation, and finally in the STR, science leads production and provides a basis for testing reality and discovering laws of development. The discovery of a 'science–technology–production cycle' is seen to create the possibility for society to consciously direct its own development, although that the STR implies a new attitude towards economic organization and development is strongly denied.[30] In East Germany, other conclusions were being drawn: the socialist planned economy was linked to the STR within the framework of a systems theory model; the aim being not so much to waste time with 'catching up' with Western technology, but to concentrate effort on developing the most sophisticated technologies to raise overall levels of efficiency. This is encapsulated in the slogan 'surpass without catching up'.

However, both of these highly 'scientized' interpretations of the role of the forces of production in the STR, were challenged in *Civilisation at the Crossroads*,[31] one of the first results of Marxist–Leninist inquiries into the probable impact of the STR upon future life, and which was conducted by an inter-disciplinary team of forty Czech scientists. Here the STR was held to be not just about changes in the *technical* forces of production, but in the social force of production as well. There were implications for the whole of civilization as the STR was a cultural revolution that would also release human potential in the effort to overcome the contradiction between the social nature of the relations of production and the fragmented nature of the production process. During its course, technology has changed both the object of labour and the subject: man has changed so profoundly that socialism will be able to prove itself a superior social order to capitalism, only if it concentrates all its attention upon the cultivation of the creative powers of man, and overcoming the alienation that occurred with the first stage of industrialization. The tendency for Richta's team to justify their claims on the basis of less orthodox texts of Marx; their stigmatization of the 'administrative-directive' system of planning and management as unable to engineer the necessary change and as holding up scientific-technological development, distinguished their work from that of the Soviet and East German theoreticians. Although they agreed that cybernetics and systems automation were the sole possible basis for modern planning and management in a socialist economy, their exploration of changes in the labour process (that will liberate human potential for participation in the 'quaternary' sphere); the hint that Leninist forms of political intervention in economic and social life might need to be reconsidered; and that the working class might react with less than enthusiasm to the reforms consequent upon the STR (with ensuing social conflict), meant that they verged on heresy.

These general views on the STR were partially related to the crisis in economic and social organization in Czechoslovakia between 1948 and 1960, but the ideology of 'socialist-humanism' that suffuses *Civilization at the Crossroads* came as a considerable challenge to the rather staid Soviet and East German pronouncements. The reaction came in the article 'Man, Science Technology' published in *Voprosy Filosofii* in 1972, and later at the Fifteenth World Congress of Philosophy at Varna in 1973, a joint Soviet-Czechoslovak paper under the same title was presented,[32] endeavouring to arrive at a consensus by providing both 'narrow' and 'broad' definitions of the STR. It was agreed that science and technology, although their scope of influence is relatively autonomous of social systems, do have negative social effects. They cannot be regarded as neutral and this means that social problems are solved by 'fixed methods appropriate to specific social systems'. The dangerous side-effects of technology were a matter for concern, but bourgeois theorists were erroneous in seeing them as capable of solution under capitalism. Rather, under capitalism social problems have become accentuated[33] and obscure the fact that in the era of State monopoly capitalism, it is the fusion of the monopolies and the State which changes the form, but not the essence of capitalist relations of production. The outcome is far from the deproletarianization of the working class: rather consciousness is raised, and there is a greater possibility of forming an anti-monopoly alliance. Thus while the STR can be a means for perfecting the structures of socialist society, it accentuates the ideological struggle between East and West.

Despite the differences between the Soviet, East German and Czechoslovak interpretations of the *consequences* of the STR in the 1960s, by the 1970s the whole concept of the STR had assumed a vital importance in the theorization of the state of conflict between the two antagonistic systems of capitalism and socialism. Under socialism, the STR will be fully used in the process of transition to communism, but in the case of capitalism, it can only go so far as to bring capitalism close to the point of transition to socialism.[34] It is at this point that the separate discussion of 'Developed Socialism', the Scientific Technological Revolution and the refutation of convergence manifest their ideological interrelatedness.

So, returning to the Soviet discussion on 'Developed Socialism', its features have been isolated onto three levels by Evans. On the economic level, the Soviet Union is presented at a higher stage of development through the achievement of the transition to 'intensive' but 'balanced' economic growth. Although by implication the startling growth rates of the earlier period were now beyond grasp, stagnating growth could be avoided by harnessing the forces of the STR. This stands in moderate contrast to the wild claims of the Khrushchev leadership (alluded to earlier). Similarly, in the sphere of social relations, there is a reluctance among the architects of Developed Socialism to endorse Khrushchev's vision of the rapid approach of the classless society. Although differences between town and countryside and between mental and manual labour were gradually being overcome, at present this resulted only in the 'strengthening of features common to all social classes and groups' (rising education levels; greater social homogeneity and cultural integration). Finally, on the subject of the political characteristics of 'Developed Socialism' in contrast to Khrushchev's prophecy of an imminent withering-away of the State, the phase of the dictatorship of the proletariat was seen to have given way to the full-flowering of the 'all-peoples' State, in which the increasing perfection of the governmental process was taking place (principally by means of applying the principle of Democratic Centralism to new spheres of State activity as was exemplified in the Soviet Constitution of 1977) but at the same time, the maximum extension of social self-management and socialist democracy was taking place with the customary proviso that a leading role would be assumed by the CPSU. The need for the CPSU to retain its ideological lead had meant that Soviet approval was necessary before any other East European country could lay claim to the achievement of 'Developed Socialism'. A joint conference of the CPSU Central Committee Academy of Sciences and the Institute of Social Science of the Central Committee of the Socialist Unity Party (SED) in Moscow in late 1971, produced a handbook for the interpretation of 'Developed Socialism' and elevated the status of SED theoreticians to the level of the CPSU. In contrast the Polish entry into the phase of 'Developed Socialism' was a long time in receiving Moscow's approval.[35]

5. Poland and the Construction of a Developed Socialist Society

While the official theoretical journal of the PZPR, *Nowe Drogi*, makes very little mention of the prospects for Polish entry into the phase of 'Developed Socialism' during the 1960s, this is more frequent by the mid-1970s. Prior to this there was some reference in the discussion of economic growth strategy to the need to move from 'extensive' to 'intensive and selective' development, but there was some awareness that this could be constrained by the absence of thorough consideration of a socialist alternative to the Western notion of industrial society.[36] Unease over, and a general anxiety to confront these problems, had by 1968 resulted in the establishment of a 'Commission on the Year 2000', by the Polish Academy of Sciences (a poor imitation of the grander scheme of Kahn and Wiener in the USA). This penchant for futurology, and a delirious belief that problems could be solved by statistical projection and economic 'modelling' produced a series of prognostic 'blueprints' after 1969. That the December 1970 events rudely intervened was a severe blow to this 'Illyrian' optimism.

At his speech to the Eighth Plenum of the PZPR Central Committee in February 1971, Edward Gierek, while acknowledging the past mistakes of the Party in losing contact with the working class, stated the firm intention of embarking upon a new stage of development not only based upon an 'intensive' economic growth strategy, but also one that would be more 'comprehensive, harmonious, programmed, and integrated'.[37] To the Committee on Research and Prognosis, 'Polska 2000', was added the newly formed Party–Government Commission for Modernization of the Economy and the State (in which 220 people working in six sub-groups were involved) and a Committee of Experts to prepare a short report on the state of education in Poland.[38] However, the Polish entry into the era of 'Developed Socialism' was a long time in receiving the approval of Moscow. At the Sixth Congress of the PZPR in December 1971, there was mention only of formulating a programme of 'socialist construction' in Poland.[39] While, at the First National Conference of PZPR activists in 1973, it was asserted that the process of transition to 'Developed Socialism' would be gradual,[40] and while there was a report of the CPSU/ SED Conference on 'Developed Socialist Society' held in Moscow in 1971,[41] it was only after the Seventh PZPR Congress in December 1975 that articles appeared in *Nowe Drogi* referring to Poland's entry into the phase of 'constructing a Developed Socialist Society', and the benefits to be gained from the STR;[42] themes later to be taken up at a Conference in Jabłonnie on 'Developed Socialism' and in a symposium on 'Science and the STR' in 1976.[43]

As to the policy implications of achieving a 'Developed Socialist Society', the intended line of development was presented in Gierek's opening speech at the Seventh PZPR Congress and in the Congress Decree (Uchwała),[44] and they closely resemble those outlined by the CPSU at its Twenty-Fourth Congress in 1971. Translating this into concrete policy objectives, in the economy it was believed that large scale organization of industrial production and priority for investment in technologically advanced industry, would facilitate scientific-technological development and modernization. Moreover, the opening up of the Polish economy to trade with and receipt of financial loans from the West would take advantage of the 'international division of labour' in both production and consumption. It was believed that the 'liberation' of the Polish working class from manual labour and the transfer of 'mental function' to automated technology would increase labour productivity.

In terms of *social policy*, the increase in social justice and equalization and *rapprochement* of class interests and opportunities with the aim of national integration,[45] was to take place by means of policies directed at the individual consumer and at collective consumption. Individual wages were to rise and the working week was to be shortened, but after 1973 there was to be an expansion of such facilities as housing, nurseries, holidays, etc., provided at the place of work (which, incidentally, would encourage greater stability of the workforce and discourage unnecessary labour turnover). In health policy the establishment of a National Health Protection Fund was to provide simultaneously, increased resources for expansion of hospitals, health centres and home care.[46] Above all, social policy was to serve the purpose of strengthening the family, and in particular large families were to be given priority for social support, especially women with pre-school age children. Education was to play an important role in the objective of integration of social class. To a certain extent the 'intellectualization' of the working class and its closer integration with the intelligentsia, had been achieved by a considerable expansion of higher education between 1971 and 1976. Hence, the entry into a 'Developed Socialist Society' now required greater emphasis upon vocational training below degree level, and on specialized post-graduate training.

The political objectives of achieving the transition to 'Developed Socialism' would require the strengthening of the leading role of the party, a reconceptualization of party organization at the grass roots, and the use of the media in propaganda activities. All this signified a desire to renovate the modes of party activity. In late 1973 a new Institute of Basic Problems of Marxism–Leninism was set up with the express purpose of modernizing the structure and operation of the PZPR. It conducted research and made recommendations on recruitment strategy, propaganda activities, and communications within the PZPR in different economic environments (such as large industrial enterprises);[47] on the change in the composition, activism, occupational location, life-style, values and political attitudes of the working class;[48] on social developments requiring theoretical elaboration in Marxist–Leninist thought;[49] and above all provided theoretical reflection upon the leading role of a Marxist–Leninist party in a Developed Socialist Society.[50] The 'strengthening and perfection' of the Polish state and the extension of Democratic Centralism to the operation of many state institutions, was exemplified in the reorganization of local government in 1973–75, a revision of Labour Legislation in 1974, and Constitutional Reform in 1976. The 'maximum extension of socialist democracy' was achieved by the reorganization of trade unions in 1973, reform of electoral law and the creation of neighbourhood self-management, and eventually by a reform of the law on Workers' Self-Management in 1978.

There is no doubt that all these objectives and their policy implications constituted an ambitious scheme for reform. However, it is ironical that at the very time that Poland announced her entry into the era of 'Developed Socialism', there were signs of weakness beginning to appear in particular policy areas. To commence with economic policy, after 1976 a major concern was the effectiveness of investment and rates of increase of labour productivity.[51] Moreover, it soon became apparent that the hope that large scale organization would facilitate scientific-technological development was illusory. Although an exercise of concentration of industrial production on a hitherto unprecedented scale took place after 1973, by 1977 the cumbersome nature of the managerial process, growth in restrictive practice, falling rates of growth of labour productivity and technological innovation, reflected adversely upon the experiment. By 1977 'small' was being hailed as beautiful, and in late 1980 the process of concentration began to be reversed.

Yet such changes in economic policy proved to be too little and too late to avoid causing considerable damage to Polish society. In terms of social structure, the liberation of the Polish working class from manual toil and the transfer of 'mental functions' to automated technology, had occurred in an unanticipated fashion. The attractiveness of white-collar status and its attendant privileges encouraged the proliferation of middle and lower level management positions with little regard for efficiency or effectiveness and promoted a continued labour intensity in the administrative process especially with respect to menial office skills. Moreover, the growing 'intellectualization' of the working class and its greater integration with the intelligentsia and subsequent class harmony, did not take the anticipated and desired course. On the one hand, the demand for higher education exceeded both the supply of full-time places and appropriate employment for graduates, and secondly access to this was found to be increasingly at the disposal of those from white-collar backgrounds. The 'intellectualization' of the working class took place under the much harder conditions of part-time and correspondence study, and fomented resentment of privilege. On the other hand, the 'proletarianization' of university educated engineers placed in posts well below their capabilities provoked both frustration with inefficient managerial superiors and disappointed aspirations.

The respect for social justice was further disturbed by the reduction in living standards that took place in Poland after the mid-1970s. Although average real wages had risen by some 40 per cent for the period 1971 to 1975, the Gierek regime, in the face of increasing indebtedness to the West, was unable to meet its commitment in house building, to expand the social services and fringe benefits provided at the workplace, or to maintain food subsidies. The need to increase labour productivity had also had its spill-over effects upon individual consumption in the form of attempted wage freezes and compulsory work on Saturday (even though a shortening of the working week had been promised in 1970 and at the Sixth PZPR Congress). Popular demands for greater affluence could no longer be satisfied, yet at a time of cut-backs it became increasingly evident that white-collar workers fared better than their blue-collar comrades (especially the peasant-workers whose work attendance record tended to be poor on account of the need to return to the land at crucial times in the year). That 'Developed Socialism' in Poland would permit working people more time to participate in creative leisure activities seemed a hollow joke to those who worked on Saturday or queued long hours for food. The anger that this aroused however, was not only confined to material issues. Protest against injustice, repression and the restrictions upon religious observance and civil liberties was after 1976, the channel into which 'creative human potential' was diverted.

Finally, the 'strengthening of the Socialist State' and the 'extension of democracy' were in reality a series of measures to extend the control of the PZPR apparatus into local government, trade unions, etc. The passage of restrictive labour legislation (the 1974 Labour Code) and a new Constitution, which was ambiguous on the subject of civil rights, were sugared by a ritualized form of consultative participation. Even the attempt by the PZPR to overhaul its methods of operation and to reconsider its leading role misfired: working class and white-collar intelligentsia discontent had been incorporated into the party which is partly why the events since the summer of 1980 have had such wide-ranging and prolonged consequences.

The PZPR either could not or would not pay heed to the danger signals emitted from social scientists among its ranks. Despite the original flush of enthusiastic articles on 'Developed Socialism' these had more or less ceased by the time of the Second PZPR National Conference of Activists in early 1978, and were replaced instead by a series of articles on the subject of social justice, moral disintegration and the revival of bourgeois values;[52] and later by an anxiety over corruption within party ranks.[53] It is ironical that the vast research network of the Institute of Basic Problems of Marxism–Leninism was not used by the leadership to illustrate the unpopularity of its policies. It comes as no surprise that one Polish social scientist could refer to Poland as a society geared towards the self-reproduction of artificial reality, where the lack of political alternatives and the ideological legitimation of argument is a trap for the ruling group; where the surreal situation prevails of a working class struggling against its own State, and where the distinctive patterns of change cannot be the planning away of uncontrolled phenomena, but only learning by crisis.[54] Another academic felt that the transition to developed socialism should be accompanied in practice by a reduction in the mode of political inter-ference associated with the modified strategy of 'imposed industrialization'; it had to be recognized that 'uncontrolled phenomena' reflecting group interests were the result of 'deficiencies in the multi-level structure of decision-making', and tensions among the workforce were due not only to the dysfunctions of the economic decision-making process, but also to the inadequacy of the political system to articulate attitudes.[55] How else could the decisions to raise food prices without consultation in 1976 and 1980 and the procrastination over measures to shorten the working week to be explained?

6. Conclusion

It was then, the absence of a role for political participation in the ideology of Developed Socialism that proved to be its greatest weakness. While there is a tendency to argue that ideological movements that are in power for a long time gradually experience the identification of ideals with reality and a consequent erosion of utopianism and emergence of prag-matism,[56] this is not the case with the Polish experience of 'Developed Socialism'. To the contrary this doctrine is tinged with utopianism and is as much a reflection of the manner in which a Marxist–Leninist party would like to develop as it is a 'pragmatic' adaptation to reality. All the discussion in the world about the intricacies of techniques such as Manage-ment by Objectives, Systems Analysis or Operations Research and their justification in assisting policy implementation or coping with unforeseen circumstances, is no substitute for consideration as to how legitimate policy goals are arrived at, reappraised and readjusted in the light of competing values. Moreover, the methodological weakness of Marxism–Leninism in ascribing the inadequacies of State socialist experience either to the technical problems of planning or to human psychological failings[57] and the confusion of possibilities with actual consequences in the comparison of East and West scientific development, have not been erased in the discussions on 'Developed Socialism' and the 'STR'.

So, if the entry of Poland, led by the PZPR, into the era of 'Developed Socialism' has been inauspicious, the demand for 'Socialist Renewal' has far-reaching implications. That so many of the elements in the twenty-one point Gdańsk Agreement had been promised earlier in 1976 and 1970, but persistently forgotten, illustrates that concern with material issues has been only one source of popular protest. As well as questions of social justice, respect for human and civil rights, a concern over the quality of the democratic process, and above all, the interpretation of and limitations to the leading role of the party, are issues that will occupy a prominent place in Polish politics for some time to come.

Notes and References

1 'Referat komitet Centralnego Polskiej Zjednoczonej Partii Robotniczej wygłoszony na IX Nadzwyczajnym Zjeździe PZPR przez Stanisława Kanie', Warsaw, July 1981, p. 6.
2 'Robotnicy w KC', interview with Jan Malanowski in *Argumenty*, No. 33 (August 1981), pp. 1, 13. Amongst manual worker delegates those who were also Solidarity members reached as high as 40 per cent.
3 See Chapter IV in this volume. Also, J. Staniszkis, 'The Evolution of Forms of Working-class Protest in Poland: Sociological Reflections on the Gdańsk-Szczecin Case, August 1980', *Soviet Studies*, 33 (1981), 204–31, especially pp. 228–31.
4 For the party/government proposal see 'Kierunki Reformy Gospodarczy', Warsaw, 1981.
5 A. Koseski, 'Budowa rozwiniętego społeczeństwa socjalistycznego', Warsaw, 1977, p. 6.
6 A. B. Evans, 'Developed Socialism in Soviet Ideology', *Soviet Studies*, 29 (1977), 404–28.
7 A. Łopatka, 'O projekcje nowe konstytucie ZSSR', *Nowe Drogi*, No. 8 (1977), pp. 39–51. '[Developed Socialist Society] is a society in which powerful productive forces guiding science and culture are created; in which there is a steady growth of national standards of living that more than ever provide favourable conditions for the all-round development of the individual. It is a society where social relations have reached maturity, which based on the *rapprochement* of all social strata and the *de jure* and *de facto* equalization of all nations and nationalities, creates a new historical community – the Soviet nation. It is a highly organized society with a high level of patriotic and internationalist idealism and consciousness on the part of working people. It is a society whose fundamental rule of existence is care of all for the well-being of each, and the care of each for the well-being of all. It 'is a society of genuine democracy whose political system ensures effective management of all social matters as well as more active participation of working people in state life, and the correspondence of real human rights and freedom with the responsibilities of citizenship. A developed socialist society constitutes a genuine step on the road to communism.'.
8 Evans, 'Developed Socialism in Soviet Ideology'.
9 Ibid.

10 M. Lavigne, *The Socialist Economies of the Soviet Union and East Europe*, London, Martin Robertson, 1974, pp. 127–41.

11 G. Leptin and M. Melzer, *Economic Reform in East German Industry*, Oxford, OUP, 1978, pp. 1–12.

12 H. H. Hohmann, M. Kaser, K. Thalheim, *The New Economic Systems of East Europe*, London, C. Hurst, 1975: see Ch. I, H. H. Hohmann and H. B. Sand, 'The Soviet System', pp. 1–42.

13 J. Danecki, 'Socjalizm a Teorie Społeczeństwa Industrialnego', *Nowe Drogi*, No. 1 (1970), pp. 27–38.

14 I. Weinberg, 'The Problem of the Convergence of Industrial Societies: A Critical Look at the State of a Theory', *Comparative Studies in Society and History*, 11 (1969), 1–15.

15 Ibid.

16 S. A. Marglin, 'What Do Bosses Do? Origins and Functions of Hierarchy in Capitalist Production', in A. Gorz (ed.), *The Division of Labour: the Labour Process and Class Struggle in Modern Capitalism*, Hassocks, Sussex, Harvester, 1976.

17 J. Goldthorpe, 'Theories of Industrial Scoiety: Reflections on the Recrudescence of Historicism and the Future of Futurology', *Euopean Journal of Sociology*, 11 (1971), 263–88.

18 M. Ellman, 'Against Convergence', *Cambridge Journal of Economics*, 4 (1980), 192–216.

19 K. Kumar, 'Industrialism and Post-Industrialism: Reflections on a Putative Transition', *Sociological Review*, 24 (1976), 439–78; K. Kumar, 'Continuities and Discontinuities in the Development of Industrial Societies', in R. Scase (ed.), *Industrial Society: Class Cleveage and Control*, London, George Allen and Unwin, 1977: K. Kumar, *Prophecy and Progress: the Sociology of Industrial and Post-Industrial Society*, London, Penguin, 1978.

20 Weinberg, 'The Problem of the Convergence of Industrial Societies'.

21 D. J. R. Kelley, 'The Soviet Debate on the Convergence of the American and Soviet Systems', *Polity*, 6 (1973–74), 176–96.

22 Ibid.

23 Ibid. Also, V. Georgescu, 'Dissident Images of Eastern Europe', *Problems of Communism* (July–August 1980), 76–9.

24 M. Rakovski, 'Towards an East European Marxism', London, Alison and Busby, 1978; G. Konrad and I. Szelenyi, *The Intellectuals on the Road to Class Power*, Sussex, Harvester, 1979; O. Sik, *The Third Way*, London, Wildwood House, 1976.

25 Danecki, op. cit.

26 J. D. Bernal, *Science in History*, Vol. 2, London, Penguin, 1969.

27 A. Bucholz, 'The Role of the Scientific-Technological Revolution in Marxism–Leninism', *Studies in Soviet Thought*, 20 (1979), 145–64; J. Filipiec, B. P. Lowe, and R. Richta, *Sozialismus, Imperialismus – wissentschaftliche-technische Revolution*, Berlin, Akademie-Verlag, 1974, pp. 12–13, 112–13.

28 J. Joravsky, *The Lysenko Affair*, Cambridge, Mass., Harvard University Press, 1970.

29 J. S. Mieleszenko, 'Niektóre problemy społeczne rewolucji naukowo-techniczne', *Studia Socjologiczne*, No. 2 (1969), pp. 83–93.

30 Mieleszenko, op. cit., and Bucholz, 'The Role of the Scientific-Technological Revolution in Marxism–Leninism'.

31 R. Richta, *Civilisation at the Croassroads: Social and Human Implications of the Scientific-Technological Revolution*, Prague, Czech Academy of Sciences, 1969.

32 L. Zacher, 'Marksistowska analiza rewolucji naukowo-techniczne', *Nowe Drogi*, No. 4 (1974), pp. 149–51.

33 N. Gauzner, 'Now zjawiska współczesnym kapitaliźmie a koncepcje społeczeństwa postindustrialnego', *Nowe Drogi*, No. 3 (1975), pp. 121–35.

34 Pavel Kovaly, 'Review Article on the Scientific Technological Revolution', *Studies in Soviet Thought*, 14 (1974), 139–48.

35 P. Marciniak, 'Rozwinięte Społeczeństwo Socjalistyczne', *Nowe Drogi*, No. 2 (1974), pp. 114–17.

36 Danecki, op. cit.

37 E. Gierek, 'Przemówienie na VIII Plenum KCPZPR', in *VI Zjazd PZPR, podstawowe materiały i dokumenty*, Warsaw, 1972, pp. 303–7.

38 J. Szydlak, 'Speech to the Plenary Session of the Party-Government Commission of the Modernization of the Economy and the State', Warsaw, 12 April 1972.

39 VI Congress, PZPR, 1971/2.

40 'Krajowa Narada, Aktywu Partyjnego i Gospodarczego: podstawowe materialy', Warsaw, 1973.

41 Marciniak, op. cit.

42 T. M. Jaroszewski, 'Rewolucja naukow-techniczna a niektóre nowe problemy materializmu historycznego', *Nowe Drogi*, No. 5 (1976) pp. 78–87; T. M. Jaroszewski, 'Perspektywa: rozwinięte społeczenstwo socjalistyczne', *Nowe Drogi*, No. 2 (1976), pp. 58–69; K. Secomski, 'Czynnik ludzki a baza materialna rozwiniętego społeczenstwa socjalistycznego', *Nowe Drogi*, No. 10 (1976), pp. 49–61; S. Widerszpił, 'Z problemów teorii rezwiniętego społeczenstwa socjalistycznego', *Nowe Drogi*, No. 3 (1977), pp. 105–21.

43 'Nauka a rewolucja naukowa-techniczna', Warsaw, 1979.

44 'O dalszy dynamiczny rozwój budownictwa socjalistycznego; o wyzsza jakość pracy i waruków życia', *Nowe Drogi*, No. 1 (1976), pp. 51–89; Uchwała VII Zjazdu, 'O dałszy dynamiczny rozwój budownictwa socjalistycznego – o wyższa jakość pracy i warunków życia narodu', *Nowe Drogi*, No. 1 (1976), pp.118–48.

45 Jaroszewski, op. cit., pp. 160–61; W. Wesołowski, and J. Wiatr, 'Nowe aspekty struktury społecznej przesłanka rozwoju demokracji socjalistycznej', *Nowe Drogi*, No. 9 (1977), pp. 119–29.

46 M. Pohorille, *Spożycie zbiorowe i swiadczenia społeczne*, Warsaw, 1975; Z. Lewandowska, *Model konsumpcji w Polsce w okresie industrializacji socjalistycznej*, Warsaw, 1979; L. Beskid, 'Tendencje i wzórce konsumpcji', *Nowe Drogi*, No. 6 (1978), pp. 145–56.

47 A. Łopatka, J. Błuszkowski, and K. Konstański (eds), *Organizacja partyjne wiełkich zakładów pracy*, Warsaw, IPPML, 1976.

48 A. Wajda (ed.), *Klasa robotniczca w społeczenstwie socjalistycznym*, Warsaw, IPPML, 1979.

49 W. Wesołowski (ed.), *Marksizm i procesy rozwoju społecznego*, Warsaw, IPPML, 1979; the problems under consideration stretched from the macro theoretical to specific aspects of development concerning life-style, political culture, values, inter-class relations, management, psychology, etc.

50 J. Błuszkowski and C. Mojsiewicz (eds), *Partia w rozwiniętym społeczenstwie socjalistycznym*, Warsaw, IPPML, 1979.

51 'Uchwała II Plenum KCPZPR', in *Nowe Drogi*, No. 2 (1976), pp. 37–40; 'Rządowa program realizacji postanowień IV Plenum KCPZPR', in *Nowe Drogi*, No. 10 (1976), pp. 6–20.

52 H. Jańkowski and J. Malanowski, 'Socjalistyczny sposob zycia a problemy moralne', *Nowe Drogi*, No. 3 (1978), pp. 83–91; Z. Sufin, 'Społeczne czynniki rozwoju', *Nowe Drogi*, No. 12 (1978), pp. 144–52; M. Pohorille, 'Problemy rozwoju konsumpcji indywidualnej i zbiorowej', *Nowe Drogi*, No. 2 (1979), pp. 72–83; W. Wesołowski, 'Interesy klas i warstw a jedność moralno-polityczna narodu', *Nowe Drogi*, No. 1 (1980), pp. 99–112; H. Jankowski, 'Z zagadnień sprawiedliwośći społecznej', *Nowe Drogi*, No. 8 (1980), pp. 101–8.

53 M. Michałuk, 'O postawie moralnej kommunisty', *Nowe Drogi*, No. 8 (1979), pp. 90–102; W. Kruczek, 'Na straży norm partyjnośći i zasad socjaliżmu', *Nowe Drogi*, No. 5 (1980), pp. 39–46.

54 J. Staniszkis, 'On some contradictions of Socialist Society: The Case of Poland', *Soviet Studies*, 31 (1979), 167–87.
55 W. Morawski, 'Socialist Industrialisation in Poland: the Doctrine, System of Decision-Making, Uncontrolled Phenomena', *Polish Sociological Bulletin*, No. 1 (1978), pp. 33–45. See also *International Journal of Sociology*, 10 (1980–81), pp. 3–11; W. Narojek, *Społeczeństwo Planujące*, Warsaw, 1973.
56 A. B. Evans, 'Developed Socialism in Soviet Ideology'.
57 K. Nyström, 'Soviet Sociology and the Scientific-Technological Revolution', *Acta Sociologica*, 17 (1974), 55–77.

2 Poland and Eastern Europe: The Impact of the Crisis

GEORGE SCHÖPFLIN

East European leaderships are understandably concerned to prevent such a line of development as has occurred in Poland since August 1980. They responded by a firm defence of the status quo – the leading role of the party – and by adopting a kind of policy of *Abgrenzung* towards Poland. Czechoslovakia and the GDR took this literally and closed their frontiers with Poland. All the countries of the Warsaw Pact, including Romania at first, were hostile to Polish developments, condemned Solidarity, reproved the Polish party and sought to show that the economic crisis there was the consequence of the unreasonable demands made by Solidarity and hostile elements. Indeed, the Soviet Union twice restated what it regarded as the essential features of a Marxist–Leninist polity, in the letter debated at the Eleventh plenum of the Polish Central Committee and in the CPSU Politburo resolution of 21 August, made after consultations with all the Warsaw Pact party leaders.[1] The first of these documents spelt out the need for resistance to 'anti-socialist forces' and 'the pressure of internal counter-revolution', which had successfully taken over within Solidarity. The letter drew attention to the Polish party's loss of control over the media, the weakening of the 'authority of law and order organs and the army', the emergence of the horizontal structures within the Polish party and the apparent undermining of the principles of democratic centralism. The Politburo resolution, which gained added weight from having been issued after the customary Crimean summit and from its symbolic associations with the anniversary of the invasion of Czechoslovakia, stressed the importance of economic co-operation within Eastern Europe and the need to avoid large scale indebtedness to the West, the strict maintenance of Leninist norms, the fostering of links with the masses, internationalism and revolutionary vigilance. Above all, as far as the last was concerned, party leaderships should be prepared to repel the onslaughts of antisocialist forces. The broad significance of these two documents is that the East European and Soviet party leaders did not see any necessity for reform of the existing political systems and had no intention of abandoning any of their monopoly. Pluralism had no place under Marxism–Leninism and autonomous trade unions were tantamount to counter-revolution. Hatches were firmly battened down.

Within the constellation of the East European polities, Yugoslavia constituted a rather special case, both in terms of its response to the Polish crisis and in respect of its strategy of political development. Unlike the Warsaw Pact countries, Yugoslavia did not join in the chorus of condemnations, but adopted a relatively open-minded attitude to Polish developments. The registration of Solidarity in November 1980 was welcomed, as a means of promoting pluralism and in July 1981, a senior party ideologist stated that in Poland the working class had become the bearer of socialist change under current conditions through the instrument of Solidarity. This generally positive attitude towards Poland was all the more remarkable in the light of Yugoslavia's own political crisis. Inflation was around 30 per cent in 1980, the integrity of the state was threatened by the eruption of rioting in the mainly Albanian-inhabited Kosovo, and the post-Tito leadership was experiencing considerable difficulties in making the system work without the integrative element of the deceased leader. In the circumstances, the Yugoslavs might have been pardoned for taking a less enthusiastic attitude towards the Polish experiment, given that the autonomy of Solidarity is not paralleled by any Yugoslav insitution.

The probable explanation for this apparent self-confidence is to be sought in the origins of the Yugoslav system. Whereas in the other East European states (Albania excepted), the Communist revolution was a foreign import with only limited support, in Yugoslavia it had genuine domestic roots. This gave the Yugoslav party, which was as addicted to its leading role as any Warsaw Pact party, a genuine legitimacy and that, in turn, gave it the self-confidence to face up to crises with something like equanimity. Above all, in this connection, the Yugoslav party had constructed a system from which society was not as completely excluded as in Poland. Although political power was firmly held by the party, a wide range of socio-economic decisions had been devolved to the local and republican levels, providing for a measure of real political participation. Against this background, the Yugoslav leadership presumably concluded that the potential challenge of an autonomous trade union–the Yugoslav unions were part autonomous, part controlled — was not as serious as in other communist party states.

In all, the 1980–81 Polish crisis must be regarded as the third occasion when the party's claim to monopoly was challenged by society. In 1956 and 1968, the challenge was beaten by force of arms. In 1980–81 accommodation was sought, and produced an awkward but apparently functioning political system in Poland, yet the official leadership response of the Soviet

Union and Eastern Europe apart, the question remains of the likely impact of all this upon the relation between domestic political systems and society in these countries. Will the ideas generated by the events of 1980–81 implant themselves elsewhere in Eastern Europe?

The countries of Eastern Europe are unique in a somewhat obvious way: they all have political systems which were for all practical purposes identical at the time when they were constrained to adopt them and, further, these political systems are popularly seen as being at variance with inherited domestic political traditions. Hence there is at times tension and at other times dissension between popular aspirations and the imperatives of the existing system.[2] In this broad context one might have predicted that the different societies of Eastern Europe would have been highly imitative of each other and would have been quick to press for reforms achieved in another state to be introduced at home. Curiously, there has been very little of this and the diffusion of ideas in this sphere has tended to be restricted.

There would seem to be several explanations for this, none of them mutually exclusive. In the first place, precisely because of the perceived tension between popular aspirations and the existing system, reformers have looked to the past or to a combination of the past and present needs when formulating their demands for change. Second, East European countries tend to be insulated from each other and to have only rather hazy notions of what is taking place in the political arena next door. Within the intelligentsia, there may be considerable information about other theoretically compatible political changes in a neighbouring country, but at the popular level this is generally absent. Third, East European societies continue to look to the West for inspiration. The welfare state model developed in Sweden is thought attractive by many people. The fourth factor, which is connected with the second and the third, is the effect of official information policy, which seeks to restrict the publication of information about reforms in other East European countries as potentially destabilizing. Fifth, there is the impact of negative stereotypes. The national tradition of every East European country includes negative stereotypes about neighbours and the result of this is often a rather prejudiced view about developments elsewhere. Finally, an important role is played, at least in the short term, by a commitment to the status quo, the fear that change will mean change for the worse, especially in the economic sphere. In this sense, the failure of every far-reaching reform programme broached in post-war Eastern Europe justifies the sceptics.

This is the theoretical background against which the impact of Poland

and the evolution of the new Polish political system in 1980–81 must be assessed. Both the experience of the past and the generalized fear for the future encouraged by officialdom have produced a rather negative response to the Polish events among Poland's neighbours. Indeed, what is striking about the 1980–81 crisis is how much more negative this response is than the experience of previous crises.

In 1956, most obviously, there was fairly widespread sympathy for the Polish reformers of that year in Hungary, and the Hungarian revolution was followed with anxiety in Poland. The proximate cause of the Hungarian revolution, as a matter of fact, was an act of symbolic solidarity with Poland. On 22 October, a group of students decided to lay a wreath at the statue of General Bem, a Polish officer who commanded a Hungarian army against the Austrians and Russians in the War of Independence of 1848–49; it was this demonstration that attracted enormous crowds into the streets of Budapest on 23 October, when the wreath-laying took place.[3] Another act of symbolic politics with connotations of international sympathy happened in 1968, when Polish students organized a march to the Warsaw suburb of Praga, to demonstrate their approval for the reform programme that was at that time being elaborated in Prague, Czechoslovakia. It is noteworthy that the common denominator of both these events was the active presence of students, who articulated a relatively sophisticated interest in the developments of another country.

The same was true of the group of party reformists associated with Wolfgang Harich in the German Democratic Republic in 1956–57. In the summer of 1956 reform was in the air in the East German party, the SED, and Harich, an academic at the Humboldt University, put together a platform of reforms aimed at democratization. He explicitly stated that he had been in contact with Polish reformers and with the Hungarian revisionist Marxist, Georg Lukács. He was clearly influenced by the Yugoslav and Polish models of workers' self-management and his proposition, that the State should reach *détente* with the Church, owed something to the agreement to this and between Gomułka and Wyszyński in Poland in October 1956. Harich's ideas found no echo outside the intelligentsia and the SED leader, Walter Ulbricht, had no difficulty in suppressing them and the group.[4]

By 1980, however, a major change had come over Eastern Europe, one which markedly softened the impact of the Polish events on the rest of Eastern Europe. This change was the informal transformation of the official ideology from reliance on Marxism–Leninism as a corpus of ideas by which society might be governed, to its petrification and replacement by consumerism and nationalism inside a shell of Marxist–Leninist language.[5] The significance of this transformation was that a corresponding metamorphosis of the means of effecting change and the basis from which the need for change was to be argued were likewise transformed.

If Marxism–Leninism had become degraded into a set of ritualistic formulae and Marxist critiques of official strategy were ignored or suppressed (the fate of the Harich group was only one instance of this), then there was little point in seeking to effect change by Marxist argumentation. Yet the aspiration for change had not disappeared throughout the area; it was merely articulated in different terms in different countries. The central, unifying factor in this process was the slow recognition on the part of the intelligentsia that pressure for change would have to be formulated in accordance with the genuine ideology of the party, as distinct from the ostensible one.

The real ideologies of the Eastern European parties include the following characteristics: the claim to a monopoly of political initiative (the leading role of the party), the monopoly of rationality in goal setting and efficiency in execution, and the propagation of traditional nationalism. Legitimation is sought − not always achieved − by a trade-off of consumerism against depoliticization, plus nationalism. The significance of this transformation of the basis of political power is that it has been localized to a far greater degree than was the case in the early 1950s. In the 1980s, local considerations govern the increasingly differentiated political systems of Eastern Europe. The consequence of this is that reformers, whether inside the system or outside it, generally look to local traditions for remedies and, therefore, there is little incentive to investigate solutions adopted in neighbouring countries.

The promotion of nationalism as an instrument of cementing loyalties between rulers and ruled has tended to accentuate this trend for the reason suggested above − the existence of negative heterostereotypes. These heterostereotypes, furthermore, are not derived exclusively from the pre-Communist period, but also from experiences over the post-war period. Thus, even before the war, Czechs and Poles generally had a rather poor mutual image, something which can be attributed to the dispute over the Teschen region. The Poles felt that ethnically and historically Teschen, an economically important area, should have been part of the reconstituted Polish state and were, therefore, bitter that Czechoslovakia should have annexed it during the 1919–20 Polish–Soviet war. This antagonism was deepened by the participation of Polish forces in the Warsaw Pact invasion of Czechoslovakia in 1968, when Polish forces temporarily occupied some of the same area. In this indirect fashion, the Teschen dispute contributed to the survival of strong negative images among Poles and Czechs. One conclusion which emerged was a marked lack of sympathy of Poland's troubles in 1980 among Czechs and disdain among Poles for Czech experiences in 1968.

An analogous state of affairs inhibited the diffusion of ideas between Poland and the German Democratic Republic. Here negative hetero-stereotypes were, if anything, even stronger than between Poles and Czechs. The historic legacy of the *Drang nach Osten*, of Prussia's part in the dismemberment of Poland in the Partitions and subsequent Polish–German antogonism in Prussian Poland, reinforced by the experience of the Second World War, have left their mark. Only among the youngest generation of Poles is the visceral hatred of everything German beginning to fade (to be replaced by anti-Russian sentiments).[6] The East German image of the Pole is no better, albeit contempt rather than hatred tends to dominate. This has tended to be intensified by the gradual rehabilitation of the Prussian legacy in the GDR. From the mid-1970s onwards, the promotion of a separate East German nationhood has sought to appropriate certain components of the Prussian tradition. Symbolically this has included the invoking of historic figures like Clausewitz and Frederick the Great, whose statue, banished from Berlin in the 1950s, was ceremonially re-erected in 1980. The particular significance of this revival of Prussia in the context of the 1980–81 Polish crisis is that the Prussian tradition contains a clear anti-Polish element and this is certainly understood by the East German population.[7]

The revival of nationalism in Eastern Europe and the impact of it on popular perceptions could be regarded, therefore, as one of the inhibiting factors in the diffusion of ideas from one East European country to another. But, as has already been noted, it was the combination of the revival of nationalism with the decay of Marxism–Leninism and the transformation of the basis of power that proved to be the most decisive in this respect. In essence, the stabilization of Eastern Europe after the Czechoslovak crisis, despite all its inherent weaknesses as demonstrated most vividly in Poland, continued to hold elsewhere.

The system of consumerism traded off against depoliticization has generally been seen as constituting a social compact which would provide East European parties with at least conditional legitimacy. The system was closely associated with Brezhnev and for that reason, it may be termed the Brezhnev blueprint. In this context, Gierek's Poland was a model of the blueprint in the first part of the 1970s. Gierek was successful in defusing the crisis of 1970–71 by welfare concessions, and what must have commended his efforts particularly was his achievement in undermining the political demands of the striking workers. The blueprint eventually failed to hold in Poland – a process which has been fully explored elsewhere in this book – but it offered the other East European leaderships sufficient room for manoeuvre to maintain their positions. What was noteworthy about the situation in 1980–81, both the collapse of the Brezhnev system in Poland and its survival elsewhere, was that in all cases local factors conditioned developments. In Poland, Gierek fell not because of a crisis affecting the whole of Eastern Europe equally, but because of the way in which developments peculiar to Poland eroded the Polish variant of the blueprint.[8] In other East European countries the reverse of this was to be seen. Thus Hungary experienced two bad years economically in 1979 and 1980 – real wages fell and there was an officially admitted inflation of over 10 per cent – yet the Hungarian party weathered the crisis, both as regards domestic developments and the potential reverberations of Poland.

This process only underlines the significance of differentiation in political development in Eastern Europe and the primacy of local factors over area-wide currents at least in the short term. Despite the universal fear of contagion from the Polish crisis on the part of party leaderships, the popular response to Poland tended to be negative. This was compounded of fear of loss of material gains, of a deterioration in the political climate, resentment that Polish 'idleness and reluctance to work' should affect the life of the population in neighbouring states and, in some countries, a kind of *Schadenfreude*-cum-envy that the Poles should be making political advances of a kind that others had failed to make. This last appeared to be particularly marked among the Czechs, understandably in the light of the very recent memories of the failure of 1968.[9]

All the above factors, therefore, would seem to militate against there being any significant fall-out from Poland to the rest of Eastern Europe. The strategy of the Warsaw Pact appeared to be one composed of containment and the expectation that the inner contradictions of the Polish experiment would eventually bring about its failure, above all, through the progressive deterioration of the Polish economy. The question, which can only be raised and not fully answered, is whether this calculation would hold for the future. Previous reforms in Eastern Europe, as already argued, had had very little impact outside the country where they were adopted. The significance of the Yugoslav experiment in the 1950s lay not in the actual institutions adopted – self-management – but in the possibility that the Soviet model of development did not have to be slavishly copied. This was in effect accepted in the early 1960s with the onset of the second de-Stalinization after the Twenty-second Congress of the CPSU. Assuming that the Polish experiment did not fail, its long-term impact was likely to be analogous to the Yugoslav reforms.

Despite the localization of political development in Eastern Europe, all the East European polities continued to share a number of features to which the Polish changes could be relevant. The most crucial of these was the disequilibrium of power between the state and society, the weakness of the mediating mechanisms between them, and the growing demand by society to exercise control over political decision making. These features appeared in different forms in the various East European polities or were latent for the time being, but it could be assumed that at some point they would begin to impinge on the existing political dispensation. In this connection, there appeared to be three aspects of the Polish crisis that could be of long-term relevance.

In the first place, that crisis was brought about by the collapse of the morale of the ruling elite and its will to rule. There have been three such instances of elite collapse since 1945 – Hungary in 1956, Czechoslovakia in 1967–68 and Poland 1980 – and each had far-reaching political consequences. However, it is far from easy to deduce from these three cases, let alone predict, which are the key factors producing a collapse. Economic deterioration is obviously central, above all in systems which rely so heavily on rationality and efficiency for legitimation. In what circumstances an analogous economic crisis might sap the will of an East European elite cannot be predicted with any claim to confidence. Deprivation on its own is clearly insufficient to bring it about – if it were, Romania would have been destabilized long ago. Hence the quality of the leadership also plays a role.

This raises the second aspect of the Polish crisis which could be of relevance to the rest of Eastern Europe – the policies adopted by the leadership towards the intelligentsia. The function of an intelligentsia in the political arena is to think independently, to elaborate alternative concepts of development, to criticize present strategies and to reinterpret the past. The problem for Communist parties in Eastern Europe has been to find the right balance between intellectual independence and stultification. If intellectuals claim and exercise excessive independence, they can easily move towards undermining the basis of the party's hold on power by demonstrating the shortcomings of monopoly rule. On the other hand, if the balance is tilted towards stultification by party control, then the party itself suffers in that the intelligentsia will be unable to perform the minimal role expected of it for fear of political sanctions. The status of the Romanian intelligentsia in the 1970s and 1980s approached this state of affairs and was undoubtedly one of the reasons for the slow pace of economic development and extensive waste in that country. The total exclusion of the intelligentsia can have another unwelcome result – it can give birth to an extra-systemic opposition, in which intellectuals attempt to exercise their functions outside the officially sanctioned framework and to challenge the regime by publishing criticism and political alternatives. This was more or less what happened in Poland in the 1970s, but the emergence of the Polish opposition was preceded by the gradual appearance of a Czechoslovak oppositional current, which can be dated from the early 1970s. The comparison between Poland and Czechoslovakia in this respect is instructive. The Czechoslovak leadership was able to contain the challenge of Charter 77 by a mixture of repression and co-optation. The majority of Czech and Slovak intellectuals preferred to remain neutral between the regime and Charter because the system appeared to be functioning adequately, the leadership had not lost its nerve, and the trauma of 1968 and after was too strong. That does not preclude the eventual resurgence of autonomous intellectual activity in Czechoslovakia, but it does suggest that such a development appears to be contingent on leadership failure.

The third aspect of the Polish crisis is the relationship between the intelligentsia and the rest of society. All three post-war East European crises suggest that radical political change is achieved when the intellectuals and the workers (the peasantry plays a less direct role in the political process) combine for a particular common purpose. Their collaboration may be tenuous, but it appears to have been sufficient for both these actors on the political scene to have challenged the regime simultaneously to produce major changes. In periods of normal party control, the regime does not appear to encounter serious problems in preventing the emergence of an intellectual–worker coalition. But the lesson of Poland is that when such a combination does arise, the regime is then obliged to retreat, presumably in the hope of being able to claw back concessions. What gives the Polish crisis potential significance is that both the intelligentsia and the workers have been able to create autonomous institutions for the defence of their interests against the state.

This has a twofold import. It can create permanent institutions for sustaining the intellectual–worker alliance and the existence of autonomous working-class institutions completely transform the nature of the post-war order in Eastern Europe. The articulation of an interest separate from and opposed to that of the party satisfies the demand on the part of society for a role in decision making for which the existing order elsewhere in Eastern Europe does not and cannot make provision. This is the long-term significance of Solidarity for the rest of Eastern Europe. It demonstrates that the leading role of the party is not a *conditio sine qua non* for stability and that − still assuming a successful outcome to the Polish crisis − Communist party rule can be reconciled with forms of social autonomy. The implication of this is that other East European societies will be able to look to the Polish example should local circumstances seem propitious.

In other words, the three aspects of the Polish events regarded as potentially relevant are interlocking and mutually interdependent and, furthermore, they are unlikely to be reproduced in exactly the same fashion anywhere else. In broad terms, therefore, Poland is more likely to be a source of encouragement than a specific model of development to be copied. The immediate impact of the accommodation between party and society is limited, but in the longer term the Polish experiences could serve as a source of ideas for other East European societies seeking a wider role than that allowed by democratic centralism.

Notes and References

1 *Pravda*, 22 August 1981.
2 A. Brown and J. Gray (eds), *Political Culture and Political Change in Communist States*, London, Macmillan, 1977.
3 Bill Lomax, *Hungary 1956*, London, Allison and Busby, 1976.
4 David Childs, *East Germany*, London, Ernest Benn, 1969.
5 See Milan Šimečka, *Le Retablissement de l'ordre*, Paris, Maspero, 1979. My own views are set out at greater length in 'The Political Structure of Eastern Europe as a Factor in Intra-bloc Relations', in K. Dawisha and P. Hanson (eds), *Soviet-East European Dilemmas: Coercion, Competition, and Consent*, London, Heinemann/ RIIA, 1981.
6 Witold Wirpsza, *Pole, wer bist du?*, Luzern, C.J. Bucher, 1971.
7 Hans Heigert, 'Polens deutsche Nachbarn', *Süddeutsche Zeitung*, 28–9 March 1981.
8 See Michael Vale (ed.), *Poland: the State of the Republic*, London, Pluto, 1981.
9 Ypsilon, in *Listý* (Rome), No. 2, 1981.

3   The Response of the Polish Communist Leadership to the Continuing Crisis (Summer 1980 to the Ninth Congress, July 1981); Personnel and Policy Change*

GEORGE SANFORD

1. Crisis Management and Leadership Conflict

The year between the near-revolution of the summer of 1980 and the holding of its Extraordinary Ninth Congress in mid-July 1981 was undoubtedly the most terrible year since the establishment of Communism in Poland for the leadership and supporting elites of the PZPR (Polish United Workers' Party). There has always been greater tension between State and society in Poland than in most other Eastern European systems where Communism has been able to establish itself more successfully. The underlying historical, political, cultural, and geopolitical reasons which caused Poland's idiosyncratic post-war development have been discussed elsewhere.[1] In this chapter I am not concerned directly with the reasons why Polish society, again, seemed to slip out of the control of the Communist State in August 1981. My primary interest will be to show how the official inquest on, and diagnosis of, the causes of the crisis proved a crucial element in producing the political programme for overcoming it.

The confrontation with the Baltic seacoast workers and the concession of the Gdańsk, Szczecin and Jastrzębie Agreements stunned the PZPR leadership. The party's organization and membership momentarily trembled on the brink of dissolution. With the emergence of Solidarity, as yet another formidable counter-force to the PZPR, alongside the Roman Catholic Church and the independent landowning peasants, many observers even considered that a state of 'dual-power' developed.

As crisis followed crisis and confrontation followed confrontation the

* This chapter is based on the following sources but limitations of space necessitates that direct citation be kept to a minimum: Official PZPR (*Trybuna Ludu, Nowe Drogi*); general Polish (*Polityka, Kultura, Rzeczywistość, Solidarność, Państwo i Prawo, Sprawy Międzynarodowe*); official Polish state bulletins (*Monitor Polski, Dziennik Ustaw, Sprawozdanie Stenograficzne Sejmu*); emigré Polish (*Kultura* of Paris and *Dziennik Polski* of London); and Western press (*Le Monde, Financial Times, Observer, Le Point*).

Communist leaders must have asked themselves whether there was any alternative to accepting the political bankruptcy of Communism in Poland. And yet the re-assertion of Communist power by brute force had been rejected by the majority of Polish Communists in October 1956, December 1970, June 1976 and as recently as late August 1980. In practice this would have meant relying on Soviet military and security-police assistance which was not as automatically forthcoming as is often presumed in the West. For various reasons the domestic sources of potential repression, especially the Polish Army, seemed both insufficient and unreliable. Did the Polish Communist leadership therefore have any other desire than to muddle through and to survive in a hand to mouth fashion from one crisis to the next? I aim to show how the top level of post-Gierek Communist leadership developed a very patient, long-term and sophisticated strategy for stabilizing, and then overcoming, the crisis by purely political methods. This strategy, and the analysis of the causes of the crisis, was outlined in general terms by Kania at the PZPR Sixth Plenum in early October. It became more radical as in order to remove Gierek's leadership elite and to rebuild a new PZPR Kania was forced to accept grass-roots' demands for the party's internal democratization. His great historical achievement, whatever the outcome of future events, was to prevent the old guard and Soviet threats from sabotaging this policy. His refusal to be provoked away from the peaceful resolution, on a one-off basis, of all the great political and social crises of September 1980 to summer 1981 undoubtedly preserved the Polish people from a national catastrophe in that period and achieved the socialist renewal of the PZPR.

The power-struggle that centred around the Polish Question after August 1980 may be regarded as a triangular one. Although neither the Soviet nor the domestic PZPR leaderships were monolithic in character, neither was Polish society. The reality of the threat of Soviet military intervention remains unclear but the evidence suggests that Soviet political pressure and Red Army manoeuvres were largely tactical in character in this period; their aim was to overawe Solidarity and the party reformists and to prod the party leaders into the appropriate responses. In my view Soviet intervention, precisely because it was an ever present possibility, paradoxically ceased to have much effect on Polish society, and on its self-defence organizations, in any particular crisis. Arcane Soviet links with, and pressure on, the domestic PZPR leaders were a totally different dimension. Their significance can only be hinted at now, given the present state of our knowledge. Soviet forbearance, however, suggests that Brezhnev and Kania were in close consultation, and probably general agreement, on the long-term strategy for overcoming the crisis by political means. This naturally does not rule out significant differences over tactical details and timing such as appeared over the CPSU letter of June 1981.

The nub of Poland's so-called 'self-limiting' revolution was that Polish society regained its autonomy, and the PZPR although humiliated and in many respects rendered impotent, was not overthrown, nor was the general principle of its rule challenged. The Polish Communist rulers after 1980 faced three sets of distinct, and yet inter-related problems. Firstly, how was the party's leading-role to be rebuilt as Polish society, especially the crucial working class, had escaped out of its control? Secondly, how was the demoralized PZPR, which faced a fundamental split between its leaders and disillusioned membership, to be reconstituted as the agent of a rejuvenated Communist hegemony? Thirdly, how could the party–State and economy be decentralized in order to allow the social activity which many hoped would solve the country's grave economic and social problems?

The key to resolving the above dilemmas was the theory that the 1980 crises had been caused primarily by the Gierek leadership's faulty and authoritarian decision-making processes and by the over-ostentatious personal corruption of its cadres which aggravated the social backlash. Gierek's officials, at every level, were therefore to be scrutinized and to be replaced by newer and uncompromised individuals. The replacement of the elite and the democratization of Polish life were prescribed as methods for salvaging the PZPR and for closing the gap between it and society. A more balanced democratic as well as centralist system would thus develop.

Leadership changes and purges of party membership are often resorted to by Communist systems, normally after the demise of a First Party Secretary, so as to allow the new leaders to build up their political clienteles and to introduce the policies which the old guard had blocked in order to maintain stability and their positions. Two strategies for the remobilization of the PZPR now competed together. The first, understandably favoured by incumbent PZPR officials, was to emulate Husak's fierce post-Soviet invasion purge of the Czechoslovak Communist Party's unreliable membership, and failed, if only because the Kremlin was reluctant to commit itself straightaway to the horrendous risks and costs involved. After some wavering in the autumn, Poland took on a directly opposite course. Leadership change, fuelled by PZPR grass-roots and popular demands for democratization and the 'settlement of accounts' with the Gierek period, became a key method of crisis-stabilization and caused the replacement of almost the entire central and provincial PZPR leadership and widespread elite-change in all walks of life except the army and police. Some continuity and a guarantee of the essentials of Communism for the USSR was provided by the retention in the top posts of Kania, Barcikowski, Jaruzelski, Olszowski, Jagielski and Jabłoński. The condemned class of Gierek officials however refused to accept their blandishments and to commit political suicide quickly and quietly. This obstructed and retarded reform and in spring 1981 Kania was forced to base his rule on the polar forces of the army and the very differentiated stratum of newly promoted PZPR activists. The manoeuvrings of Kania and his supporters however, enabled the PZPR to renew its unity and legitimacy to some extent and to survive the first, year-long, stage of the crisis.

2. Personnel and Policy Change and the Struggle for the Renewal of the PZPR

The period from August 1980 to the Ninth Congress in mid-July 1981 was crammed full of dramatic crises, confrontation and alarums. One can discern the following main periods of political history:

  (i) August to early October saw the fall and removal of Gierek and his immediately compromised associates who were replaced by what I term Gierek's 'pall-bearers'. The PZPR elite, still reeling from the shock of its capitulation in August, only began to pull itself together at the October Plenum.
 (ii) October to mid-December saw the first stage of the intra-party struggle between those who, like Kania, were convinced of the necessity of of accepting and implementing the Gdańsk and associated agreements, and hardliners who attempted to hold up, if not sabotage, the process.
(iii) The fall of the more compromised hardliners at the Seventh Plenum in early December did not end the obstruction of the promised reforms and the hindering of co-existence with Solidarity by the residual party–State old guard until after the Bydgoszcz events and the Ninth Plenum in late March. Simultaneously, the debate over the party statute, programme and electoral rules reflected the rise of more reformist, pro-Solidarity inclined elements within the PZPR.
(iv) In the last phase, from April onwards, the hardliners were swept away by the secret and democratically contested voting procedures for Congress delegates and for the PZPR provincial and lower-level executives. Kania, Barcikowski and Premier Jaruzelski survived the last fling attempts by the hardliners and their Soviet patrons to replace them at the Tenth and Eleventh Plena and to postpone the Congress. The victory of Kania's, now more radical, centrism, was assured at the

Ninth Congress on 14–20 July 1981, by the rejection of both hardline and radical wings in the voting to the Central Committee and by the election of a new and politically virgin Politburo.

(a) The Factions and Reform

After Gdańsk the more intelligent and realistic Polish Communists realised that a prerequisite for stabilizing the situation was a PZPR leadership which could convince society of its reforming intentions and capacities. The two aspects of leadership, personnel and policy-programme, were linked but not entirely so, as the October Plenum reform-line was accepted verbally by almost the entire PZPR. A period of intense in-fighting then commenced as the Communist leaders, at every level, manoeuvred to evade responsibility for their actions in the 1970s and attempted to catch the new currents. The Communist *sauve-qui-peut* of late 1980 was initially more individualistic in character than the earlier PZPR factional conflicts of the late 1940s, 1956, and the 1960s, although basic policy divisions later on caused more distinct groupings to coalesce.[2] One can also do no more than touch on the very fluid relationship between political labels such as 'reformer' or 'hardliner' borrowed from bourgeois-democratic usage and often indiscriminately and misleadingly applied by Western journalists, and the behaviour of Communist politicians especially of such chameleons as Olszowski or Werblan.

Kania at first played a quiet, unassuming, back-seat role. The leadership was very 'collective' in character right up until the Ninth Congress although the influence of different individuals waxed and waned over time. The post-August leadership had to regain the confidence of Polish society and of the disillusioned PZPR grass roots. Almost a third of the latter joined Solidarity, not in order to take it over, but to better express their demands for reform and democratization. Kania also had, at the same time, to convince the Soviet leadership and their hardline allies, Czechoslovakia and East Germany, that Communism had survived in Poland and that it could be rebuilt on a new basis.

The main initial problem was, however, one of personnel and personalities. The Fourth to Sixth Plena in August to October merely cleared out Gierek's inner leadership team. Power passed into the hands of figures who had built their careers under Gierek but who were just a notch outside his magic circle. Figures such as Żabiński, Wojtaszek, Waszczuk and Pińkowski and even the intra-elite critics such as Olszowski, Grabski and Tejchma were called derisively the pall-bearers (*pogrobowcy*) of the Gierek regime. They now declared their support for the reform-line but the problem was that their political pasts paralysed the implementation of the reforms and maintained old attitudes towards Solidarity and the post-August realities. Their attempts to prevent or redefine the registration of Solidarity led to a protracted and serious confrontation in October and November and to their eventual humiliation. Other attempts to reassert their authority such as the arrest of two Solidarity printers in Warsaw or the harassment of Solidarity in Częstochowa in late November likewise provoked conflict, confrontation and then defeat for the authorities. The attempt to stabilize the situation on the basis of limited, but by no means negligible, leadership change and to define the limits of reform from above, between September 1980 and the Ninth Plenum in late March 1981 therefore failed. It opened up the way in spring to summer 1981 for the humiliation and almost complete replacement of Gierek's political class. Nevertheless the postponement of the Ninth Congress initially from December until March/April and finally mid-July 1981 meant that the sympathizers of the Gierek Central Committee elected at the February 1980 Eighth Congress prolonged the crisis for many months and remained unnecessarily long as a brake on the credibility of the Communist reformers.

Turning to the analysis of the crisis the proponents of decentralization now argued that the crisis stemmed from much more than just the mistakes of incompetent, corrupt and megalomaniac leaders.[3] The faulty political and economic mechanisms had allowed the manipulation of events and processes, the stifling of discussion and criticism and a slanted presentation of events, which was condemned as the 'propaganda of success'.[4] The top decisions were often taken in an unprepared and voluntaristic manner and were monopolized by Gierek and his small team of lieutenants.[5] The problem now was to renew social confidence in Communist leadership and to provide the necessary institutional guarantees against a renewal of the previous pattern of reform promises followed by political degeneration.

The best guarantee for the democratization of Polish public life would be that of the PZPR itself, as symbolized by its wholesale acceptance of the free, contested and secret election of party delegates and officials by party members between May to July 1981 and not their *de facto* nomination by the party officials as in the past. In this way the crisis would be stabilized and contained and the PZPR would gain a new legitimacy which would enable it thereafter to define the new limits of what was to be considered politically acceptable in Poland. The leadership would then be capable of assimilating the more moderate and economic-minded Wałęsa wing of Solidarity into the transformed political system, while isolating the 'political' and 'KOR' (Workers Defence Committee) elements in the free trade unions. Just as Church–State or regime–intellectual confrontations had been contained within the 1956–80 framework so now confrontations with trade unions and social organizations would be managed within a reformed Communist party political hegemony. This would be accepted by the Soviet leadership as a vastly preferable alternative to continuing chaos and crisis or a national uprising and the sweeping away of all bar 'panzer-Communism' in Poland. Future developments might also allow the clawing back of the 1980 concessions. Ideologically the workers' revolt could be justified as a return to the party's proletarian roots and as a reaction against Gierek's more national-patriotic and elitist-technocratic postures. The dangers were, of course, that the PZPR might be paralysed by its internal divisions, the old Central Committee might sabotage the democratization movement, even provoke a Soviet invasion in order to save itself, or alternatively the grass-roots democratic move-ment might really capture and control the Politburo, Secretariat and Central Committee.

Kania and his few close personal advisers, such as the politics professor Jerzy Wiatr, must have mulled over such possibilities from September onwards. In the event Kania managed to maintain balance between the factions from the outbreak of the crisis right up to the Congress. He resolved the confrontations on an *ad hoc* basis and removed Gierek's political class from the scene without provoking either a domestic counter-revolution, or a Soviet invasion or a Solidarity-led uprising. By July 1981 Kania's new political consensus within the party seemed to confirm the view that one should not neglect 'the proven capacity of a First Party Secretary, given time, to gain control gradually of the various levels of power in the Party and State'[6] although the new mechanisms appeared to make him barely a *primus inter pares*.

(b) The Purge of Gierek's Supporters

I now wish to concentrate on the purge of Gierek's leadership personnel and the functional use of the scapegoating of the old elite to legitimize the new leadership and to stabilize the crisis. The period between the Fourth Plenum on 24 August 1980 and the Ninth Congress in July 1981 saw one of the most extensive and wide-ranging turnovers of leading personnel at all levels and in all walks of public life which any Communist state has ever undergone.

The key to understanding these developments is that the PZPR hoped that it would be allowed to reconstitute its leading role over Polish society if the following two conditions had been achieved before the Ninth Congress.

(i) There would have to be a genuine *rozliczenie* or settlement of accounts with the Gierek period. In practice this meant that a sufficiently large number of individuals in directing positions in the later Gierek period would have to be replaced in order that the new authorities should appear uncompromised and capable of starting out with a clean slate.

(ii) The PZPR would have to democratize itself in order to carry out the above, to motivate its grass-roots membership and the working-class core and to provide institutional guarantees against the reversion to more orthodox Soviet practices.

The above process took almost a year to achieve as Kania had to maintain the continuity of the PZPR as well as to transform it. It was also not inevitable that he would win out against the opposition of the condemned Gierek official class and the doubts of the Soviet leadership.

The changes at the very top were initially the most dramatic and the most rapidly executed. Only seven out of the nineteen members of the Politburo, and one out of the Secretariat of eight, elected by the Eighth Congress in February 1980, remained at the end of 1980. A mere five of these original members of Gierek's Politburo (Barcikowski, Jaruzelski, Kania, Jabłoński and Jagielski) survived until the Ninth Congress and only the first three were re-elected to the Politburo there (see Tables 3.1 and 3.2). The Ninth Congress re-elected only eighteen of the outgoing Central Committee to be full members in the new one and maintained another five, all army officers, as candidates. Over 90 per cent were therefore newcomers. Between September 1980 and July 1981 almost all of the forty-nine provincial First Party Secretaries were changed, in some instances twice. Only Fiszbach in Gdańsk, Kruk in Lublin and Dąbrowa in Kraków survived as major regional party bosses, although important roles were played by the new appointees (Żabiński in Katowice, Czechowicz in Łódź, Kociołek in Warsaw and Opałko in Tarnów). Paradoxically, for reasons explained by Kolankiewicz in Chapter 4 of this book only 10 per cent of the PZPR membership left in this period so the change in the party was a qualitative one in terms of leaders, internal processes and attitudes rather than a quantitative one.

The extent and pace of the leadership changes affected all walks of Polish life and can only be touched on here. Given the problem of finding trustworthy and experienced, as well as not-too-compromised cadres, a vast rotation around as well as turnover of ministers, deputy-ministers, and chairmen of State-agencies had taken place by July. The Council of Ministers changed its character in no less than six major reshuffles, some posts such as the Chairmanship of the Planning Commission, changing

Table 3.1 The PZPR Politburo and Secretariat

1. Elected by the Eighth Congress, 11–15 February 1980.	2. Elected by the Extraordinary Ninth Congress, 14–20 July 1981.

(a) The Politburo

Full Members	*Full Members*
Edward Gierek	Stanisław Kania
Edward Babiuch	Kazimierz Barcikowski (186)
Zdzisław Grudzień	Tadeusz Czechowicz (170)
Henryk Jabłoński	Józef Czyrek (187)
Mieczysław Jagielski	Zofia Grzyb (177)
Wojciech Jaruzelski	Wojciech Jaruzelski (189)
Stanisław Kania	Hieronim Kubiak (150)
Alojzy Karkoszka	Jan Łabęcki (162)
Stanisław Kowalczyk	Zbigniew Messner (176)
Władysław Kruczek	Mirosław Milewski (167)
Jerzy Łukasiewicz	Stefan Olszowski (186)
Jan Szydlak	Stanisław Opałko (168)
Andrzej Werblan	Tadeusz Porębski (170)
Tadeusz Wrzaszczyk	Jerzy Romanik (166)
	Albin Siwak (133)

Candidate Members	*Candidate Members*
Kazimierz Barcikowski	Jan Główczyk (151)
Józef Pińkowski	Włodzimierz Mokrzyszczak (126)
Tadeusz Pyka	
Emil Wojtaszek	
Zdzisław Żandarowski	

(b) The Secretariat

First Secretary: Edward Gierek	Stanisław Kania (defeated Barcikowski by 1,311 votes to 568; 60 voters crossed off both names)
	Kazimierz Barcikowski (187)
Stanisław Kania	Józef Czyrek (189)
Jerzy Łukasiewicz	Hieronim Kubiak (164)
Józef Pińkowski	Zbigniew Michałek (183)
Jerzy Waszczuk	Mirosław Milewski (178)
Andrzej Werblan	Stefan Olszowski (187)
Andrzej Żabiński	Marian Woźniak (178)
Zdzisław Żandarowski	

Members of Secretariat

Zdzisław Kurowski
Zbigniew Zieliński

Numbers in brackets denote votes received out of a maximum 191 for full Politburo members and 192 for candidates and Secretariat members. Not elected: for Politburo members – Mieczysław Maksymowicz (42), Kazimierz Miniur (57), Józef Mitak (45), Stefan Paterek (35); for Politburo candidates – Stanisław Kałkus (46), Jadwiga Nowakowska (49).

Table 3.2 Main Leadership Changes in the PZPR (August 1980–July 1981)

Politburo
(Outgoing members in brackets, * = Candidate Members)

24/8/80	Fourth Plenum:	Stefan Olszowski, Józef Pińkowski, Jerzy Waszczuk*, Andrzej Zabiński* (Edward Babiuch, Jerzy Łukaszewicz, Jan Szydlak, Tadeusz Wrzaszczyk, Tadeusz Pyka*, Zdzisław Żandarowski)*
6/9/80	Sixth Plenum:	First Secretary: Stanisław Kania (Edward Gierek) Kazimierz Barcikowski, Andrzej Żabiński
5/10/80	Sixth Plenum: (continued):	(Zdzisław Grudzień), Władysław Kruk*, Roman Ney*
2/12/80	Seventh Plenum:	Tadeusz Grabski, Mieczysław Moczar, Tadeusz Fiszbach*, (Władysław Kruczek, Alojzy Karkoszka, Stanisław Kowalczyk, Andrzej Werblan)
30/4/80	Tenth Plenum:	Zygmunt Wroński (110 votes, out of 123 cast), Gerard Gabryś (111 votes); (Józef Pińkowski), Józef Masny* (107 votes); (Emil Wojtaszek)

Secretariat

24/8/80	Fourth Plenum:	Stefan Olszowski, Emil Wojtaszek (Łukasiewicz, Pińkowski, Żandarowski)
6/9/80	Sixth Plenum:	Tadeusz Grabski, Zdzisław Kurowski, Jerzy Wojtecki
5/10/80	Sixth Plenum: (continued):	Kazimierz Barcikowski (Żabiński). Member of Secretariat Stanisław Gabrielski
2/12/80	Seventh Plenum:	Roman Ney (Andrzej Werblan)
30/4/80	Tenth Plenum:	Kazimierz Cypryniak (87 votes); (Emil Wojtaszek, Jerzy Wojtecki, Zbigniew Zieliński)

Central Committee

The Fourth Plenum co-opted Grabski. The October Plenum dismissed ten members and appointed twenty-three new ones (including Gabrielski, Masny, Ney, Opałko, Romanik and Siwak). The Seventh Plenum dismissed Gierek and two others and the Eighth Plenum another eight.

---

hands twice. Between August 1980 and July 1981 there had been almost fifty ministerial changes including a major, but somewhat botched up, amalgamation of industrial ministries in June. Over half the provincial Governors (twenty-six) and their deputies had gone as had innumerable chairmen of subsidiary political parties, co-operatives and other apparats such as the Youth Movement. University and polytechnic rectors were now being elected by their Senates in genuine and contested elections. People's Councils took on a new life while the ferment in the factories and trade unions is a subject in its own right.

Intra-party struggles are normally difficult to document but the remarkably frank discussion at the Fourth to Twelfth Plena enables us to identify the various stages by which the foregoing leadership transformation was achieved.[7]

Gierek's Politburo team were cleared out at the Fourth Plenum on 24 August as his promises of economic concessions and the implied threat of police-repression (or even Soviet intervention) failed to defuse the industrial unrest which culminated in the Baltic seacoast factory occupations. His major critic Olszowski returned to the Politburo and Secretariat while Pińkowski replaced Babiuch, Gierek's right-hand man as Premier. The Baltic strikers were unmoved by these sweeping personnel changes as they considered that they had been fooled by Gierek's promises in 1971. So they now held out for written agreements backed up by institutional guarantees such as the right to strike and to organize 'free and self-governing' trade unions (*Niezależne i Samorządne Związki Zawodowe*). Their conditions arguably represented the greatest humiliation which any ruling Communist party has ever accepted, after which Gierek's position became untenable. The rapidity of his replacement by Stanisław Kania at the Sixth Plenum on 5–6 September, seems in retrospect to have nothing to do with the gravity, or otherwise, of his heart attack. Kania, a Central Committee Secretary since 1971, was a quintessential apparatus man who, designated by Moscow, gained the unanimous support of the PZPR central *aktyw*. This apparently dull, but experienced and unassuming party bureaucrat, was an ideal compromise choice to guide the PZPR through the crisis.

The September Plenum limited Kania, as it did not give him a Politburo majority and promoted individuals who had merely acquiesced in his election. The deadlock was relieved slightly at the October Plenum with two rank newcomers Kruk and Ney becoming Politburo candidates, while Barcikowski became a Central Committee Secretary. The wholesale condemnation of the Gierek period at this Plenum tilted the political balance in favour of the reformers. The PZPR there recognized the need for systemic changes involving the wholesale democratization of Polish life. The corruption and expensive lifestyles of some Communist functionaries provided an obvious source of elite scapegoats, the most notorious being Maciej Szczepański who headed Polish radio and television in the 1970s and Kazimierz Tyrański, an industrial manager, who despite widespread political connections received a fifteen-year jail sentence.

The activities of the *Twardogłowi* ('hardliners') were paid for at the Seventh Plenum. Discredited Politburo figures were replaced by Moczar, Grabski and Tadeusz Fiszbach, the First Party Secretary in Gdańsk who had gained the strikers' confidence and who emerged as a major reform-spokesman. This party-personnel strand up to the end of 1980, can be rounded off by noting the following developments. Firstly, the October Plenum unprecedentedly appointed twenty-three new Central Committee members to replace the ten Gierek lieutenants and compromised officials dismissed at the same time. Gierek was suspended but not dismissed from the Central Committee until the Seventh Plenum, while ex-Premier Jaroszewicz, who had been dropped at the Eighth Congress, was dealt with now in far harsher terms than Gierek. Secondly, Kania reshuffled the Heads of the crucial Central Committee Departments, appointing Józef Klasa to Press, Radio and Television. Thirdly, twenty-two of the provincial PZPR First Party Secretaries were replaced by the end of 1980. Lastly, the Central Party Apparatus decentralized the nomination of the Chairman of the provincial People's Council to local pressures quickly and without fuss. These posts were now separated from that of the First Secretary and contested in secret elections which proved a precursor of the 'free-elections' of 1981.

Although many individuals dropped out for good, public opinion was struck by the extent to which office-holders were being rotated around according to what became colloquially known as the leadership 'carousel'. The participants in the process, however, felt that it was more like riding an unsafe and heady rollercoaster without a definite stopping-point. Among the conflicting trends in the earliest appointments the most significant was the political comeback of individuals associated with Gierek's initial reform period up to about the First National PZPR Conference in 1973. Some had been shunted off to diplomatic posts like Kociołek to Belgium, Klasa to Mexico and Olszowski to East Germany, but what was normally the last stop before the Communist political graveyard now proved to be a resting place for a return to power. However, the mere moving up one step by officials who were next in line, such as the Żabińskis and Wojtaszeks of Polish political life, was widely regarded as irrelevant.

The Seventh Plenum appointed a 218 strong Congress Commission, whose presidium set to work under Olszowski's chairmanship but the Congress itself was only vaguely scheduled for March/April 1981. December, marked by the unveiling of the Gdańsk monument to the 1970 victims, was fairly quiet but January to March then witnessed the outbreak of strikes, factory and office occupations, and widespread social unrest all over Poland on a far larger scale than that of summer 1980, as well as potentially explosive confrontations between Solidarity and the Government. These developments undermined Kania's moderate reform-consensus achieved in tandem with Moczar and Olszowski at the Seventh Plenum. Kania's efforts were undercut by the inertia of the party middle-rank apparats and by the provocative activities of the residual hardliners who now attempted to reassert the PZPR's power and prestige. On the other hand more radical and pro-Solidarity inclined elements within the PZPR began to organize themselves and to present their demands more forcibly at provincial, factory and cell level and within the Congress Commission. Their pressure, the gravity of the social crisis and the cold shudder of fear and anger which ran through Poland after the beating up of three Solidarity activists in Bydgoszcz, finally inclined the battered PZPR leadership to take another, but this time more fundamental, lurch towards reform and the implementation of democratization at its Ninth Plenum on 29 March 1981.

The Polish 'Hot January' of 1981 saw direct social action over a wide variety of issues. The attack, as in the case of the Rzeszów peasants, was usually two-pronged, a local or professional issue being coupled with indignant attacks on the corruption and privileges of Gierek's elite. The striking workers who occupied factories and municipal and other offices, most notably in Nowy Sącz, Zielona Góra, Wrocław, Łódź and Jelenia Góra were mollified by local agreements covering the handing-over of offices, including party and police ones, for social use such as housing, schools and hospitals, the dismissal of unpopular officials and compromise packages over the economic issues.[8] The biggest regional crisis was in Bielsko-Biała where about a quarter of a million workers in 400 factories went on strike. The local issues were however overshadowed by a national confrontation between Solidarity and the Government over the issue of 'free Saturdays', which had been conceded in the Gdańsk Agreement. Although the Government, headed by Pińkowski and Jagielski, had economic rationality on their side, their inept handling of the matter caused the maximum of acrimony, which forced them to collapse again after long negotiations with Wałęsa on 1 February. It was also agreed that Solidarity should publish its weekly newspaper and have regular access to the mass-media.

The hardliners, as well as becoming the targets of public hatred, also had to face attacks from within the PZPR, and not only from its reform-wing. The ex-Partisans latched on to the popular call for the settlement of accounts in order to refurbish their political image and to compete under the new conditions. Moczar expressed the representative view that all the officials who were responsible for the crisis and who did not accept 'the great revolution, as well as the new views, ideals and activities of the great mass of the people' would have to resign their positions in order to avoid more social outbursts.[9] On the other hand if the aim of the reported

Olszowki-Grabski-Pińkowski hardline offensive in January had been to gain Soviet and PZPR apparat support by demonstrating that Kania's conciliatoriness was weakness, it rebounded on them in the masterstroke of Jaruzelski's appointment as Premier. The regime's climbdown after that enabled Solidarity, which had been accused by Kania of aspiring to become a political opposition, to start forging a new institutionalized relationship with the Communist state. Wałęsa and his moderate, more economic wing began to act as social 'firemen' in resolving political and economic disputes and in mediating the return to work.

(c) Balancing Between the Extremes; the Army Saves the Day

The Eighth Plenum decided to replace Pińkowski as Premier by General Wojciech Jaruzelski who remained as Minister of Defence. His appointment was designed to reassure the Soviets, to raise the authority of the Government in dealing with social conflicts and the economic crisis, and to suggest that the right man was now in the right place if force was required. The support of Jaruzelski, and of the army, which he had kept scrupulously neutral since 1968 in all the PZPR factional disputes, was also designed to circumvent party apparat opposition to Kania's and Moczar's desire to continue the purge of directing-personnel.

The party attacks on radical and political activists within Solidarity (such as KOR) began at the Seventh Plenum and were repeated more sharply by the ever aggressive Grabski in the Politburo Report to the Eighth Plenum. The political line of division, he claimed, was not between the PZPR and Solidarity but ran within Solidarity itself. He called on all PZPR members to rebuff attempts to turn the free trade unions into political forces. The Plenum was dominated by discussion of the continuing social conflicts, what the PZPR policy should be towards Solidarity, and the official branch unions and Moczar's earlier call for the dismissal of Gierek's officials who were sabotaging Kania's policy. The fluid state of the party reflected in its final resolution was symbolized by the exchange between the Gdańsk shipyard worker, Jan Łabęcki, who defended the policy of dialogue and Zygmunt Wroński from Ursus who demanded a strong party counter-attack.

Jaruzelski moved the bid for compromise on by calling in the Sejm on 12 February for a ninety-day moratorium on strikes, by promising a social dialogue and collaboration with the Church and by appointing Mieczysław F. Rakowski (Editor of *Polityka* since 1958) as a Deputy-Premier heading a new committee of the Council of Ministers for co-operation with the trade unions and Solidarity in particular.[10] Control of this hot seat was to prove crucial for the reformers in the coming months. Rakowski's positive role, stressing the need to collaborate with Solidarity and the new social forces soon made itself felt.[11]

Yet Kania did not only need to secure support at home so he had already assured the Twenty-sixth CPSU Congress in Moscow that the PZPR would be able to resolve its problems by political means on its own. Despite criticism at the Congress he apparently succeeded in persuading his hosts that he still controlled events. On his return to Warsaw he received increasingly strong demands from the other end of the political spectrum for new electoral rules which would allow the secret and democratic election of PZPR officials at every level. That the domestic situation was potentially explosive was shown by the immediate and strong public reaction to even minor matters such as the Łódź hospital dispute, while major demands such as those of the Radom workers for the punishment of officials responsible for the 1976 repression caused even more furore.[12] The situation reached a crisis with the beating up of Rulewski and his two colleagues in Bydgoszcz on 20 March. Although the run-up to these events was described in incredible detail subsequently, one can only presume that the police acted on the orders of a section of the highest level of the apparat, which were transmitted to them by Mach, the Deputy-Premier on the spot. The party authorities, despite incredibly heavy pressure, have stubbornly refused to reveal who was responsible, which suggests that there might have been more of a division of labour between alleged hardliners and conciliators in the Politburo than is often supposed. The threat of a national strike was barely averted by long and arduous negotiations between Rakowski and Wałęsa, which produced an agreement on 30 March. The same day Stefan Bratkowski, the Chairman of the Association of Polish Journalists, circulated an Open Letter to the Party, attacking the conflict-ridden approach of the hardliners. He declared that Bydgoszcz constituted 'the last chance crisis for those who wanted to turn back our party from the road of social understanding and to guide our state in this manner on to the path of an unavoidable catastrophe.'[13]

It is unclear whether Olszowski, Grabski and the ambiguous Ney really attempted to overthrow Kania at the Ninth Plenum on 30 March by the highly original expedient of submitting their resignations. It is more likely that they wanted to strengthen their positions or even that they were ordered by the Politburo majority to divert attention in this way. The Central Committee, however, glossed over any factional conflict by voting confidence in the entire leadership and the resignations were withdrawn. Although personnel questions were not resolved crucial policy decisions were taken at this Plenum. Firstly, it was decided to hold the Ninth Congress by 20 July and that delegates to it should be elected in a vigorous election-report campaign according to revised rules, which had been fought over bitterly since December. Secondly, the policy-line of dialogue was confirmed in the final resolution, which opened the way to agreement over Bydgoszcz. Thirdly, Barcikowski diagnosed the main cause of the 1980 outburst as lying in 'the inadequacy of intra-party democracy, of rank and file criticism and control, in distortions in the system of electing the leadership and a faulty cadres policy'. His report marked a watershed in the Kania leadership's conversion to democratization and it was a crucial guide to its aims in preparing the Ninth Congress. Its political significance was that the opposition of the Communist Ultras had pushed the more realistic and far-sighted leaders on from moderate reform aims to far more radical paths.

Kania and his supporters had thus succeeded in out-manoeuvring the hardliners but the reactivization of the grass roots and the spread of horizontal structures within the PZPR meant that Poland's allies now had to be reassured. Leaving the heady atmosphere of the Ninth Plenum, Olszowski led the PZPR delegation to the Sixteenth Congress of the Czechoslovak Communist Party in Prague, where things were still done in the proper Soviet manner. Western press reports that the Soviet leadership was opposed to, and at the very least wanted to brake, the democratization movement in Poland and that the much, and wrongly, maligned Olszowski, had offered his services as an alternative hardline leader are unsubstantiated.[14] Brezhnev, as was his wont, expressed his confidence that the PZPR would defeat the enemies of socialism and overcome their difficulties.

Brezhnev's confidence was reinforced when Barcikowski soon afterwards assured the SED Congress in East Berlin that the PZPR 'was and would remain the leading force in the Polish state'. This was no idle boast, but within limits, a statement of fact. The Kremlin, in my view, all postures to the contrary, were convinced by Kania that the strategy of Socialist Renewal and the peaceful resolution of conflicts would allow the survival of Communism in Poland at the cheapest cost to themselves. On the other hand they certainly wanted guarantees that the process would not get out of hand and their demands caused Kania many domestic difficulties. Suslov flew to Warsaw on 23 April to check the situation but, although the USSR continued to attack revisionist and anti-socialist elements in Poland, the exercise assumed a largely tactical and modest character.

(d) A Disciplined Democratization? Preparing for the Ninth Congress

That Kania, although he had moved to the left, was still balancing in the new centre, was confirmed at the Tenth Plenum on 29–30 April by attacks by conservatives such as Putrament and Siwak on his leadership for con-ceding too much, and by reformers for not carrying through democratization quickly and fully enough. Kania's keynote theme was that now that it had been decided to hold the Congress between 14–18 July, unity and dis-cipline were essential if the PZPR was to exercise its leading role success-fully in the democratization process. The leadership changes at this Plenum were, however, nowhere as significant as expected but the resignation of discredited officials swung the balance in Kania's favour in the Politburo and Secretariat. Their replacements were voted on by the Central Com-mittee for the first time since the Eighth Plenum in October 1956 (see Table 3.2).

The explosive and deteriorating political atmosphere in Poland worsened further in May and June with the frequent daubings of Soviet war memorials, the aggravation of the food and other shortages, and with outbursts of violence such as the burning of Otwock police-station near Warsaw. Above all the great sadness and emotion aroused by the death of Cardinal Stefan Wyszyński, the Primate of Poland since 1948, and by the attempt to assas-sinate the Pope, Wojtyła, a fortnight earlier in mid-May, must have acted as a cold douche to the unrealistic hopes generated the previous summer.

Although the run-up to the Congress was dominated by the reformers the hardline and nationalist elements within the PZPR also made last ditch efforts to organize themselves.[15] Soviet concern over Polish develop-ments, expressed in the strongly worded CPSU letter of 5 June to the PZPR Central Committee, provoked the unexpected holding of the Eleventh Plenum on 9–10 June.[16] The letter attacked counter-revolutionary elements within Solidarity and the growing wave of anti-Communism and anti-Sovietism in Poland. It claimed that the class-enemy had gained control of the mass media and that the election campaign to the Congress was being dominated by revisionists and counter-revolutionaries, but called on all the healthy forces in the party and society to rally together to defend the socialist order. Was the letter a call to the PZPR Central Committee to replace Kania by a more reliable hardliner? Or was it a Machiavellian ploy designed to strengthen Kania by bringing the opposition to him out into the open, thus demonstrating the futility of this hardline swansong?

Whatever the truth, the PZPR Central Committee knew that the over-whelming majority of its members would not be re-elected at the forth-coming Congress, but more than their mere positions was at stake. Kania set the tone for the Plenum by declaring that the Socialist Renewal would continue but that the party would now take a stronger line against counter-revolutionary and anti-Soviet forces. Olszowski remained silent, probably as a result of a deal with Kania which ensured his longer-term political survival. He left the main attack on the leadership to Tadeusz Grabski who, supported by Olszewski, the ambassador to Moscow, accepted the validity of the Soviet charges. Grabski attacked the slide from one compromise to the next since the Sixth Plenum and doubted whether the Politburo under Kania was capable of leading the country out of the crisis.

Interrupted by the cat-calls and desk-banging of his opponents, Rakowski however won over the Plenum; 'there is no sensible alternative to continuing the renewal, therefore we must continue it further and confirm the reforms at the July Congress'. Warm support came from Fiszbach, Barcikowski, Jaruzelski and the genuine worker representatives. As to Grabski's charges, Kania declared that he and his colleagues demanded an individual vote of confidence; anyone who received less than half the votes would resign. The Central Committee however backed down from this challenge. It decided instead to have a single vote of confidence on the Politburo as a whole, over-ruling Kania's proposal by eighty-nine to twenty-four with five abstentions. Hardline threats were thus fended off. The final resolution balanced between confirming the party's will to continue the renewal and to implement the earlier decisions concerning the Congress and the condemnation of the subversive activity of the previous weeks.

After the Tenth Plenum the provincial party organizations discussed the reports, agenda and proposed changes in the statutes prepared for the coming Congress and voted out their executives at a previously unheard-of pace. Between the middle and the end of June no less than twenty-one provincial First Party Secretaries were replaced in secret ballots on multiple candidatures. Re-elected incumbents normally also faced challenges. Two or three candidates were proposed in most cases but the number went as high as eight in Sieradz and six in Zamość.

The real struggle took place over the election of Congress delegates as the failure to get nominated meant disqualification from the future Central Committee. A mere seventy-one out of the 236 members of the old Central Committee became delegates. Moreover the outgoing Politburo and Secretariat notables faced varying degrees of difficulty in getting nominated, although sixteen eventually did so. Only Kania's personal appeal that certain hardliners should be nominated ensured Grabski's election in Konin after his rejection in Poznań and Olszowski's in Warsaw.[17] The ferment was not restricted solely to developments within the PZPR. The extent to which Polish political and intellectual life was changing at this time can be gauged by the official celebration of the twenty-fifth anniversary of the Poznań uprising in late June. Much literature appeared celebrating it as a justified workers' revolt.[18]

Besides the crucial question of delegate selection to the Ninth Congress the months of May and June were also occupied with the final 'settling of accounts' with Gierek and his officials. The PZPR leaders hoped that this would now close the question for good and allow them to move off the defensive to concentrate on managing Poland's appalling economic problems and the revised relations with society. As Grabski, the chairman of the Commission charged by the Tenth Plenum with accelerating the appraisal of responsibility, said, the process was to be completed by the Ninth Congress in order 'to free the majority of cadres from unjustified suspicions, from the psychosis of the continuous witch-hunt and to oppose determinedly the attacks and slanders on people who are fulfilling their obligations well.'[19]

Since September 1980 the party's Central Control Commission (CKKP) had set to work to cleanse the PZPR of individuals who had abused their offices for personal gain but it had also, less publicly, made great efforts to maintain internal party discipline. A string of CKKP communiqués from April 1981 onwards revealed the detail of the more glaring cases of corruption as well as the global proportions of the weeding-out process.[20] The most glaring scandals concerned the use of public resources for building, the buying of State property at artificially low prices and the taking of bribes in the allocation of flats and car-vouchers.

Grabski's fifteen-strong Commission had acted as the Communist equivalent of a Royal Commission, although it only had a few weeks and eight well-publicized sessions in which to interview the key figures of the Gierek period, to assimilate a wide range of party, NIK and academic evidence and to submit its report for confirmation by the Twelfth Plenum just prior to the Congress. Its conclusions were fairly standard ones by then but the condemnation of the Gierek leadership was unqualified and easily understood by the public. On its initiative the Congress expelled Gierek, Babiuch, Łukasiewicz, Pyka, Szydlak and Żandarowski from the party and requested the Council of State to deprive them of their offical decorations while criminal proceedings were recommended against Jaroszewicz for his economic bungling.

Grabski's Commission had enunciated three unclear and contradictory criteria for assessing responsibility. The most glaring cases of corruption were doubtless clear enough but the secondary everyday cases depended upon chance, personal factors and the protection afforded by the party apparat. Grabski summarized the *rozliczenie* process statistically as follows. The CKKP had investigated 16,014 cases, confirmed accusations in 4,990 instances and cleared the remainder. NIK, the State Control Chamber, had investigated 7,149 individuals and confirmed charges in just under half the cases causing the dismissal of 427 officials. The judicial process was however infinitely slower and the procuracy had only charged 59 individuals and carried out the preliminary investigation of 146 cases involving 285 persons by July. Grabski summed up these confusing and parallel party, State and judicial inquiries with the statement that charges had been confirmed against 12,000 individuals, 3,400 of who had been in directing positions, out of the grand total of 26,000 cases investigated.[21]

3. The Ninth PZPR Congress: The End of the Beginning of the Crisis

The Ninth Congress between 14–20 July 1981 confirmed the reform analysis of the causes of the crisis and put its imprimatur on the democratization process. The scale of the leadership renewal which it carried out after protracted procedural wrangles over nomination and ballot procedures for the Central Committee of 200 full and seventy candidate members was breath-taking as only Kania, Barcikowski, Jaruzelski, Olszowski, and another fourteen colleagues from the old Central Committee were re-elected to the new one. However the contest for First Secretary was restricted to two very similar figures and the Congress duly elected Kania by a two-to-one majority over Barcikowski. The outcome suggested that Kania and Barcikowski underwritten by Jaruzelski, had not only accepted democratization since the Ninth Plenum, but had also been quite successful in guiding, perhaps even directing, the process. They were thus able to keep both the Grabski and Fiszbach extremes off the Central Committee and, more surprisingly, to exclude Rakowski from the Politburo. The new Politburo and Secretariat members appeared somewhat second-rank as they were chosen for their experience and skills rather than as spokesmen of political tendencies (although they represented a wide enough range of post-August realities). Apart from the few major survivors of the Gierek period (Kania, Barcikowski, Jaruzelski, Olszowski), there were four obvious worker representatives (Łabęcki, Romanik, Siwak and Zofia Grzyb, the first woman ever to enter the Politburo), two apparat-representatives (Milewski, police, and Czyrek, Foreign Affairs), three academics now turned politician (Porębski, Kubiak, Messner) and the remainder were hitherto, moderately known figures (Główczyk, Editor of *Życie Gospodarcze*, Woźniak, Czechowicz) and rank newcomers (Opałko, Mokrzyszczak, Michałek).[22]

I have argued that there were two distinct yet at times, overlapping, strategies within the PZPR for overcoming the crisis. One current, voiced first by Moczar in October, aimed to appease the PZPR grass roots and Polish society and wanted to cleanse the party morally and politically, so that it could make a new start after the Ninth Congress by settling accounts with the Gierek generation both in individual and political terms. The *rozliczenie* movement became frankly demagogic when it fell into Grabski's hands in spring 1981, as he wanted to save as much of the Communist official class as possible by the draconian treatment of Gierek and his immediate associates. By doing so he hoped to undercut the real democratization drive, which shared with it a common analysis of the causes of the crisis, but which offered genuine democratic prescriptions rather than insincere slogans.

The Ninth Congress appeared, at the time, to have succeeded in renewing the PZPR in a manner acceptable to the Soviet leadership and to the bulk of its own members. It had also produced the conditions for a manageable co-existence with Solidarity, although their relationship was doomed initially to be crisis-ridden. Whether the new legitimacy gained by the institution of internal party democracy and the renewal of the political leadership, which has been described in this chapter, would enable the PZPR to reform Poland's administrative and economic structures, to overcome the economic disaster and to lead Polish society out of the crisis then became the key question of the political agenda.

Notes and References

1 Although much has been written about Poland in English the literature is somewhat uneven. Surprisingly there is, as yet, no adequate government and politics textbook. As a guide consult; R.F. Leslie (ed.), *The History of Poland since 1863*, London, CUP, 1980; G. Kolankiewicz and R. Taras, 'Poland, Socialism for Everyman' in A. Brown and J. Gray (eds), *Political Culture and Political Change in Communist States*, London, Macmillan, 1977; G. Sanford, 'The Polish People's Republic' in B. Szajkowski (ed.), *Marxist Governments; a World Survey*, London, Macmillan, 1981, Vol. 3, Ch. 20; G. Sanford, 'Polish People's Republic' in G. Walker (ed.), *Official Publications of the USSR and Eastern Europe*, London, Mansell, forthcoming).

2 On the significance of 1956 and the political framework for factionalism which then emerged see G. Sakwa, 'The Polish "October"; a Reappraisal through Historiography', *Polish Review*, 33 (1978), 62–78.

3 For an interpretation of the Communist regime's greater willingness to allow political institutions such as Sejm elections to work more freely in unsettled crisis periods and the light which this aspect throws on the periodic regime–society confrontations see G. Sakwa and M. Crouch, 'Sejm Elections in Communist Poland; an Overview and a Reappraisal', *British Journal of Political Science*. 8 (1978), 403–24.

4 See the full record of the October Sixth Plenum in *Nowe Drogi*, No. 10–11 (1980).

5 The political history of Gierek's rule is covered by G. Blazynski. *Flashpoint Poland*, London, Pergamon Press, 1979. For the most penetrating analyses of the strains of the late-1970s see the two DiP (*Doswiadczenie i Przyszłość* – Experience

and Future) reports published in English in *International Journal of Politics* (Summer–Fall 1981).

6 G. Sanford, 'Gierek's Downfall and the Response of the Polish United Workers' Party to the Social Crisis (August–December 1980)', paper presented to the Annual Conference of the National Association of Soviet and Eastern European Studies (Cambridge, Easter 1981), pp. 15–16.

7 I have used *Trybuna Ludu* for the initial reports on these Plena and *Nowe Drogi* for the full record. In addition the PZPR publishing House, *Książka i Wiedza* (KiW) published full versions from the Seventh Plenum onwards in mass-circulation brochure form. The reader is asked to bear these documents in mind as each Plenum is covered in the text:

VI Plenum KC PZPR, 5-6 września, 4-6 października 1980r (77 pp.); *VII Plenum KC PZPR, 1-2 grudnia 1980r* (182 pp.); *VIII Plenum KC PZPR, 9 lutego 1981r* (109 pp.); *IX Plenum KC PZPR, 29-30 marca 1981r* (139 pp.); *X Plenum KC PZPR, 29-30 kwietnia 1981r* (298 pp.); *XI Plenum KC PZPR, 9-10 czerwca 1981r* (139 pp.).

8 By mid-April, 1,160 offices had been re-allocated for social use as private dwellings, 132 for health and social-care purposes and 43 for educational ones (see *Trybuna Ludu*, 21 April 1981).

9 M. Moczar, 'Historyczne tradycje PPR a współczesność', *Trybuna Ludu*, 27 January 1981.

10 *Sprawozdanie Stenograficzne Sejmu*, Eighth Sejm, sitting of 12 February 1981.

11 See M.F. Rakowski, 'Szanować partnera', *Polityka*, 17 January 1981 and his Seventh Plenum speech, *VII Plenum KC PZPR*, op. cit., pp. 66–9. Rakowski, by conceding university autonomy and an independent students' organization was instrumental in ending the widespread student sit-ins, especially in Łódź.

12 The Radom officials resigned but the PZPR leadership prevented the political rehabilitation of the riots although they accepted that the workers' protests against the price-rises were justified. Cf. Marian Turski, 'Radom 1976' in *Polityka*, 27 June and 4 July 1981. Kania, personally absolved Prokopiak, the Radom First Secretary in 1976, of any blame in handling the situation *Trybuna Ludu*, 11–12 July 1981, p. 4).

13 Cited in *Dziennik Polski*, 27 March 1981.

14 Ibid., 7 and 8 April 1981.

15 Note the earlier organization of the *Grunwald* Patriotic League by the police and ZBoWiD (war-veterans), the launching of a residual Partisan dominated weekly *Rzeczywistość* (Reality) and the organization of well-publicized Forums, especially in Katowice and Poznań, by small groups of little known neo-Stalinists.

16 For the Eleventh Plenum see *Nowe Drogi*, No. 7 (1981). The Soviet letter is reproduced on pp. 29–32.

17 The half-hearted support for party notables was shown by Olszowski's mere 246 votes out of a possible 426 in Warsaw (see *Trybuna Ludu*, 30 June 1981). Grabski was reported as having called these proceedings an *amok wyborczy* or electoral murderous frenzy (*Polityka*, 4 July 1981).

18 See in particular a series of articles and reminiscences in *Polityka* (30 June 1981, 6 July 1981, 13 July 1981). The main literary event however was the publication of J. Maciejewski and Z. Trojanowicza (eds), *Poznański czerwiec*, Poznań: Wydawnictwo Poznańskie, 1981. Calls for the truth to be revealed about March 1968 fell on stonier ground (J. Holzer, 'Doświadczenia marca 1968r', *Kierunki*, 17 May 1981).

19 Twelfth Plenum speech, *Trybuna Ludu*, 11–12 July 1981.

20 Ibid., 27 April, 29 April, 8 May and 26 May 1981.

21 Ibid., 11–12 July 1981. See *Sprawozdania: Komitetu Centralnego PZPR: Centralnej Komisji Rewizyjnej PZPR: Centralnej Komisji Kontroli Partyjnej PZPR: za*

okres od VIII Zjazdu do IX Nadzwyczajnego Zjazdu PZPR, Warsaw, Nakładem 'Trybuny Ludu', July 1981.
22 For the official biographies of the new Politburo and Secretariat members see *Trybuna Ludu*, 20 July 1981.

4   The Politics of 'Socialist Renewal'

GEORGE KOLANKIEWICZ

'Democracy is not in the gift of the authorities . . .'
(S. Kania, VI Plenum KCPZPR)

The emergence and establishment of NSZZ 'Solidarność' (Solidarity) in
the aftermath of the July–August strikes of 1980 masked an equally
revolutionary change, indeed not unrelated to the former, in the ranks of
the PZPR. Superficially it appeared that, following the examples of 1956
and 1970, the party would shed a proportion of its membership, apply
some political cosmetic and continue largely unaltered. Analyses indicate
that in the years 1957–58 the party's net membership fell by 275,200, or
from 10.2 per cent to 6.3 per cent of the occupationally-active population.
In particular, working-class membership dropped from 60.5 per cent in
1948, to 40 per cent in 1959. Beginning in 1960, party membership grew
so that by 1970 it was 2,319,900 or 12.7 per cent of the working-age
population. This had fallen to 12.1 per cent by 1971, with a loss of
137,542 members, but a net loss of only 59,404. The upturn in working-
class party membership really took off in 1973, so that by 1979 46.2 per
cent of the 3,037,000 membership were manual workers, and 14 per cent
of the occupationally-active population had joined. At the time of the
Extraordinary Ninth Congress of the PZPR, in July 1981, membership
was 2,870,000 with major losses in the ranks of the working class, who
between May 1980 and May 1981 accounted for 60 per cent of the
305,858 party cards handed in (as opposed to expulsions).

Astonishingly, therefore, a crisis that had almost seen the disintegration
of the PZPR, had passed-off with the loss of only approximately 10 per
cent of its membership.[1] Whilst deploring the exit of old working-class
members, the leadership admitted to recruitment campaigns aimed at
'selectively incorporating'[2] key groups of the population, with scant regard
for ideological criteria. Indeed the PZPR set quantitative recruitment plans
in the polity in much the same manner as those for the economy.

If the periodic loss of disaffected members had served the interests
of continuity during the 1960s and 1970s, the novelty of post-1980
Poland was that sufficient numbers remained within the party, resolved

to radically transform and restrain it with 'institutional guarantees' which would, once and for all, put a stop to the convulsions within the party and society at large. It was made abundantly clear to the newly ensconced Stanisław Kania that the party unity he immediately demanded after the Sixth Plenum was to be bought at a much higher price than he had originally bargained for.

Far-reaching democratization within the party was seen as a necessary prelude to the democratization of society. Democracy was nothing however without *accountability*, which in turn entailed the free nomination and election of party leaders, powers of recall, the extrication of the party from its over-involvement in societal management, and the unrestricted articulation and aggregation of rank-and-file initiatives, etc. Whilst at the first session of the Sixth Plenum, the PZPR perhaps started from the principle of how much democracy might be offered to the party masses, by the time of the second session of the Sixth Plenum was held, a month later, it was apparent that it would be more a case of how much democracy could be kept from the demanding grasp of the party rank and file. The discussions at the Sixth Plenum raised most of the key demands the leadership were to contend with during the coming months, and also represent a unique insight into the malfunctioning of a Communist party. The final outcome, in terms of a 'reconstituted' party, provides a model for possible developments in other ruling Communist parties.

1. 'We Are a Party Serving the Rulers, Not a Ruling Party'

The preface to all demands addressed to the party was that the perpetrators of Poland's economic, political and moral ignominy should be brought to book, as an indispensible pre-condition to the party regaining any credibility both amongst its own membership and in society at large. The major substantive thrust however was for an extraordinary Ninth Congress to be held as soon as possible. Given that it was the highest statutory authority in the party, it alone could change the Central Committee inherited from Gierek. The major task of this Congress would be to endorse new party statutes and election regulations governing party practice. Again the sophistication of the demands articulated at the Sixth Plenum, only two months after the signing of the Gdańsk agreement, pointed to the intensity of the internal party debate both before and immediately after the Polish August. Whilst Kania offered such palliatives as a clearer definition of the powers of the Politburo, Secretariat and First Secretary (powers so ostentatiously abused by the previous leaderships) as well as a more general subordination of the party apparatus to the elected bodies at all levels, the rank and file of the party, through the few spokesmen they had at this stage on the Central Committee, were more specific. In particular the elected and co-opted full-time party apparatus came under fire as a major *structural* cause of the crisis.

Not only was there to be a limit set on the period of office for elected party functionaries, but 'careers' in the apparatus could no longer be taken for granted. Those with occupational experience in other walks of life could be drafted into the apparatus on a temporary basis working on problem commissions and thus injecting into the party the experience of their respective milieux. The party apparatus, which had expanded with the administrative reforms of the mid-seventies, now numbered some 11,600 full-time employees (although those engaged in some commission, group of other elected function numbered 550,000). Thus what constituted an 'apparatchik' proved difficult to define.[3] That a career in the apparatus was now the norm was made all too obvious by an analysis of the educational background and career path of the typical organization person. They were usually men who worked through the party–State hierarchy, rarely had manual work experience (although they were generally of working-class origin), normally had a higher education in politics, administration or some other such area, which did not make them easily employable elsewhere, and which therefore provided an increased incentive for the construction of a secure career hierarchy.[4] This in turn made the apparatus more responsive to their superiors, upon whom promotion depended, rather than to the organization they were to service. It led to a filtering and distortion of information to make it more acceptable to their masters, but in the process this stifled the critical voice of the grass roots, thus creating an 'apparat party'. The further *economization* of the apparatus during the stage of 'imposed modernization', where detailed interest in economic affairs led to even the lowest levels (KD) of the apparatus having specialist economic departments, was symptomatic of the *deideologization* of the party. This is portrayed by the bald statistic that only three Plena of the KCPZPR were given over to ideological matters during the 1970s. This same apparatus controlled a *nomenklatura* of some 180,000 management positions stretching from the ministerial level down to the position of factory chargehand. The consequences of such a system are now well publicized, but 'negative selection', where the wrong people joined the party for the wrong reasons and were thereby given access to key *nomenklatura* positions, did much not only to bring the party into disrepute but undermined the very economic goals it espoused.[5] Furthermore any attack on the economic policy of the Politburo was easily misconstrued as politically motivated.

Evidence of the latter was provided by a statement at the Sixth Plenum to the effect that two-thirds of all changes in party personnel in *all* the socialist bloc countries were accounted for by the 'carousel' of positions in the Polish party. Differences of opinion, particularly on economic policy could not be tolerated.[6] As the term 'carousel' makes plain, this was no turnover of elites. It was a system of political musical chairs within a central committee where 75 per cent of members were drawn from a narrow band of party apparatchiks and economic administrators, who constituted only 4.3 per cent of the party as a whole, whilst over 80 per cent of top economic-management apparatus were party members.[7] To this deformation in party life was attached the term 'bureaucratic centralism', which by the time of the Ninth Congress in July 1981 was fairly common currency for a shorthand analysis of the 1970s.[8]

Put another way, if the manual working class were 46 per cent of PZPR membership, they constituted 10 per cent of the central party leadership and only 2–3 per cent of discussants at KC Plena![9] Needless to say the demand for a physical limitation on the size of the apparatus was often a disguised formula for limiting the prerogatives it had usurped. In the formidable attack on this apparatus which emerged after the Eighth Plenum, conservative elements within the leadership were wont to equate an attack on the apparatus with an attack on the party itself.[10] The fact that many members of the higher apparatus had translated political power into material privilege only gave further support to the case for making the apparatus into a strictly *service* organization, and for unequivocal subordination of the executive to fully elected bodies at various levels. Again, the legislation concerning the privileged pension rights of the higher party and State functionaries and their 'extended families' (available after only five years service and enacted in 1972) gave credibility to those who argued that a quasi-class of bureaucrats-technocrats had emerged.[11]

'Bureaucratic centralism' and the rule of the apparat-party required the *structural atomization* of basic party organizations (POP) vertically integrated through a systematic hierarchy from Factory Committee (KZ) to Ward Committee (KD), Village Committee (KG), Town Committee (KM) or a hybrid (KM–G), to Regional Committee (KW) or large city party committees, (e.g. Warsaw, Kraków, Łódź) right up to Central Committee. Information manipulation, 'staged' consultations (particularly with key enterprises under direct Central Committee supervision) local party leaders 'brought in a briefcase' and installed from above, as well as the so-called 'election key', were the institutional accoutrements of apparatus rule. The 'election key', was an advanced form of political tokenism involving a crude statistical notion or representation whereby quotas of particular age-groups, socio-occupational milieux, economic sectors, or sex were imposed in all 'elections'. Whilst being representative of the make-up of the PZPR (e.g. 20 per cent of the KCPZPR were women, representing the 20 per cent of PZPR members who were women), they in fact *represented* no one but themselves.[12]

The response of the apparatus was to complain that it had been ignored by the centre and that economic advisers on the central committee had been treated as an 'opposition' by the State organization such as the Planning Commission or the Central Statistical Office. Jarosziewicz indeed was accused of forbidding information to be passed from the ministries to the Central Committee. A closer examination of party-State relations during the 1970s may indicate the extent to which the *party* was made into another arm of the State bureaucracy and party membership amongst bureaucrats was no guarantee of their subordination to the central committee, providing rather, a suitable cover for the pursuit of sectional interest.[13] The initial response of the party apparatus in the aftermath of the Sixth Plenum was to replace its severely compromised members by new functionaries. These again were nominated from above, rather than elected by the appropriate plenary body, indicating that the apparatus had not taken to heart the lesson of August 1980, namely that it was not so much individuals but 'structures' which had to be changed.

2. 'The Authorities Must Learn Humility'
(Kołodziejski, Gdańsk Wojewoda)

Democratic election of all levels of the party structure was not just an expression of the re-appropriation of power by the individual member and the basic party organizations, but acted as a *rite de passage* for those committed to the 'Socialist Renewal'. These elections represented the reconstruction of the party from its base. The condition that only those with mandates as delegates from a basic party organization may proceed further up the hierarchy indicated that everyone would have to be accountable to some party organization or another. It had been the introduction of nominees at middle levels of the apparatus that had fostered the 'voluntarism' and irresponsibility of the higher apparatchiki.

The Seventh Plenum at the beginning of December 1980 conceded the growing pressure for democratic elections, but confined it to the *factory* level (whereas these had already spontaneously taken place in the key factories and attention had meanwhile shifted to the regional apparatchiks). The percentage of freely nominated candidates was increased from 15 per cent to 50 per cent, which whilst it represented '35 per cent more democracy' was nevertheless not complete democracy.[14] Likewise the distinction between 'passive election rights' (i.e. the right to be elected) and active election rights (i.e. the right to elect) was maintained, providing a loophole for nominations to be introduced from amongst those who were not mandated delegates of a lower party organization. The right of nomination by superior organs was viewed as a key feature of traditional democratic centralism and treated accordingly by each side.[15] The Ninth Plenum at the end of March finally lifted the limit on the number of nominations from the body of the delegates (one delegate, one nomination) whereas the outgoing Central Committee hung grimly onto the principle that 'invited guests' or 'Politburo nominations' should be allowed to stand as candidates for delegation to the Party Congress, and successfully reaffirmed this principle at the Eleventh Plenum in May 1981. Democratic elections required a secret ballot to be obligatory in voting at all levels. Article 27 of the existing statutes permitted secret voting but this was generally applied to the election of whole committees, whereas open voting was the rule when electing the real power bodies such as the executive, First Secretary, Politburo, etc., and here most pressure was applied.[16] Election regulations which had hitherto been the prerogative of the Central Committee and had remained intact since 1971 would now be incorporated into party statutes to be amended only by the party Congress. Simultaneous elections to the Congress as well as to regional party organs were seen as essential, since an unreformed regional apparatus could jeopardize a democratic Congress and vice versa.

Elections in turn were given a powerful impetus by the ever more strident demand for bringing the previous local and central elites to account. The Central Committee, as each Plenum came and went, became more transparently a resting place for displaced or soon to be displaced local leaders, ex-ministers, 'functionless' functionaries, who represented no one but themselves and who obstructed the reform movement as best they could. Thus by March 1981 there were thirty regional ex-First Secretaries and Ministers on the KCPZPR. Furthermore as the Central Pre-Congress Commission, established at the Seventh Plenum ostensibly to prepare the ground for the forthcoming Congress, was composed largely (83 per cent) of representatives of the outgoing apparatus, its role seemed primarily to delay the Congress rather than ease its passage.

Free elections not only served to cleanse the party organization of discredited apparatchiks, they also initiated and provided a forum for an intense discussion of internal party life. The *mechanisms* and *procedures* of election were essential ingredients of democracy for the party member, and activated them in a manner which even the most critical observers of

'Renewal' found moving. Guarantees of members' rights to hold and voice critical opinions based upon realistic information were the natural adjuncts to popular party democracy. Whereas the reformers wished to see a party with a free exchange of views and alternative competitive programmes of action, the conservative elements argued that the party was not to be reduced to a 'discussion club' but required unity for action. Equally the definition of the party's 'leading role in society' and its 'directive role in the State' saw a divergence in opinions. On the one hand there were those who felt the party's role should be inspirational: more that of a neutral arbiter than of one of the combatants. It would be an organization which would wield power through the influence and authority of its members, in industry, agriculture and education, rather than through power instruments such as the *nomenklatura*. On the other hand there were those who saw this as an attempt to undermine the 'constitutionally' defined position of the party by neutralizing it and reducing it to one of many forces within society. A related issue concerned the presence within the PZPR of those with a non-Marxist–Leninist view of the world, i.e. the estimated two-thirds of members who were to a greater or lesser extent Roman Catholics. It was argued that since the PZPR was an aggregate of Polish socialist traditions, it must of necessity incorporate the religiosity of those same traditions, this being one of the unique features of Polish socialism.[17]

Others retorted that it was the party's pervasive control of occupational career mobility through the *nomenklatura* that made party membership essential to 'normal' promotion, inevitably diluting the party world-view by this 'careerist' intake.[18] In essence the reformers felt that criteria for party membership should be the acceptance of its *political* programme and the conscious support of its goals, but not the private, idiosyncratic questions of world-view. To others however, the party was a political movement with certain ideological credentials and there had to be a distinction between a party member and a 'sympathizer', ideological dilution weakened the party, gave the apparatus its head under the materialist slogan of 'enrich yourselves' and again reduced it to 'discussion club' status.[19] After all, if it was found to be necessary, room for those of non-Communist world-views could be provided by extending genuine participation to members of other political parties and organizations, e.g. activating and extending the role of the National Unity Front (FJN).

The argument around the 'religiosity' factor in the PZPR high-lighted concern not just over the intellectual bankruptcy of Marxism–Leninism since the crushing of 'revisionism' in 1968, but also over its loss of *ethical* drive and appeal to a younger generation. At the same time it emphasized the gap between the PZPR's desired role as a 'national-patriotic' party and the evident superiority of the Church and Solidarity in appealing to nationalistic sentiment. Some compromise and co-operation over this was essential 'since a battle of world-views with the Church cannot be won'.[20]

3. Horizontal Collectivism vs. Bureaucratic Centralism

It is doubtful whether the militancy within the ranks of the party inspired by the Polish August would have culminated in the eventual calling of an Extraordinary Party Congress and in the detailed re-writing of the party statutes if the political atomization of apparat rule had not been neutralized by the emergence of the so-called 'horizontal movement'. This was a qualitatively new form of political association, which was the complete antithesis to vertical, bureaucratized political participation and which was to prove to be a major democratic internal control mechanism within the PZPR.

The essence of the 'horizontal consultation and agreement commissions' was the creation of direct unmediated sideways links between basic party organizations, so that the power of the apparatus was checked. It grew out of the perceived inadequacy of the apparatus during the August days, when basic party organizations were thrown back onto their own initiatives in dealing with the tide of popular discontent. The blueprint for such association was provided by the regional horizontalism of the inter-factory strike committees, which co-ordinated, consulted and negotiated directly with the authorities. As an expression of self-organization and political self-management, the horizontal consultation movement represented a collective response to the stultifying inertia and organizational paralysis of the middle-level party apparatus, whose only reflex appeared to be to look upwards and wait for directives that never came.[21]

Where and how it originated is still a matter of dispute. The regional pre-Congress Commissions, set up in Gdańsk and Kraków (the latter on 13 October 1980) to collect and process the flood of demands, proposals and projects being thrown up by the grass-root organizations, were seen as the initiators of this exchange of ideas, experiences, aspirations for renewal etc., as they prepared for the Extraordinary Congress already demanded in August by the Kraków Marxist discussion club 'Kuźnica'.[22] The commissions were from the outset under the direct auspices of the more enlightened regional party leaderships. However where the opposition to party renewal was more open or where co-optation was less subtle or too late, then the rank-and-file response hardened into an oppositional structure.

4. The 'Toruń Disease'

Such was the case in Toruń. Whilst associated with the peculiarities of the internal party relations in the region and in particular with the personality of one Z. Iwanow, the 'horizontal structures' which emerged elsewhere were based on the Toruń ideal-type, around which the stereotypes, misinformation and scaremongering focused. Set up on the 27 October 1980 on the initiative of the party organization at the Institute of Social Sciences in the University of Nicolaus Copernicus, it brought together initially eight of the largest factory party organizations in concert with the University party group, into the so-called 'Komisja Konsultatcyjno-Porozumiewawcza POP'. This alliance was repeated in those regions where the horizontal movement was active, e.g. the Cegielski works and University in Poznań. Internal democracy, open meetings, free exchange of views and information, and a commitment to transforming the structure and practices of the party along genuine Marxist–Leninist lines, appeared to be the hallmarks of this movement.

Iwanow, the First Secretary of the local marine engineering factory, was a declared Roman Catholic, an arden supporter of Solidarity, but probably the first factory organization First Secretary to be elected by free ballot after the August days. On 24 November 1980 he was summarily expelled from the ranks of the PZPR by the regional party control commission, a decision subsequently upheld by the central party control commission. In the case against him were encapsulated many of the problems facing the party in crisis:

(1) Accused of 'undermining the Marxist–Leninist world-view' he nevertheless had sufficient authority amongst his comrades for them to refuse to accept the expulsion ruling and to be nominated as their delegate to the local town party conference;

(2) That he aired his views to the foreign press and elsewhere indicated that he believed the party had to wash its dirty linen in public if it was to gain any credibility;

(3) That he refused to subordinate himself to the orders of his immediate superiors was due to their perceived illegitimacy, i.e. the discipline of democratic centralism could only be imposed by superiors freely elected from the grass roots;

(4) The most serious charge of 'factionalism' again raised the question of how far could individual party members and organizations proceed in *organizing* dissent from the political line of the party, without being accused of undermining party unity, and of seeking to usurp power within the party;

(5) The personalized and bitter attacks which he instigated against the local leadership was a sign of the level of disenchantment with, and alienation from, the local apparatus on the part of the grass roots;

(6) Finally, the manner of his exclusion, without recourse to his 'maternal' party organization, was indicative of the disdain and insensitivity of this party apparatus, to the albeit limited *sovereignty* of the basic party organization which had freely elected him.[23]

The Seventh Plenum in December 1980 was really concerned with the emergence of these horizontal structures, as the caustic attack on Iwanow in the party press indicated.[24] Kania himself warned against the creation of 'extra-statutory organizational structures', insisting that fractionalism would not be tolerated.[25] 'Horizontalism' however, was spreading, particularly to party organizations within particular occupational or professional milieux. For example, employees in design offices, representing some 15,000 party members, wished to formulate their own propositions for the Congress to consider. Radical university party organizations had also met and developed a programme by early January.[26] The horizontal movement was however not just about programmes and proposals but also about action.

Not content with simply waiting for official permission to carry out new elections to the local party leadership, the Toruń horizontalists, who now represented some thirty local party organizations, were able to gather the statutory one-third of party members and demand an election conference to the Toruń city party committee. In this they anticipated the eventual endorsement of this by the Tenth Plenum some four months ahead of time.[27] This in turn was indicative of the highly charged emotions within the party and the *resolution* of horizontalists, who bolstered by the self-assurance that came with free elections in their party organizations, could indeed accuse the local party leadership of being 'political corpses', representing no one.[28]

Elsewhere, in Kraków and Gdańsk, the local party organizations were also preparing for election campaigns. Solidarity for its part gazed favourably, though from a suitable distance, at the election movement within the party, recognizing that the reconstruction of the authority of the party and the emergence of a 'genuine' partner in negotiation, was only possible through democratic elections.[29] Lobbying on the two points of regional party elections and the announcement of a Congress date, the horizontalists emphasized the need for the latter to be held as soon as possible, initially January, then March/April and finally an outside date was set by the Ninth Plenum for 20 July. The leadership for their part

argued that the Congress had to be 'successful', i.e. well-managed, pre-
dictable in outcome etc., indicating just how great was the rift between
those who saw the Congress as a 'working Congress', providing a forum
for the genuine resolution of party problems, and those who stuck firmly
to the 'choreographed Congress'. It was made clear to the latter, however,
that the longer they postponed the Congress the more difficulty the
majority of the old leadership would have in finding themselves elected
as delegates. Already critical attention was shifting from those with pre-
August guilt to those sabotaging post-August renewal. The 'mafia-like
discipline' of the horizontal movement, as the Warsaw First Secretary
Kociołek called it, was as disconcerting to the authorities as that of the
strikers in August 1980 — and indeed it appeared that many of the old
leadership were so ideologically bankrupt that they could not countenance
that the grass-roots party movement still believed in socialism!

5. The Bydgoszcz Provocation

It came as no surprise that the provocative beatings in Bydgoszcz on
19 March served to mobilize the rank-and-file movement even further
(along with the 'free Saturdays strike' and confrontations at the regional
level such as that in Bielsko-Biała). This was clear evidence of the irresponsibility, indecisiveness, and saboteur provocations of the 'rump' Central
Committee, who had to be removed as soon as possible. Having worked
hard to re-establish their credentials with the population at large, by such
means as internal free elections, the working out of employee self-
management schemes (where they wished to extend their influence without resort to institutional means), by integrating branch and Solidarity
union members in the party organization, the rank-and-file membership
again had to bear public opprobrium for the actions of their Central
Committee.

The 'horizontalists', now more actively than ever, mandated their
previously supine representatives on the Central Committee to express
their anger, to call for an immediate Congress and to demand the heads
of those responsible for the Bydgoszcz incident. Many spoke of the crude
attempts by the Politburo decision of 22 March to create a rift between
party members and the working class by forbidding them to strike on the
27 March. In fact more than one Central Committee member made it plain
that they would. Over 350 resolutions were telexed by basic organizations
to the Ninth Plenum indicating the level of militant scrutiny to which the
latter were now subjected.

The issue of *accountability* had penetrated the Central Committee proceedings, and the Politburo were mandated to present their case individually to the party organizations in the large factories. Whilst the reformers and their erstwhile protagonists such as Werblan, the ex-director of the Institute for the Fundamental Problems of Marxism–Leninism, were attacked by hardliners like Grabski,[30] the 'horizontalists' had held parallel meetings during the Plenum; a practice to be repeated subsequently. In Toruń the representatives of two hundred factory party organizations met at the University and drafted resolutions which they directed at the Central Committee in Warsaw.[31]

Cautious voices were, however, already being raised against 'idealizing' the Congress; against seeing it as a panacea for all ills. Also it was clear that by the Ninth Plenum only 12 per cent of party organizations had carried out 'free' elections. This highlighted the limited scope of the reform movement (if not its intensity), rooted as it was in the large factories and urban centres. The provincial organizations were on the whole quiet, waiting for orders, and very much an unknown quantity.[32] The nurturing of the core working-class membership (i.e. the 205 key enterprises) during the 1970s and post-August period by the party leadership was to some extent inevitably creating a rift between the former and other party organizations. Nevertheless the meetings between the individual Politburo members and the core working class posed enough of an eye-opening experience for the leadership to alter their perception of the grass-roots fervour for reform. In particular Kania and Olszowski, in their separate ways, were made aware of grass-roots party sentiment towards their activities. Kania likened his meeting with the Lenin shipyard party organization 'to a university experience'.[33]

Other party figures such as Fiszbach and Rakowski were already submitting themselves, successfully, to popular party election mandate at grass-roots level. The Toruń horizontalists for their part had, in anticipation of manipulation, restricted delegate status to those who had belonged to their party organization *before 1 January 1981* — so that elections could act as a verifying sieve and not be bypassed by the centre finding 'amenable' party organizations. Perhaps the essence of grass-roots concern over the ultimate accountability of all those who hold party office at whatever level came in a question presented to Kania at the Lenin shipyard: 'Does comrade secretary consider it appropriate that he belongs to a party organization in Płock, is an MP for Gdańsk, and works in Warsaw?'[34]

6. Dual-power Within the Party

The disenchantment with the statements and inactivity of the Central Committee Ninth Plenum found expression in what was the symbolic apotheosis of the horizontal movement, namely the 'Party Consultative Forum' held in Toruń on 15 April 1981. Organized by the Toruń KKPOP — which now contained forty party organizations — twelve other regional horizontal organizations (Bydgoszcz, Białystok, Gdańsk, Kraków, Łódź, Olsztyn, Pabianice, Szczeciń, Włocławek, Wrocław, Katowice, Poznań) were for the first time openly brought to Toruń. The venue was enough to have the Forum described by the hardliners as 'that factional conventicle',[35] for whilst many other horizontal organizations had achieved more in the way of reforms, Toruń had become for the conservative party opposition a symbol of all that was bad.[36] The Forum however, was officially recognized by the Central Committee who sent a member of the organization department to be present. Although Kania himself had reportedly half-promised to attend, the leadership cooled markedly as the date of the Toruń Forum drew closer. Sixty journalists were present, including *Newsweek* magazine, which was disparagingly seen to be acting 'as an arbiter of "Leninist" norms in the functioning of a communist party'.[37] Not surprisingly perhaps, little internal national coverage was given to the event since the resolutions which emanated from it were highly critical of the path taken since the Sixth Plenum (thus providing further evidence that the party apparatus was still in control and was blocking information as usual). It was claimed that the Central pre-Congress Commission as well as many regional Commissions, were manipulating and distorting grass-roots postulates. Duplicity in action was evident on the part of the CC, which whilst declaring that party and state functions should be separated, nevertheless at the Ninth Plenum nominated a central committee secretary to be Minister of Agriculture. It appears that the Forum was now putting pressure on the Tenth Plenum, demanding that regional ex-Secretaries be removed and replaced by worker candidate-members, that there be direct broadcasting of the proceedings of the Tenth Plenum and that the physical presence of observers from the Forum be permitted at its plenary sessions. A tightening of election regulations ought to be introduced with delegates to the Congress elected at the levels closest to the rank and file. The Congress should be a multi-session affair, dealing first with elections and then with the working out of a party pro-gramme and new statutes. Finally an accurate picture of the state of the party, of the reform movement, should be communicated to 'fraternal party organizations'. It was intended that this was to be the first of a series of sessions running parallel to the apparat-controlled preparations for the Congress. As it happened, the Gdańsk, Poznań and Łódź organizations did not fulfil their promises of staging such a forum, since Central Committee sanction was not given to a repeat performance, and much of the impetus was anyhow taken out of the movement by the announcement at the Tenth Plenum of the election campaign culminating in the Extraordinary Congress to be held on 14 July.[38]

Needless to say, the Forum observers, referred to as 'Hetman Iwanow's pickets', were not allowed into the plenary meetings of the Tenth Plenum. A series of 'party alerts' had however been called by the horizontal movement to monitor the progress of the meeting and instruct their by now accepted mouthpieces with appropriate directives. Working in shifts, using all the means of information transmission available to them, assisted by the committed journalist members of the Association of Polish Journalists, who had played a crucial role in opening up the proceedings of such plenary meetings, the plenipotentiaries of the horizontal movement comprised as they were of the party executives or plena, were able to take immediate decisions on resolutions, demands and instructions at the Tenth Plenum.

An example of the benefits of such monitoring came when the resolutions of the Plenum concerning the election regulations for the pre-Congress Campaign were claimed to have been 'consulted' with the large factory organizations. The Toruń 'alert' immediately checked this and discovered that nothing worthy of the name 'consultation' had taken place.[39] Whilst the Tenth Plenum predictably mounted another attack on the horizontal structures, Weblan, Rakowski and others pointed to the creative energies, ardour, and authentic Communist idealism generated by this youthful movement and which was at last stripping away 'layers of Stalinist bureaucracy'. The conservatives such as Siwak, however, now changed the direction of their attack to one of the *consequences* of the 'horizontalist' inspired election campaign, namely the absence of working-class respresentatives in these, the first democratic elections in the Polish party.[40]

Indeed, the first results from factory and local elections in Toruń and Kraków, for example, indicated that whilst some 70 per cent of First Secretaries were new to the job and 50 per cent of party executives were new, only 25–30 per cent were manual workers, and 75–80 per cent of delegates to the City party conference were white-collar.[41] Nevertheless at the Tenth Plenum, as a foretaste of things to come, the two new members of the Politburo were elected by secret ballot.

7. 'What is Important, is that Workers Elect, Not that they are Elected'.

After the Tenth Plenum attention of necessity shifted to the election process, which became dominated by questions of *procedure, personalities* and *programmes*, in that order. Learning democratic procedures did not come easily, particularly in the atmosphere of mutual suspicion within which they took place. By early May the first results were emerging from the large industrial enterprises, which along with the university organizations alone were given the 'privilege' of directly electing delegates to the Congress in the ratio of one delegate to 850 members. This was partial concession to the 'horizontalists' demand that elections take place at levels closest to the rank and file, but was essentially a continuation of the 1970s process of privileged representation for those key-enterprises which employ some 480,000 of all party members. As mentioned, workers were not being elected; instead managers, engineers, technicians and white-collar employees were being thrown up by these intense election meetings. In response to this the reformers insisted that the very working-class origins of managers and engineers made them sensitive to working-class interests and indeed better able to represent them articulately at the Centre. It should perhaps be added that attitudinal surveys and studies of inter-generational mobility had indicated that attitudes of engineers to workers were 'more positive' than that of other non-manual groups and that 'social barriers between the working-class and technical intelligentsia [were being] erased'.[42]

This distinction between worker and non-worker was seen as a political attempt to create cleavages within the reform movement and to invalidate first, the election process, secondly the delegates thus elected, and ultimately the Congress itself.[43] On another level many party election conferences spontaneously and illegally elected delegates directly to the Congress rather than go through the hierarchy to the regional conferences. This represented the frustrations with the bureaucratic subordination experienced by certain active party organizations within the system and the desire of key party milieux to be heard directly at the Congress.

At the end of the day, 22.3 per cent of delegates elected to the Extraordinary Ninth Congress were manual workers directly employed in production, transport, construction and services. More importantly, of the 1964 delegates, 568 were secretaries of basic party organizations, in factories and institutions, a major indication of the effects of the reform movement during the election campaign, and the redistribution of power from the top to the party depths'.[44] However, bald sociological statistics hide the other major unanticipated consequence of the democratic elections, namely the electoral annihilation of the 'horizontal' activists.

8. 'The Revolution Devours its Own Children'

The regional (Wojewodztwo) election conferences in Toruń, Gdańsk, Włocławek, Olsztyn, Poznań and Kraków, highlighted the internal animosities and suspicions *within* the grass roots of the party as much as that between the latter and the leadership. Delegates representing the highly radicalized urban party organizations were often 'mowed down' by the more numerous provincial and rural party organizations. The explanations suggested were many. Obviously not all party organizations had gone through the 'post-Bydgoszcz and Ninth Plenum' cleansing process. At the same time the higher the level of selection the more Solidarity party members were selected out, and the more the extremes were eliminated at the secret ballot box. In a situation where few delegates knew much about each other, the highly publicized activities of some of the 'horizontalists' made them a natural target for 'deletion' from ballot sheets. In fact the very activities of the horizontalists often alienated them from their less motivated 'country comrades' who felt that they were being politically patronized, manipulated and in some cases, as in Toruń, subjected to 'over-organised' election tactics. Contrary to the expectations of the activists, there was no guarantee that those who had made the 'Socialist Renewal' possible should now reap the rewards in terms of popular election mandates. In the Toruń region, for example, instead of the forty representatives in the local party committee which its share of party membership demanded, the Toruń city party organization, which was the home of the 'horizontalists', received only four mandates.[45] It appeared therefore that the 'negative selection' and de-ideologization of the 1970s had finally proved too much of an obstacle to the reform movement within the party. The Congress, more and more, promised to be a far cry from that event heralded as the most important in the history of Polish Communist movement. When Bratkowski was quoted by his arch-rival, the soon-to-be-elected Politburo hard-liner Siwak, as describing the Congress delegates as largely consisting of 'magma', this geological analogy (referring to a 'crude pasty mixture' or 'fluid strata') seemed peculiarly appropriate.[46]

9. The Congress as the Collective Wisdom of the Party

It is not difficult to detect the experiences of the preceding election campaign in the proceedings and outcomes of the 'historical Congress', the highest forum in the party. From the outset the Congress would not allow itself to be manipulated either in its agenda or in such crucial matters as leadership elections. The sovereignty of the plenary body of elected delegates was re-affirmed as it had been so often at lower levels. Aware of their wider audience, the delegates kept in touch with their base organizations and ensured that their 'mandated' positions were stated either at the full plenary session, where one delegate from each region spoke, or at the working sessions. Democracy meant on the one hand behind the scenes election deals and campaigns of slander and insinuation, but on the other hand it also saw the so-called 'hour of frankness' where candidates to leadership positions were subjected to vigorous, intensive and often embarrassing questioning about their views, actions and material possessions. Again the election process brought unanticipated consequences, which in turn reflected the spirit of the reform movement. The separation of party and State was made clear in that only five members of the Government were elected to the Central Committee of whom two subsequently resigned their Government position. Of twenty-eight regional First Secretaries who stood for Central Committee membership and who previously could have been guaranteed a seat, only eight were elected — ostensibly on the principle that they were powerful enough already.[47]

A new mode of political interest aggregation will now have to emerge where, as at regional level, so many obvious power centres have not found physical representation on the Central Committee. Finally, whereas the regional election campaign saw workers electing a largely 'intelligentsia' Congress, the latter promptly voted in a 'worker–peasant–military and lower party apparatus' Central Committee. It is the increased representation of these groups at the expense of higher party–State representatives, involving almost a total 'renewal' of the leadership, as well as the more homogeneous geographical distribution or central committee members, giving a greater voice to all regions, which are the major consequences of democratic elections.[48] But the workings of the newly constituted party organization will be largely dependent upon the draft statutes produced by the Congress. Controversial to the end they contain eighty-eight paragraphs compared to the sixty-two in the old statutes. Highly detailed but with many compromises, they reflect the desire that no loopholes remain to be exploited by a future renegade leadership yet also the acceptance that certain key issues cannot be unambiguously resolved.[49]

10. Guarantees Against What?

Eight major changes were carried out on the projected statutes and given over to inter-party consultation, although the Congress resolutions were more explicit on key issues than the relevant statutes. (i) The directing role of the party in the State was to be implemented through the activities and influence of party members upon State administrative and social organizations, being based upon widespread consultation *within* the party and between the party and society. (ii) These party members could include individual 'believers', although the party *as a whole* supports a 'scientific world-view'. This withdrawal of the party from direct interventionism and the focus upon an openly broader recruitment base is further highlighted by the (iii) statutory limits upon the simultaneous holding of State and party functions at the same level and upon the limited tenure of such office. (iv) The executive bodies of the party are firmly subordinated to the elected plenary meeting and the apparatus is clearly reminded of its 'service' function. (Although the one major set of postulates concerning organizational changes and a reduction of apparatus levels, e.g. the KD, was rejected.) This 'service' will be mainly to facilitate widespread consultation, based upon free-flowing information, with the basic party organizations. Their powers in turn are considerably enhanced, not least by (v) the new election regulations and by the retention of delegate mandates during inter-Congress/Conference periods. (vi) Whilst the party control and review commissions are given greater powers these cannot be so easily abused in dealing with dissenting voices, since such terms as 'factionalism' have been more closely defined. (vii) Thus 'inner-party democracy, the freedom of discussion and criticism cannot be constrained and restricted as likewise it cannot be exploited for goals contrary to party ideology and policy or to its political and ideological unity. Activities of a "factional" nature are particularly inadmissible, this being defined as the creation of formalized groups within the party which propagate a separate programme, party line and organizational principles and create an autonomous command centre as against the statutory party authorities'.[50] This fairly broad-ranging definition provides the 'horizontal movement' with considerable scope, particularly as basic organizations are also given the (viii) right of co-operation, common party meetings, the exchange of experience, etc.

The internally reconstituted party now faces the task of re-establishing itself in a society which in the intervening period has changed beyond recognition. Statutes, after all, only bind those associated within the party, whilst election regulations, however democratic, affect only party members. Positive resolutions concerning the party's commitment to:

(i)   Strengthening the position of the Sejm;

(ii) Widening the rights of local councils (RN);

(iii) Broadening the activities of the FJN;

(iv) Supporting the functioning of independent trade unions

have been accompanied by the consolidation of the 'orthodox' opposition within the party grouped around the Katowice Party Forum and similar conservative 'horizontal' associations of the 'Marxist-Leninist core'.[51]

Whilst this may simply be a clarification of positions in the aftermath of the Congress, it poses the very real threat of a major internal vertical cleavage within the party should external pressures, such as the activities of Solidarity increase significantly.

Notes and References

1 J. Olbrycht, 'Raport o Stanie partii', *Żołnierz Wolności*, 9 August 1981; L. Gryzbowski, 'Robotnicy w PZPR: 1948-1975', KiW, 1979; and *Nowe Drogi*, No. 8 (1981).

2 G. Kolankiewicz, 'Bureaucratized Political Participation and its Consequence in Poland', *Politics*, 1 (1981), pp. 35-40.

3 'Styl pracy partyjnej', *Życie Partii*, No. 2 (1981).

4 *Perspektywy*, 27 March 1981.

5 'Gospodarka w nomenklaturze', *Życie i Nowczesność*, 561, 16 April 1981.

6 'VI Plenum KCPZPR', *Nowe Drogi*, Nos. 10-11 (1980), p. 256.

7 'Spór o demokracje', *Kujawy*, 17 December 1980.

8 S. Swiątek 'Uwaga! Struktura!' *Nowości*, 3 May 1981.

9 M. Heyza, 'Forum wymiana poglądów', *Gazeta Pomorska*, 11 March 1981.

10 Plenum Komitet Warszawski PZPR, *Życie Warszawy*, 18 February 1981.

11 Dziennik Ustaw, 7 October 1972, No. 42 Decree 270 of 5 October 1972. 'O zaopatrzeniu emerytytalnym osob zajmujących kierownicze stanowiska polityczne i państwowe oraz członków ich rodzin', pp. 410-12.

12 M. Rymuszko, 'Klucz', *Prawo i Życie*, 48 (842), 30 November 1980.

13 *Nowe Drogi*, Nos. 10-11 (1980), p. 293.

14 P. Moszyński, 'Sprawa Wyborów', *Polityka*, 7 March 81.

15 'W sprawie regułamina wyborczego', *Życie Partii*, No. 3 (1981), p. 8.

16 L. Winiarski, 'Propozycje poprawek statutowych', *Gazeta Pomorska*, 23-5 January 1981.

17 S. Bratkowski, 'Pięć polskich odrębności — ku czemu idziemy', *Życie Warszawy*.

18 K. Jakubowski, 'Czy wierzący mogą należyc do partii?' *Życie Warszawy*, 3 February 1981.

19 R. Bryla, M. Karwat, 'Partia dla wsystkich', *Trybuna Ludu*, 6 February 1981.

20 K. Kłopotowski, 'Gdzie biją źródła wartości?', and also A. Kołakowski and J. Migaciński, 'Luzoryczne Tęsknoty', *Literatura*, 26 July 1981.

21 L. Witkowski, 'Partia: Zjednoczenie w działaniu', *Polityka*, 9 February 1981.

22 L. Winiarski, 'Odnowa wymaga mobilizacji "Kuznica" ', *Życie Partii*, No. 12 (1980); J. Piekarczyk, 'Zanim doszło do zjazdu', *Gazeta Krakowska*, 15 July 1981; B. Holub, 'Oddział zakaźny', *Polityka*, 14 February 1981.

23 W. Pawlowski, 'Werifikacja', *Polityka*, 8 November 1980.

24 J. Kraszewski, 'Dyskusja a jedność dzialania', *Trybuna Ludu*, 2 December 1980.
25 S. Kania, 'Zadania partii w walce o socjalistyczny charakter odnowy zycia społecznego', *Nowe Drogi*, No. 12 (1980), pp. 8–24, especially pp. 16–18.
26 *Gazeta Pomorska*, 15 December 1980; *Gazeta Pomorska*, 8 January 1981, 'Głos universytetów w dyskusji przedzjazdowej'.
27 *Nowości*, 13 January 1981; 'Przewodzic, ale jak?', *Gazeta Pomorska*, 17 January 1981; 'Prawdziwie robotnicza, prawdziwie marksistowska, prawdziwie demokratyczna', *Fakty*, 14 February 1981.
28 J. Czula 'Sprawa Iwanowa, czyli rowna pochyła', *Życie Partii*, No. 7 (1981). A particularly bitter attack on Iwanow containing the weight of the establishment case against him.
29 E.g. S. Swiątek 'Pęknięcie, rozłam, przepaść', *Nowości*, 9 February 1981.
30 Ninth Plenum KCPZPR, *Nowe Drogi*, No. 4 (1981).
31 *Gazeta Pomorska*, 30 March 1981.
32 B. W. Olszewska, 'Dyskusja', *Polityka*, 4 April 1981.
33 J. Bijak, 'Twarzą w twarz', *Polityka*, 18 April 1981; W. Kozyra, 'Robotnicze gwarancje', *Życie Warszawy*, 13 April 1981.
34 M. Bacciarelli, 'Czy odnową mamy zrobic sami?' *Fakty*, 18 April 1981.
35 Tenth Plenum KCPZPR, *Nowe Drogi*, 5 June 1981, p. 70.
36 M. Księzarczyk, 'Instrumenty i orkiestra', *Życie Warszawy*, 13 April 1981.
37 *Nowe Drogi*, 5 June 1981, p. 70.
38 M. Księzarczyk, 'Forum porozumienia partyjnego w Toruni', *Życie Warszawy*, 16 April 1981; 'Stanowisko Przedzjazdowego Forum Porozumienia Partyjnego w Toruniu', *Nowości*, 16 April 1981; M. Wesołowska and P. Moszyński, 'Żyć własnym życiem', *Polityka*, 25 April 1981; M. Kruszko, 'Od dolu – do gory', *Fakty*, 9 May 1981; 'Mowi Z. Iwanow', *Wolne Słowo*, No. 44, 9 June 1981.
39 J. L. Ordon, 'Dyżur nadzwyczajny', *Fakty*, 16 May 1981.
40 *Nowe Drogi*, Nos. 5–6 (1981), p. 85.
41 *Nowości*, 16 March 1981.
42 M. Wojciechowska, 'Co to znaczy byc trzyocznym?' *Kultura*, 4 January 1981; K. Zagórski, *Rozwoj, skruktura i ruchliwość społeczna*, 1978, p. 133.
43 For a discussion of the causes of this 'abstention from power' see Z. Sufin, 'Nie chcą czy nie są wybierani', *Życie Warszawy*, 3 June 1981; M. Anasz, 'Czy nie chą byc wybierani', *Trybuna Luda*, 16 June 1981.
44 'Sprawozdanie Komisji Mandatowej', *Trybuna Luda*, 16 July 1981, p. 3.
45 *Gazeta Toruńska*, 25 June 1981; S. Lipiński, 'Wojewodzka konferencja w Gdańsku', *Życie Gospodarcze*, 16 June 1981; M. Baciarelli, 'My, Włocławek', *Fakty*, 13 June 1981.
46 *Życie Warszawy*, 20 July 1981.
47 *Gazeta Krakowska*, 23 July 1981.
48 J. Sadecki, 'Jawne i niejawne spięcia na zjezdzie', *Gazeta Krakowska*, 24–26 July 1981; also Z. Szeliga, 'Naprawdę nowa ekipa', *Polityka*, 25 July 1981.
49 Z. Kurowski, 'Sprawozdanie komisji statutowej', *Trybuna Luda*, 21–22 July 1981.
50 'Wyrosły z życia', *Nowości*, 31 July–2 August 1981; 'Uchwala IX Nadzwyczajnego Zjazdu w sprawie opracowaniu perspektywycznego programu PZPR', *Nowe Drogi*, No. 8 (1981).
51 P. Moszyński, 'Miesiąc pózniej', *Polityka*, 22 August 1981.

5 Political Consequences of the Changes in Party–State Structure under Gierek

PAUL G. LEWIS

1. Pressures for Institutional Change

The changes with which we are concerned were those made by the Gierek leadership to improve party leadership and control of Polish society and its economy and to enhance decision-making mechanisms and the organizational means by which the decisions taken were implemented. The structural reform which took place in Poland between 1972 and 1975 concerned firstly, measures to centralize on a local plane the system of state administration and party supervision in the countryside, secondly, to strengthen party leadership over the People's Councils (hitherto combining functions of self-government with those of administration) whilst stripping them of their administrative responsibilities, and, thirdly, to streamline the structures of both party and State by transforming the three-tier system into a two-tier one. By these means it was intended to enhance the implementation of centrally taken decisions, to form institutions adequate to manage and direct an increasingly complex and developed industrial economy, to stimulate the growth of agricultural production, and to improve the system of social self-government. Yet five years after these reforms were completed Polish industry was grinding to a halt with uncontrolled growth of investment, lack of raw materials, low productivity and declining output. Food shortages were reaching catastrophic proportions, whilst self-government was achieved only at the cost of a massive wave of strikes and the defeat of the government and party leadership. In themselves the institutional changes made in Poland were not particularly radical nor exceptional within the context of Eastern Europe. A variety of other factors were relevant and some more significant for the collapse of the Polish leadership. But the consequences of the changes in party–State structure also contributed to the development of the crisis that erupted in 1980 and to the weakening of party leadership in Poland.

The need for certain reforms was announced by Gierek soon after his assumption of power in 1970. This was to be expected following the experiences under Gomułka during the sixties when the Party had become distant from the people; its leadership became faction-ridden, economic reforms had been drawn up on several occasions and then shelved, and the population was increasingly worse served by the rule of the party and its management of the economy. The institutional changes discussed here thus formed part of a general process of reform which was publicized in the early seventies and which concerned various areas of Polish social life. These included industrial production and the economic administration, industrial relations and closer party links with the workers, education and – in common with the Soviet Union and other allied countries – the promulgation of a new Constitution which was to regularize the system of party rule. The introduction of a series of relatively conservative institutional reforms also accorded with the approach of other East European leaders at this time. Following the salutary experience of Czechoslovakia and the menacing consequences of the diverse forms of economic reform discussed though only partially implemented, leaders saw a more satisfactory solution to their problems of slowing economic growth and popular restiveness in more efficient administration and more dynamic forms of party control and leadership. In Poland great stress was placed on the gradual improvement of the economy, which foresaw 'the introduction of a complex conception of changes in the methods of planning, direction and adminstration of the national economy (which) will take place gradually, successively, commencing with pilot organizations'.[1] In the Soviet Union hope had been placed since the beginning of the seventies on the techniques of the 'scientific and technical revolution' whose spread within Communist society led to 'the growing role of the party in the period of the building of Communism. And it is this growing role that calls for improving the forms and methods of party leadership, specifically for optimally combining and delineating the functions of party and State bodies'.[2] Elsewhere in Eastern Europe hesitant reforms had been made in Romania, where steps to unify the party and State hierarchies had been taken in order to improve the system of party control.[3] State and party organization had also been streamlined in Slovakia in 1969 by switching from a three-tier to a two-tier structure, following a similar example in Bulgaria.[4]

The Polish reforms thus generally followed a tendency of institutional change prevalent in Eastern Europe, although they did carry their own particular emphasis. A formal textbook gives the following as the objectives of the reforms – in the case of the first and second stages (the establishment of the larger rural commune and the introduction of a State executive separate from the People's Councils) 'the acceleration of socio-economic development, the better satisfaction of people's needs, the enhancement of socialist democracy, and the further strengthening of the role and authority of People's Councils and local organs of State administration as well as the supervision of their activities'. The economic objectives are more strongly emphasized in the case of the third stage (the introduction of the two-tier structure):

> adaptation of the administrative division of the country to the needs of accelerated socio-economic development, the establishment of conditions for more efficient administration of the national economy and for the functioning of the organs of power and State administration in the intention of better satisfying society's growing needs . . .[5]

The economic motivation behind the reforms was also stressed immediately before the implementation of the third stage by the Prime Minister, who pointed out that the development of the State was lagging behind that of the economy, creating obstacles in the implementation of party policy and giving rise to 'bureaucratism'.[6] As Dobieszewski makes clear, though, the speeding up of socioeconomic growth and the better satisfaction of social needs definitely took precedence over other features of the reform.

There were particular reasons why this should have been so. In contrast to Gomułka, who had neglected the economy to the extent that living standards in Poland during the sixties rose more slowly than in all other Comecon countries, Gierek inaugurated a policy of rapid growth based on extensive foreign investment. Following the stagnation of the sixties and with the massive use of foreign capital it was imperative to make productive use of the resources available and to improve production efficiency. Moreover, while earnings and the extent of new plant rose quickly, the expected growth in industrial output was not materializing as expected. It was therefore increasingly essential to raise productivity, improve the degree of effectiveness of industrial investment and generally boost the operation of the economy if wage growth was to be sustained and a start made on repaying foreign debts. The rapid rise in earnings and the requisite supply of goods to be purchased had to be maintained also for political reasons as the policy of consumer satisfaction was one of the few strategies open to Gierek to maintain a degree of support and secure and adequate level of political compliance. Thus as the economy ran into increasing and ever deepening difficulties the effectiveness of the reforms gained greater political as well as economic significance and the consequences of the measures taken in 1972–75 made their own contribution to the economic and political crisis of 1980. Before discussing their consequences, however, let us look more closely at what the institutional changes involved.

2. Structural Reform 1972-75

At the Sixth Congress of the PZPR (Polish United Workers' Party) in December 1971 a number of principles were established which clearly reflected the new leadership's awareness of the need for institutional change and political and administrative reform. In keeping with the slogan launched by Gierek that the 'party leads and the government governs' the ground was laid for a realignment of party–State relations, clarification of the competence of the different tiers of administration,

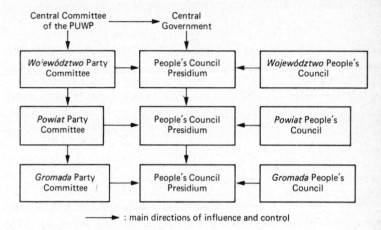

→ : main directions of influence and control

Fig. 5.1 The pre-1972 system

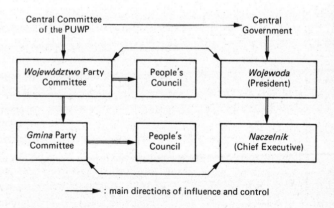

→ : main directions of influence and control

Fig. 5.2 The post-May 1975 system

overall modernization of the State administrative structure and the formation of a better qualified and more competent executive staff. This was
designed to sweep away the obstacles to effective local management and
the exercise of central control inherent in the pre-1972 administrative
system (see Figure 5.1). Such obstacles hinged on the ambiguous status
of People's Council Presidia as the executive organ both of elected Councils
and of central government, imprecise definition of the party's leading role
vis-à-vis the Councils and Presidium, the lack of adequately trained personnel in the proliferating bureaucracies of party and State, and the excessive *de facto* power of the local party secretary – both within the local
political system and, with regard to the status of the *Województwo* Party
Secretary, in relation to the central party leadership. Initial legislation was
passed in 1972 and the first measure of institutional change was introduced on 1st January 1973. This concerned the lowest of the three tiers
of administration as it existed in the countryside (as will be clear from
Figure 5.1 at the beginning of the decade the line of command from the
central authorities ran through the *województwo*, or province, to the
powiat, or district, and the *gromada*, which comprised on average some
eight or nine villages and had a population of three to four thousand).
Instead of the *gromada* the considerably larger *gmina*, or commune, was
established. The new commune was approximately twice as large and,
at least in intention, endowed both with personnel and powers sufficient
to establish it as a unit of self-government and as a service centre to meet
the needs of local peasant farms and their proprietors. Most significant
from the political point of view was the introduction of the post of
naczelnik, or local manager, who was appointed as chief executive and
representative of the state authorities. Previously such functions as he
performed had been shared by the Presidium of the local People's Council
(the unified state structure which had combined executive and legislative
functions) and by higher authorities located at *powiat* level (compare
Figures 5.1 and 5.2). The establishment of a stronger executive figure
in the rural commune thus represented a measure of administrative
decentralization and a shift away from the conception of the *powiat* as
the central authorities' base in the countryside. This turn towards stronger
one-man local management in the state structure may suggest, as it did to
Taras, a likeness to local prefects 'correspondingly roughly to the most
influential offices in the French local government system'.[8] In view, however, of the subsequent souring of peasant-*naczelnik* relations this post
may also be seen as a contemporary copy of the office of 'land captain'
as instituted in 1890 in Russia. But in comparison with the situation
that had emerged under Gomułka the introduction of the *naczelnik* also

represented a stronger commitment, on the part of the state, to control and stimulate agricultural production on private peasant farms.

A second change made later in 1973 tackled a further inadequacy of the People's Council structure: that concerning its role as an organ of self-government. In order to strengthen this aspect of its activity it was suggested at the National Party Conference in October that the first secretary of the appropriate party committee act as chairman of the local People's Council. This, it was felt, would enhance the self-governing, 'social' side of the Councils' work and give concrete expression to the role of the party as the leading force in *society*, rather than appearing to all intents and purposes as a body of full-time apparatchiks barely distinguishable from the chief authorities within the state bureaucracy. Since at the time of the proposal the introduction of the one-man executive had taken place only in the *gmina*, elsewhere in the system the Councils and their Presidia continued to combine executive with self-governing tasks. Consequently the implications of this change for the declared policy objective of drawing a clear distinction between party and State structures and their activities seemed rather muddled. Somewhat clearer, however, was the intention of giving formal recognition to the leading role of the party in the organs of the State and in the exercise of governmental authority. This was already established to a certain extent in the new electoral law (also promulgated in 1973) but was not to be consolidated within the Constitution (and then only after considerable controversy) for several more years. Some of the confusion concerning party–State relations was in fact soon dispelled, as before the Conference recommendation could be acted upon, and the party secretaries 'elected' as Council chairman, the system of one-man executive management already established in the *gmina* was extended to cover the rest of the state structure. In the seventeen provinces (*województwo*) the chief executive was established under the historic title of *wojewoda*, for example, whilst in the five major towns which had *województwo* status he was called the president of the city. This, then, clarified party–State relations to a certain extent, in that State executive authority was concentrated in the person of the *naczelnik*, *wojewoda*, etc. of the particular sphere of administration, whilst the People's Councils were now divested of their executive responsibilities and even more emphatically 'led' by the PZPR (see Figure 5.2). Executive authority was thus clarified and apparently strengthened but social initiative in public affairs and self-government was also to be enhanced. The sphere of institutional activity of chief State executive and dominant party authority became more easily identifiable. Formerly the party had had no formal status within the structure of the State and, however inappropriate the placement of the party secretary at the head of the non-executive Councils and however misleading the pretence that the structure of State authority was separate from that of the party, at least some structural delineation was attempted of State authority and party leadership. This gave some concrete meaning to Gierek's slogan 'the party leads and the government governs' and, it was hoped, cleared the way for more effective supervision over the implementation of governmental decisions and for the development of a more effective State administration with greater capacity to direct an advanced economy and social system.

The final stage of reform occurred in 1975 and, doubtless because it represented the most politically radical of the reform measures, its introduction took place immediately following the passage of legislation and virtually without public foreknowledge (although the possibility of such change had been foreseen and earlier discussed).[9] It was later said of this: 'It originated purely "from above" and was not the subject of consultation with society . . . The very implementation of the reform proposals also aroused grave reservations'.[10] It involved the transformation of the three-tier structure of administration into a two-tier one (see Figure 5.2). The intermediate, *powiat* tier was eliminated altogether and forty-nine smaller *województwa* were set up to replace the previous larger provincial units. In theory the *powiat* had been the lowest effective organ of state power in Poland, but by the mid-seventies it had become quite clear that this claim was no longer valid. In fact the legislative designation of the *powiat* as the basic unit of State administration had been adopted in 1958 but never fully implemented, as numerous functions and activities formally devolved from the centre had been blocked by the *województwo* and had continued to rest at that level.[11] With the enlargement of the lowest administrative units (*gminy*), the extension of their powers and the introduction of one-man management at that level the functions and authority of the *powiat* and its staff became even more tenuous. The new local executive, with greater resources and more staff at its disposal, was able to act with considerable independence and had taken over many of the activities formerly concentrated on the *powiat.* Whilst for many *powiat* towns the third stage of the reform implied some kind of diminution in formal status as only a small number could become the seat of the new, smaller *województwo* authority, in material terms the position of other former *powiat* towns was actually improved due to the tendency of the old, stronger *województwa* to monopolize funds and protect their own interests.[12] In several ways the final stage of the reform can be regarded as the most politically significant, as it involved a major change in the structure and (certainly in intention) functioning of the party itself as well as that of the State administration and People's Councils. In theory the existence by this stage, some thirty years after the establishment of People's Poland, of sufficient numbers of qualified cadres who could be relied upon to perform the roles of administration, management and leadership meant that the heavy weight of central control, with its inevitable problems of bureaucracy and institutional sluggishness, could be lightened and the party–State structure streamlined to the advantage both of economy and effectiveness.

Thus, in tackling what Prime Minister Jaroszewicz had described as the lag of party and State organs behind the development of the economy an attempt was being made to modernize Poland's institutional framework and to adapt it to the demands of a modern economy and 'developed socialist' society. Indeed, the package of reforms as a whole had considerable political significance and was seen as reflecting the attainment of a new stage of development:

> the reform, although it is concentrated on organs of self-government and administration, goes in reality far beyond the levels of local government, and also beyond problems of the State apparatus itself. It has in fact embraced the mechanism of authority in the broadest sense of the term, and particularly two very important aspects of it: (i) the question of mutual relationship between the Marxist–Leninist Party as the leading force in society and the organs of authority and administration, (ii) the questions of the methods and forms of activity of central administrative organs . . . [13]

Thus despite their apparent concern with the structure of the People's Councils, improvement of the mechanisms of State administration and the enhancement of State authority, the reforms also represented an explicit attempt on the part of the party leadership to adapt the party structure and its leading role to a new set of conditions, a task which Gomułka had not faced and the avoidance of which had contributed to the onset of the direct events of December 1970. I shall now suggest that the way in which the Gierek leadership tackled the need for institutional change equally made its own contribution to the dramatic events of 1980.

3. Party–State Relations

One of Gierek's earliest slogans popularized on his assumption of the party leadership was, as noted earlier, that 'the party leads and the government governs'. This slogan was accepted as one of the guiding principles in the process of reform and underlay such measures as the party's direct assumption of leadership over the People's Councils and the establishment of a separate state executive, as well as the switch to a two-tier executive and the intended reduction of bureaucratic complexity and overlapping functions. By emphasizing the separation of State and party activities it was intended to strengthen party control over State organs and thus enhance party leadership. However, it seems this was done without paying due attention to the organization of the economy and the structure of economic administration. Whilst economic reforms were carried out – most notably in extending the number and powers of the WOGs (*Wielkie Organizacje Gospodarcze*: Large Economic Organizations) – changes in ministerial powers and organization were not made, although they did form part of the original conception of the reform process. Whilst changes were not made in this area the reforms that were made contributed to a weakening of party control and to the overburdening of the State executive. The availability of investment funds, allocated by central ministries and at the disposition of the agents of central government, further served to bolster the relative position of plant directors and the economic administration and to increase their autonomy *vis-à-vis* the local party authorities. The peculiar relationships that had developed between the chief representatives of party and State at national level only served to exacerbate these problems.

So, whilst the new party–State structure may have been intended to take account of the spatial distribution of industry and related geographical aspects of socioeconomic development it harmonized less well with the structure of economic adminstration and in particular with the forms of plant and enterprise autonomy that had developed under Gierek. This conflict was clearly expressed in criticisms made by the Kalisz *wojewoda* (formerly First Secretary of the *powiat* and town party committee) at a Central Committee meeting held two years after the new structure had been in operation:

> The experiences of more than two years point to the necessity of returning to the question of the role, position and competence and – in this respect – responsibility of the *województwo* authorities for the development of their territory. The organization of enterprises and institutions should be more boldly fitted into the *województwo* framework than has been the case so far . . .[14]

Co-ordination of economic activities was obstructed where enterprises were controlled by agencies outside the *województwo*; production plans of key enterprises were being altered by the directors of associations (*zjednoczenia*) with no reference to *województwo* authorities. In particular, the KW (*Województwo* Party Committee) Secretary from Wałbrzych, stated that the 'main failure we are experiencing at *województwo* level lies on the investment front. This is largely due to the fact that we have not yet worked out a well organized system of party control'.[15]

Such criticism received no direct reply in Gierek's closing address to that plenary session, although he did state that 'We expect considerably more from directing cadres at all levels. They must be more closely supervised in the execution of their duties than has been the case so far'.[16] The effectiveness of local co-ordination was therefore open to much doubt: the relationship between local and central planning was not a close one and local plans were criticized for their vagueness and were for this reason frequently ignored by the central authorities.[17] Whilst endorsing the beneficial consequences of the reforms in terms of feedback from regional organs (particularly significant in view of the 'known tendencies towards disharmony under socialism') another writer was equally sceptical about the practice of local control. This arose from the lack of specialized expertise at regional level, the importance of hierarchical supervision, the trend back towards earlier methods of economic regulation following the economic difficulties that had surfaced in 1975, and the general inappropriateness of the new *województwo* structure in cases where inter-departmental requirements had to be harmonized, as they frequently did within the developed socialist economy.[18] The need for greater local control had, indeed, been indicated three years earlier as a partial counterpoint to the role of the increasingly large and autonomous units of industrial organization (including the associations), which were described as representing the interests neither of enterprises nor of the State.[19] In this sense Gierek's reorganization of economic life had already contributed to the spread of bureaucratic autonomy. One aspect of this was quantified by the Wrocław *wojewoda* at the Sixth Plenum of the Central Committee in 1980 when he stated that his office consumed and produced eight tons of paper each year. In this process the 'function of the *wojewoda* as representative of the government suffered a deformation, and the *województwo* administrative apparat became something like the *województwo* association of the national economy'.[20] In the situation of the late seventies the state executive was thus overwhelmed by the demands and powers of the economic administration.

The relative autonomy of the plant director with regard to the local authorities was further enhanced by the favourable attitudes to industrial investment initially shown by the Gierek administration in contrast to the relative parsimony towards apparently unproductive social investment (a Communist gloss on 'private affluence and public squalor'). While industrial investment more than doubled (up by 113 per cent) between 1971 and 1976, funds available for investment in the social infrastructure rose by only 70 per cent. On average by the mid-seventies industry was funding some 25 per cent of expenditure on the material production of community services, although in certain areas the level could be as high as two-thirds.[21] After 1970 10 per cent of industrial investment was supposed to flow automatically to People's Council officials to fund the provision of the necessary attendant social facilities, but a significant proportion (30 per cent was estimated in one province) never arrived. In one southern mining region investments of 3,000 million złoty were made during this period, which provided a sharp contrast to the total budget of 200 million złoty available to one of the two councils charged with the administration of the area.[22] Given this imbalance and the desperate social needs of many areas of Polish society it is not surprising that the influence of plant directors over the local authorities was often disproportionately strong. Somewhat disingenuously one director is reported as saying 'the town never refuses our offers'.[23] In the light of the pressures to which the plant director was subject, in particular the pronounced labour shortage (at least under the conditions in which Polish industry operated), his concern for the provision of strictly non-productive facilities was quite understandable if the plant was to be accessible to transport and was to attract the necessary labour force. The enterprise, it was stated, 'is also a social group which may satisfy needs concerning culture, recreation and housing, etc. which go far beyond solicitude just for the efficient performance of production functions'.[24] Moreover, if the provision of such necessary facilities and services could be used to gain the support of the local authorities in, say, some action of doubtful legality but of vital importance to the achievement of production targets, so much the better from his point of view.

In view of the reduced institutional checks on his activity following the reforms, the degree of freedom enjoyed by the plant director was difficult to curb if exercised irresponsibly or in unacceptable directions. It now appears clear that such abuses occurred with increasing frequency in the latter half of the seventies and several examples confirm the view expressed above that local authorities, including the party secretary, were themselves powerless to correct them. One such case concerned the refusal of the Industrial Construction Association in Wrocław province to build workers' flats, choosing instead to provide individual houses for the director's close colleagues. In 1977 the KW Secretary wrote an article pointing out 'our *województwo* is one of the few in the country where since 1974 the number of housing units made available has fallen in proportion to the formation of new households'.[25] A year later the reasons for this decline, which included the impotence of the authorities at *województwo* level, were made public. In the effort to rectify the situation, it was stated, 'requests and threats from the *województwo* authorities did not help'. Resolutions passed by the party committee achieved no more (in fact it was only when removed from his post in the economic administration that the director was also expelled from the party committee) and it was only through the actions of central figures, the Minister of Construction (himself fired in 1980) who was then also Vice-Premier, that remedial action was taken.[26] Such an example demonstrates, among other things, the illusory nature of the decentralizing reforms. The reduction in the size and status of provincial party organizations, far from bringing effective political leadership closer to the local community, simply reduced the party's capacity to supervise and control economic activity at the local level and necessitated cumbersome approaches being made through the central government apparatus. Similar mechanisms had to be brought into operation within the party itself when matters raised by a Primary Party Organization (POP) concerning the disciplining of management for various abuses could not be dealt with by the *województwo* control commission because the individual's competence extended over several provinces and had to be processed by the central control commission.[27] Certainly in this respect the reforms did not enhance the practice of party leadership. The failure to extend the reform to the economic adminstration and central ministries compounded problems of co-ordination and party control already raised by concentration on the WOG strategy of industrial development.

4. Institutional Change and Party Authority: 'Particularism' and Corruption

Central government recognition of the drawbacks of the institutional changes, their deleterious effects on the economy, and their tendency to weaken aspects of the political system, came at a relatively late stage. In early 1980 Wrzaszczyk, head of the Planning Commission, admitted that the reform process, and particularly the development of the new administrative structure, could not 'be regarded as completed, nor the results achieved as optimal'.[28] Babiuch, having taken over as Prime Minister in February 1980 after the dismissal of Jaroszewicz (who had presided over the misfortunes of the Polish economy since 1970) also stressed the importance of strengthening the role of the *województwo* authorities in controlling economic activity.[29] Yet it soon emerged that not only was party authority too weak to enforce its decisions at plant level, but also that the central party leadership had been unable to impose its will on Jaroszewicz's government. Paweł Bożyk, head of a group of scientific advisers assembled by the First Secretary in 1977, described how 'the government introduced an informal prohibition on the passing of information to Central Committee workers, including the group of advisers, and some members of the government used the term "opposition" as a kind of humorous description of them'.[30] The information also later emerged from the President of the Republic that the remedial Economic Manoeuvre adopted in 1976 had been disowned by the Prime Minister himself, who 'frequently expressed his disapproval of the Manoeuvre and later even held that it was the root of our problem'.[31] A majority of the Politburo had, it transpired, been in favour of his removal but had been overruled by Gierek. Thus conflict within the central leadership also served to create conditions for the weakening of party authority. By the time Jaroszewicz was removed in 1980 many sectors of the economy had been running out of control for some years and a system which had emerged on an *ad hoc* basis to further the cause of individual and group 'particularistic' interests was now well entrenched.

As suggested above, the direction of Polish economic reform had led to organizational fragmentation and the autonomization of different organs of the central administration, giving rise to a confused situation of 'multiple power'.[32] Strong criticism of the burgeoning structure of 'local empires' had been launched in 1975 but little had been done about it. The result was that plant directors often acted as local potentates and petty dictators who acted as the main guarantors of local subsistence and in return demanded compliance and submission from the workforce.[33] Moreover, whilst the reforms had reduced the influence of the local authorities on the organization of plant activities from the outside, industrial reorganization had further weakened the remaining elements of worker self-government within. The growth of the WOG network in the industrial sector had created a new organizational structure which still found no reflection in 1978 in the organs of self-government, which remained in the form of the moribund Self-Government Conference and offered even according to official statements virtually no possibility of influencing the actions of central management.[34] Conference resolutions, formally of a binding character, were being overridden without the Conference delegates even being informed; indeed, the legislative definitions adopted some twenty years earlier were not even applicable to the contemporary situation.[35] The disproportionate influence of economic management cadres not only reflected political inequality and the uneven distribution of power in the locality and the factory, but they also were said to give rise to 'subjective factors' which made it far harder to deal with the already considerable problems arising from the 'objective' economic situation.[36]

On one side it was questioned whether the degree of authority held by the director was simply not too great for him to exercise effectively, weighed down as he was by all the details of plant operation. Directors themselves, however, were understandably reluctant to divest themselves of any of their responsibilities and the large number of deputy directors and administrative subordinates merely served to slow down the process of management.[37] On the other hand the freedom of top management to pursue its interests encouraged particularism and frequently led to the involvement of a whole circle of allies in blatantly illegal activities and often included the whole work-force in an open conspiracy. The consequences of this were socially and economically disastrous: acting on the principle of 'minimum effort, maximum profit' supervisors would tolerate shoddy work and underwrite low productivity by artificial pricing, the introduction of fake 'new' products, etc.[38] To those in on the deal this could be quite lucrative. One director was found to have falsified work orders and reports to arrange for average wages to rise by 27 per cent in one year, whilst productivity declined by 17 per cent.[39] What, however, was most telling about the social climate of Poland under Gierek was that the revelation of these machinations in no way detracted from the director's reputation for dynamism and responsibility towards his work-force, and even official condemnation was only half-hearted. Jaroszewicz's statement in 1975, that territorial reform would 'facilitate the elimination of manifestations of particularism and the co-ordination of central and local activities in the execution of the tasks contained in the State plan' thus turned out to be pathetically wide of the mark.[40] With the introduction of the Economic Manoeuvre in 1976 and the attempt to restrain investment and concentrate resources on priority areas, criticism of particularism increased. The Minister of Finance explicitly linked its growth with the 'excessive profits enjoyed by enterprises' and the decentralization of the pricing policy.[41] It was clear that the new structures of administration and party guidance had weakened control over the economy and given freer rein to existing tendencies towards particularism and the misuse of economic resources. But as awareness of such unrestrained egoism spread, and numerous unanswered appeals were made for its eradication, it became increasingly obvious that the party was largely powerless to counteract this. The weakness of the party in this situation played a large part in undermining its authority and encouraging public cynicism about the pronouncements of its leadership. Whilst the reforms had weakened the position of the party they had in fact done little to bring about a clearer separation of the role and functions of party officials and members, and economic administrators. The damaging effects of this on the position of the party were pointed out in 1977 by the editor of the party's theoretical journal:

> We realise that the party is blamed for all evils if it does not wage war against them. This is what the ordinary citizen believes whether we agree with it or not. The only way in which the party can avoid the blame for negative phenomena is to fight them under the banner of the party . . . [42]

But surprisingly little action was taken in this direction.

That the problem of particularism was so intractable and had such harmful consequences for the operation of the economy and for social morale was due not just to the weakening of party control following the reforms. The involvement of adminstrators and officials at all levels in financial abuses and other forms of conspiracy to defraud served to hide individual wrong-doers and those who were merely inefficient. Zanussi's film *Camouflage* brilliantly demonstrated how the self-seeking individual blended harmoniously into a pervasive framework of corruption and mutual self-protection, which was of course why it became a topic of considerable political controversy on its release in 1977. Subsequent trials and sentences of central officials, including the disgrace of Glazur and Lejczak (Ministers of Construction and Coal-mining until late 1980), merely suggest the proportions of the corruption and particularism that developed during the seventies. At the very least, many central government officials and administrators had little interest in or motivation to curb the excesses of management or decision makers at the local level. Frequently such officials also held major positions within the party as well. If the main problem on the government side, given its tolerance of uncontrolled investment and its participation in the use of industrial funds, was that the central authorities turned a blind eye to local abuse, in terms of the party the lack of control can be characterized by the leadership and central apparat being willing and able to turn a deaf ear. There existed no means by which countervailing pressure could be effectively exerted by lower party organs on the leadership. It was not simply a matter of com- munication — the leadership apparently did not want to hear the bad news transmitted from local levels concerning the state of the membership and its inability to control the processes which had taken over Polish society and its economy. Minister of the Interior Kowalczyk, referring to the intelligence channels of the security organs as well as those of the party, described the situation in relatively mild terms:

> The situation underwent a change in the mid-seventies. We began to receive a stream of disquieting information about the growth of social criticism concerning the methods of rule and social perceptions of the discrepancy between the official programme and actual practice. We systematically informed about these matters as well as about growing dissatisfaction resulting from inadequate (social) provision and the declining standard of living of the population. This content tallied with that coming from many *województwo* committees. Unfortunately it was not always adequately comprehended . . .[43]

Further contributions to the sixth Plenum following on from the August 1980 events were more direct. One stresses the divorce of leadership from rank-and-file party members in terms of the lack of consultation before the taking of such decisions as that to raise food prices in 1976, which sparked off workers' demonstrations. Advice and informed comment were not only disregarded but projected increases in prices were further raised: 'Thus was broken the fundamental principle according to which the party leadership functioned. As consultation with society, and even that with the *województwo* committees, degenerated into farce so the basic social compact made after the events of December 1970 was broken'.[44] A *województwo* party secretary also adds his comment on the central importance of the leadership's 'lack of faith in the capacity and abilities of the leading organs at *województwo* level and that of the primary organization'.[45] Certainly the leadership eventually began to have forebodings concerning the mood of the population. At a Central Committee meeting held in 1979 three months before the Eighth Party Congress a *województwo* secretary reported that 'the favourable political atmosphere which we observed during the (electoral) campaign has given rise to a certain anxiety amongst the *aktiv* as to whether all the problems current in society were really articulated at the meetings'.[46] The fact that such currents had been unable to impress themselves upon the awareness of the leadership for some years meant that the problems they referred to had grown even more grave and more difficult to solve.

The erosion of party authority can thus also be linked with the failure to establish institutional means by which the behaviour of the leadership could be changed by pressure exerted on lower and intermediate party organs. Indeed, the downgrading of the status of the individual KW and the *województwo* secretary in 1975 lessened the political pressure on the party leadership and reduced the threat of competition from powerful local secretaries (a major factor in the closing years of Gomułka's rule and, of course, the route by which Gierek had reached the party leadership). But the institutional changes not only diminished the role of the *województwo* party committees and reduced their capacity to influence the leadership. There is also evidence to suggest that the disruption involved in the reform undermined the effectiveness of the committees and local organizations in performing even the reduced role they were now entrusted with. It has been suggested that the reform contributed to the furore caused by the 1976 price rises by disrupting channels of communication.[47] This has to some extent been supported by more recent statements of ex-leaders.[48] There were other indications that the staff changes, intended to improve the quality of personnel and enhance institutional effectiveness, in fact proved quite disruptive. In general, considerable care was taken to ensure continuity and experience in the leadership of the new *województwo* party committees. Thus in *województwa* relatively unchanged by the boundary shifts involved in the reform, eleven first secretaries remained in post and four existing second secretaries were promoted. In newly established *województwa* twenty-one out of the thirty-two new first secretaries came directly from apparat posts, in the majority of cases from organizations which had been responsible for the area from which the new province had been carved out.[49] Whatever the general care taken, though, there can be little doubt that party control was weakened not only by the structural configuration of the reform but also by the disruption involved in the change and associated staffing problems.

One local report, for example, notes that party cells in a *gmina* were behaving in a quite unacceptable fashion with regard to the Peoples' Council and continued to do so because *województwo* authorities did not notice and failed to take action, being absorbed for some time in introducing elements of the political and administrative reform.[50] A more common complaint concerned the quality of the staff placed in some parts of the new structure. Thus with the introduction of the *gmina* network there were often insufficient numbers of experienced party workers available or willing to work in it and the new secretaries were often *powiat* instructors for whom the placement was their first job within the party apparat.[51] A similar point was made following the territorial redivision when the same reporter noted that many posts attached to the new *województwo* committee in Radom were being filled by apparently dynamic young cadres who were, however, lacking in experience, and that certain difficulties were being caused by this.[52] The First Secretary in Radom was himself relatively inexperienced in party work and Krall, it appears, wrote a later report on the basis of her experiences during the workers' demonstrations and subsequent riots telling of the secretary's inability to respond to the crisis and his dependence on central instructions. This, however, did not pass the censor and was not published.[53] The fact that the secretary had not worked in the apparat before and was by occupation a Warsaw-based construction engineer must have contributed to the loss of party control in Radom under these conditions, although the exceptionally poor socioeconomic situation in the area must also have played a part.[54] More detailed information was also published on one *województwo* party organization, Toruń, which has recently seen some of the sharpest conflict between central and provincial party authorities. Of the 170 members of the party apparat there, only one half had been in the party at all for more than ten years whilst a hundred had been in equivalent apparat posts for less than three years.[55] It does therefore appear that the post-reform party was staffed in many cases by relatively inexperienced cadres, a factor which has been lent greater weight by recent complaints that during the seventies many experienced revolutionary activists were needlessly thrust out of active party work.[56]

5. Conclusion: Past and Future Reform

This brief discussion of some of the implications of the Polish reforms for the performance of the party of its leading role, and for its ability to control economic and social processes, does suggest that the attempt of the party to adapt to new requirements of socioeconomic management had major consequences for the operation of the political system as a whole. In particular this concerned the lack of correspondence between the structure of the party and, to some extent, the State executive with that of the economic administration. As a result the streamlining of the party–State structure led to a weakening of party control in this area and to the growing autonomy of the economic administration, which was increasingly beyond the guidance both of the party and of the community as a whole. The specific international political and economic climate of the seventies in combination with the policy espoused by Gierek also provided an opportunity for the well-established Communist weakness for indulgence in industrial investment to be exercised to an unprecedented extent. This permitted the entrenchment of self-seeking, particularist groups which served the interests both of local officials and branch administrators and further prevented the exercise of co-ordinated management. The emergence of domestic problems with the economic strategy in 1975 coincided with severe recession in the international economy intensifying the crisis faced by the Polish leadership. The gravity of the situation in which it found itself meant that conflicting views on how it might be tackled (e.g. the Economic Manoeuvre) were the subject of bitter conflict and remained the source of leadership dissension for the rest of the decade, thus providing further conditions for the perpetuation of institutional disharmony at local level and the further weakening of party leadership. Meanwhile party leaders themselves showed remarkable equanimity in the face of these problems, a response which can be partly attributed to the result of the reforms in insulating the central leadership from pressures conveyed by the party machine within the country as a whole. Certain problems encountered in organizing staff for the new party structure may also have raised some doubts about the reliability of the new organizations. However, also entering this situation was the extremely limited range of action open to the leadership resulting from the tenuous relationship in which the party stood *vis-à-vis* Polish society and to its persistent problems of political legitimacy.[57]

This combination of problems left Gierek's heirs with a crisis so serious that even the Kremlin was inspired to an unaccustomed show of tolerance. One of the most significant factors in the recent domestic crisis has been that the weakening of the party leadership and the apparent refusal of the central authorities after 1975 to take steps to halt the national decline has undermined the role of the party in the political system. The deafness of its leaders to warnings from the rank and file and *województwo* committees over the results of its policies has hardened the resolve of local activists to oppose all further leadership moves which in their view do not strengthen the mass base of the party. This tendency has been strongly expressed since early 1981 and was much in evidence in contributions of working-class Central Committee members at the Seventh Plenary Session.[58] Indeed, in early 1981 it remained questionable how dedicated the authorities were to what was called the Renewal Movement. This helps to explain the head of steam behind the demands for inner-party democracy, for free elections to and within the Extraordinary Ninth Party Congress and also the signs of growing impatience and radicalism within the union Solidarity. Certainly there was much dissatisfaction with the way that central ministries and branch organizations continued to run the economy, more or less as they did before 1980. Equally new conceptions of economic reform announced in early 1981 received only a luke-warm reception and were criticized for being over-influenced by the heads of the existing economic administration, those who (with a few spectacular exceptions) had formerly run the economy into its present state of shortage and declining output, with its attendant features of particularism and abuse of office. Stated one writer nine and a half months after the beginning of the strikes: 'Nothing so far has changed in the methods by which ministries run the economy or in the mentality of the administrators. No signs that any attempts are being made by the administration to adapt to the new situation are visible'.[59] Accounts of ministerial resistance to change which would mean economizing on staff, dispersal of monopolistic power and curbs on their unrestricted authority recall similar resistance to the remedial Economic Manoeuvre of 1976 which attempted to save the economy from the disaster it encountered in 1980. It was, stated one report, 'a public secret that in the majority of ministries there is not even a shadow of any plan of action apart from propaganda intending to convince people of the indispensibility and utility of the department'.[60] The most obvious sign that no basic change in the economic system had yet taken place was the fact that investment funds appeared to flow in the unrestricted fashion characteristic of the previous few years and that competition for them continued unabated.[61]

Certain changes in party–State structure have already been made, although it is too early to tell how important their consequences have been. It was, however, significant that the 1972–75 changes had gained such notoriety that during meetings of Politburo members with local activists the leaders were directly questioned as to whether there were any plans to reverse them.[62] Party leadership of the People's Councils came under strong criticism at the second session of the Sixth Plenum of the Central Committee (October 1980) and a decision to end this practice of leadership selection was announced at the Seventh Plenum in December. At the Eighth Plenum (March 1981) Kania stated that *Województwo* People's Councils had already elected their chairmen whilst the process of election had nearly been completed in councils at lower levels.[63] Certain steps had also been taken to enhance the position of the *województwo* Party committee. Politburo members had attended their sessions and the frequency of meetings of *województwo* secretaries with Central Committee workers had also intensified 'to ensure an accurate assessment of the situation'.[64] The most serious problem in Gierek's legacy to Kania, however, remained the gap between the leadership and the party rank and file. During the early summer of 1981, nearly a year after the beginning of the strike movement which gave birth to Solidarity, the commitment of the leadership to renewal and genuine political reform remained in doubt. Continuing scepticism about the leadership had encouraged the creation of party 'horizontal organizations', which involved direct contact and collaboration between local party groups rather than the practice of following orthodox procedures of directing all communications through higher organizational units. Such scepticism concerning the outlook and intentions of the party leadership continued to be expressed most force-fully by working-class members of the Central Committee. Thus Gajewski, from the Warsaw steel works, reported that his organization was

> deeply worried by the tardy and superficial course of the renewal process and the reckoning carried out with those responsible for the existing sociopolitical crisis. In our opinion decisions taken up to now are only half-measures which do not receive general approval. The lack of concrete and decisive action on the part of party organizations and the administrative authorities is responsible for a continual decline in trust in the party and its leadership.'[65]

Similar sentiments were expressed by a mining delegate at the subsequent meeting of the Committee (Ninth Plenum) who reported declining attend-ances at party meetings and suspicion of the party apparat.[66]

Such statements lend credence to the conclusion that 'In June 1981 the political leaders of the country cannot claim to have regained the con-fidence of the working class'.[67] Much in this respect was expected of the Extraordinary Ninth Congress of the party. When it was eventually held in July 1981 elections to and within the Congress were conducted in accord-ance with the demands for greater recognition of democratic practices voiced by the party rank and file. Freely elected delegates voted a new Central Committee on which sat only eighteen members of the former, 146-strong Committee constituted in February 1980. Very few regional secretaries and no heads of Central Committee departments were included on the new Committee — thus reflecting general fears of a self-perpetuating elite of party functionaries and the desire for a parliamentary-style Com-mittee which would control the apparat rather than being the expression of it. Whether such aspirations will provide the basis for the reformation of the Party and its re-emergence as a viable political institution capable of genuine social leadership will depend, as Kania emphasized in his closing address to the Congress, on results:

> Action and only action can assure whether we find our way out of the crisis. Much depends on whether we can now emerge from the phase in which has been dominant discussion of the effective action which our situation demands. Only the renewal of work can pull Poland out of crisis. Otherwise we shall go down in history as those who talked Poland to death.[68]

Notes and References

1 *Polityka*, 2 June 1973.
2 G. Shakhnazarov, *The Role of the Communist Party in Socialist Society*, Moscow, Novosti Press, 1974, p. 54.
3 M. E. Fischer, 'Participatory reforms and political development in Romania', in J. F. Triska and P. M. Cocks (eds), *Political Development in Eastern Europe*, New York, Praeger, 1977, p. 226;
4 J. Służewski (ed.), *Terenowe organy administracji i rady narodowe po reformie*, Warsaw, Wiedza Powszechna, 1977, p. 129.
5 A. Dobieszewski (ed.), *Organizacja polityczna społeczeństwa socjalistycznego w Polsce*, Warsaw, Książka i Wiedza, 1978, p. 477.
6 *XVII Plenum KC PZPR*, Warsaw, Książka i Wiedza, 1975, p. 32.
7 Dobieszewski, op. cit., p. 477.
8 R. Taras, 'Democratic Centralism and Polish Local Government Reforms', *Public Administration*, 53 (1975), p. 420.
9 S. Lotarski, 'Reform of Local Adminsitration', in A. Bromke and J. Strong, (eds), *Gierek's Poland*, New York, Praeger, 1973, p. 120, and R. Taras, 'The Process of Reform in Post-1970 Poland' in J. Shapiro and P. Potichnij (eds), *Change and Adaptation in Soviet and East European Politics*, New York, Praeger, 1976, p. 74.
10 W. Michalski, in *Nowe Drogi*, No. 3 (1981), p. 165.
11 S. Gebert, *Władza i administracja terenowa po reformie*, Warsaw, Książka i Wiedza, 1978, p. 15.
12 A. Strońska in *Polityka*, 4 December 1976.
13 S. Zawadzki, 'The Reform of Local Government in the Polish People's Republic', *Polish Roundtable Yearbook 1976-77*, Warsaw, Ossolineum, 1977, pp. 14–15.
14 *IX Plenum KC*, Warsaw, Książka i Wiedza, 1977, p. 59.
15 Ibid., p. 70.
16 Ibid., p. 94.
17 A. Zarajczyk, in *Nowe Drogi*, No. 5 (1979).
18 W. Madurowicz, in *Nowe Drogi*, No. 4 (1979), p. 98.
19 S. Jakubowicz, in *Polityka*, 8 May 1976.
20 *Nowe Drogi*, Nos. 10–11 (1980), p. 210.
21 *Polityka*, 8 May 1976.
22 K. Zielińska, in *Polityka*, 22 November 1975.
23 Ibid.
24 J. Bafia, in *Nowe Drogi*, No. 9 (1979), p. 51.
25 L. Drozdż, in *Życie Partii*, No. 5 (1977), p. 18.
26 J. Fastyn, in *Życie Partii*, No. 3 (1978), p. 17.
27 *Zycie Partii*, May 1980, p. 4.
28 T. Wrzaszczyk, in *Nowe Drogi*, No. 5 (1980), p. 15.
29 E. Babiuch, in *Nowe Drogi*, No. 4 (1980), pp. 22–3.
30 P. Bożyk, in *Nowe Drogi*, Nos. 10–11 (1980), p. 294.
31 Ibid., p. 269.
32 J. Zielinski, 'New Polish Reform Proposals', *Soviet Studies*, 32 (1980), p. 19.
33 J. Maziarski, in *Polityka*, 15 November 1975.
34 L. Winiarski, in *Życie Partii*, No. 8 (1978), pp. 1–2.
35 J. Maziarski, in *Polityka*, 27 May 1978.
36 Ibid.
37 A. Kopeć, in *Nowe Drogi*, No. 4 (1978), p. 65.
38 J. Maziarski, in *Polityka*, 15 November 1975.
39 J. Fastyn, in *Życie Partii*, No. 6 (1977), p. 13.
40 *XVII Plenum KC PZPR*, Warsaw, Książka i Wiedza, 1975, p. 36.

41 *IX Plenum KC PZPR*, Warsaw, Książka i Wiedza, 1977, p. 78.
42 *VII Plenum KC PZPR*, Warsaw, Książka i Wiedza, 1977, p. 65.
43 *Nowe Drogi*, Nos. 10-11 (1980), p. 262.
44 Ibid., p. 256.
45 Ibid., p. 233.
46 *XVI Plenum KC PZPR*, Warsaw, Książka i Wiedza, 1979, p. 35.
47 See R. R. King and J. F. Brown (eds), *Eastern Europe's Uncertain Future*, New York, Praeger, 1977.
48 According to E. Babiuch (*Polityka*, 16 May 1981) there was simply 'insufficient time' for reliable consultation.
49 *Polityka*, 21 June 1975.
50 A. Zarajczyk, in *Życie Partii*, No. 5 (1977), p. 35.
51 H. Krall, in *Polityka*, 8 February 1975.
52 H. Krall, in *Polityka*, 29 May 1976.
53 *New Statesman*, 9 January 1981.
54 W. Grochoła, in *Polityka*, 28 June 1975.
55 Z. Machowski, in *Życie Partii*, No. 5 (1977), p. 13.
56 *Nowe Drogi*, Nos. 1-2 (1981), p. 355.
57 These are explored in P. G. Lewis, 'Obstacles to the Establishment of Political Legitimacy in Communist Poland', *British Journal of Political Science*, 12 (1982).
58 *Nowe Drogi*, Nos. 1-2 (1981), especially pp. 8, 21, 24, 41.
59 A. Paszyński, in *Polityka*, 11 April 1981.
60 Z. Szeliga, in *Polityka*, 18 April 1981.
61 A. Mozołowski, in *Polityka*, 9 May 1981.
62 D. Zagrodzka, in *Polityka*, 11 April 1981.
63 *Nowe Drogi*, No. 3 (1981), p. 29.
64 Ibid., p. 26.
65 Ibid., p. 100.
66 *Nowe Drogi*, No. 4 (1981), p. 140.
67 G. Mink and J. Y. Potel in *Problèmes politiques et sociaux* (La Documentation Française), 19 June 1981.
68 *Życie Partii*, No. 8 (1981), p. 4.

PART II   POLICY

6   The Degeneration of Central Planning in Poland*
GEORGE BLAZYCA

1. Introduction

Unlike the situation in the West where political leaderships, if they reach power, expect to do so on the back of a popular mandate or, less positively, thanks to popular indifference, in Poland major political change appears to have more to do with social protest. Major social disturbances will lead to immediate and fundamental shifts in social and economic policy as recent Polish history reveals. However, it also shows that the changes in policy may not be deep enough to overcome basic problems, or not as deep or enduring as first appears. In fact, in the case of Polish economic policy in the 1970s, upon which we wish to dwell in this chapter, all three of these deficiencies will be encountered. To give away the ending of the story at the beginning we will argue:

(i) that the economic policy developed by the Gierek team in the early seventies was internally inconsistent and did not overcome the defects of the traditional central-planning system;

(ii) that some well publicized aspects of economic policy relating to economic reform were hardly implemented; and

(iii) that both the broad economic policy changes of the early seventies and the more specific economic reform were whittled away as the decade progressed.

To make matters worse, all of this happened in the context of an economy operating less and less effectively and over which the central planners progressively lost real control. Indeed, the unsatisfactory nature of the economic policy of the Gierek team bears much of the responsibility for the huge deterioration in economic performance in the second half of the 1970s.

---

*The flow of the argument has benefited from many suggestions made by Charles Clift and Professor W. Brus, and remaining inelegance is solely the responsibility of the author.

2. The Polish Economy before Gierek

One of the most unfortunate consequences of traditional central planning was that by the 1960s it became clear that the planning model was operating increasingly ineffectively. That is to say, in most countries of Eastern Europe growth rates of output were decelerating (in Czechoslovakia a small slump occurred in 1963) despite the acceleration in growth of production inputs. Each unit of output was becoming more and more expensive in terms of input requirement. Of the variety of statistical measures one could select to capture this effect the data in Table 6.1, showing the slow down in the rate of growth in total factor productivity in industry, is representative.

Table 6.1 Productivity of East European Industry

	Annual average percentage growth rate of total factor productivity*			
	1951–55	1956–60	1961–65	1965–70
German Democratic Republic	–	5.9	2.7	3.7†
Czechoslovakia	6.7	6.2	1.8	4.2
Hungary	4.2	2.4	2.5	2.1
Poland	6.4	5.3	3.7	3.0
Bulgaria	5.3	3.3	3.8	2.7
Romania	5.9	5.3	5.0	3.8
Soviet Union	6.2	3.9	1.9	3.5
Unweighted average	5.7	4.6	3.0	3.3

Source: Structure and Change in European Industry, UNECE, 1977, p. 159.

*Total factor productivity is defined as output per combined unit of capital *and* labour.

†1966–68

Given the diversity among countries exhibiting this declining effectiveness the common factor of central planning drew attention to itself. As the late Janusz Zieliński put it, 'From East Berlin to Bucharest, from Sofia to Prague, the existing mechanism of planning and management was singled out as the main cause of East European poor economic performance.'[1] Alongside economic deterioration, interest grew in the possibility of reforming the traditional planning mechanism to purge it of its 'anti-effectiveness' features and instil it with a 'pro-effectiveness' dynamic. East

European economists also developed the theory that economic growth was either of an 'extensive' or 'intensive' nature with growth of the former type relying almost entirely on growth of inputs and the latter relying instead on increased productivity.

With the exception of Hungary, the late 1960s was not a period noted for successful economic reform. Poland over this time was typical of the majority of East European economies. Growth rates were certainly faltering but the Polish authorities subscribed to no clear idea of the appropriate direction economic reform should take. In the absence of any well-defined development programme in which reform could play a part, the idea of timid changes to traditional planning advertised as 'economic experiment', to use the then fashionable description, predominated in Poland.[2]

As far as economic policy in the broad sense was concerned, in the absence of alternative conceptions the Polish authorities fell back on traditional instruments in what eventually turned out to be a very costly attempt to increase sluggish growth rates. The central planners' response to the slow-down of economic growth was to attempt to secure even greater central control over the economy and to restore high growth by committing greater volumes of inputs to production. Labour participation rates, already high by international standards at the start of the 1960s, were stepped up.[3] Wages were held down as the authorities squeezed consumption to find more resources for investment. Real wages grew at only 1.8 per cent per annum over the 1960s – the lowest rate of increase in any centrally planned economy while the investment ratio increased from an average of 16.9 per cent of national income in the 1950s to 21.1 per cent in the 1960s.[4] This involved such a squeeze of consumption that further attempts to maintain the accumulation process by curbs in living standards (the food price increases of December 1970) were fiercely, and successfully, resisted.

The economic policy followed by Gomułka in the 1960s failed completely to halve the decline in the growth rate. In the first half of the 1960s national income grew on average by 6.4 per cent per annum and in the second half of the decade by 5.8 per cent per annum. This was in spite of an acceleration in input growth, especially of fixed assets from 4.6 to 6.2 per cent per annum.[5] The growth rate of labour productivity fell from 5.0 to 3.9 per cent per annum between 1961–65 and 1966–70.

The only 'success' of the 1960s was that the authorities managed to control inflationary pressures by holding the growth of wages in industry to around 70 per cent of productivity growth.[6] If a tight incomes policy was the hallmark of Gomułka's approach to managing the economy and if that sort of economic policy making could lead to an outburst on the

December 1970 scale then there could be no doubt that the lessons would not be lost on Gierek. Indeed, as we shall see, the complete absence of any effective policy to control incomes was the first and a lasting characteristic of the Gierek approach to the problems posed by economic development in the 1970s.

3. The Evolution of a Modern Economic Policy and Reform Blueprint

Gomułka had failed to lead the Polish economy to the virtuous path of intensive growth. Without any clear idea of how to achieve this higher stage of economic development the central planners retreated to the increasingly inefficient instruments of policy which at least had the virtue of familiarity – detailed economic commands. Central orders were, however, fundamentally incapable of encouraging growth through greater efficiency. The economy and policy making became locked in a vicious circle where any deterioration in performance elicited further and ever more detailed central commands and injunctions, which in turn encouraged even poorer economic results.

Gierek was well aware of the basic problems of the Polish economy. He knew too that the only solutions worth considering were those tailored to facilitate the transition of the centrally planned economy from extensive to intensive growth, from low to high productivity, from inefficiency to efficiency. The lack of major developments in economic policy and indeed, in economic planning theory, in Poland in the 1960s meant that ready solutions in the form of a new programme of economic development were not to hand for Gierek.[7] It was also clear that channels of communication between the workers and the leaders of the Polish United Workers' Party had somehow become fouled. Uncertainty over economic policy and the lack of trust suggested, indeed insisted, that widespread social discussion should be the means by which a 'socialist renewal' would be carried throughout society and a suitable economic policy for the years ahead would also be collectively determined. That the programme for the seventies would have to be thrashed out in public added to the appeal of the Gierek regime.

The discussion was quickly initiated. Throughout 1971 debate raged fiercely in the press on the two critical issues of the day: how had things come to the sorry state revealed in the previous December; and how to ensure that those events would not be repeated? Almost immediately a consensus of opinion was plainly revealed. This suggested that economic reform could no longer be postponed and that an economic policy which shifted the burden of adjustment, in the process of trying to maintain a high tempo of growth, onto the working people via restrictive wages policy was a basic mistake. Incomes policy would have to be adapted to suit new conditions and in particular to blend with other aspects of economic policy or reform aimed at fostering permanently higher rates of growth of productivity.

In the early months of 1971 the emphasis of social discussion rested, for quite understandable reasons, on the deficiencies of previous wage and consumption policy. At the congress of the Polish Economic Association held on 7-8 January 1971, Josef Pajestka, an economist and Government Minister argued that:

> In development policy it is not permissible to consider consumption only as a question of its share in the national product. Faster consumption growth is an economic and social condition of faster growth in general. It was precisely the lack of understanding of this fundamental issue which was harmful in our country in the recent period.[8]

Over the next few months the point was reinforced as more economists and others pointed the finger at wages policy as a major source of the tragic December events.[9]

Table 6.2 Annual Average Percentage Growth of Real Wages in the Socialized Economy

1961-70	1971	1972	1973	1974	1975
1.8	5.7	6.4	8.7	6.8	8.5

Source: Rocznik Statystyczny 1976 Warszawa, GUS, 1976, p. 80.

As far as immediate policy measures were concerned Gierek was forced in the early months of 1971 to rescind the price increases of the previous December and the brake was taken off wages growth. Real wages which had grown by less than 2 per cent per annum over the 1960s and only by 1.7 per cent in 1970 grew by 5.7 per cent in 1971. The trend was reinforced when at the Sixth Party Congress held in December 1971 the Prime Minister, Piotr Jaroszewicz, stated, 'The main aim of this plan [for the five years to 1975] is an acceleration in the growth of living standards in comparison with the past ten years'. This commitment was followed up in 1972 by an official decree sanctioning widespread centrally authorized wage increases.[10] Throughout the early seventies real wages did grow quickly, as can be seen from the data in Table 6.2, which also indicates the dramatic change that had taken place in incomes policy.

Thus the main thrust of immediate economic policy measures was aimed at relieving the tensions caused by the previously restrictive policy towards consumption. If political survival was a concern of the new leadership there was no room for compromise; living standards had to be improved and the sooner the better. In a sense, the immediate policy changes that had to be executed were so obvious that the new leadership was in no position to worry about whether or not the right decisions were being made. Economic reform was not so easy to handle. Nor, indeed was the choice of broader economic policy which had to be designed to accommodate both consumption growth and reform as major objectives.

Acknowledgement that the December crisis was not simply the product of any maliciousness on the part of the Gomułka leadership was given in the speed with which the new team instituted a formal discussion on the possibilities of reforming the traditional planning system. After only a few weeks at the helm a Commission was set up to organize work on economic reform under the chairmanship of Jan Szydlak (then a Politburo member and a rising star in the Gierek firmament). An initial report of the Commission on the directions of reform was presented for discussion to the Sixth Party Congress in December 1971. By then a general direction of the embryonic reform became clear as also did the official explanation for the failure of past reform attempts

The public discussion of reform as reported in the colums of *Życie Gospodarcze* focused at first on two main themes, neither of them surprising given what had been said about economic policy and central planning in the 1960s. These were: (*a*) wages, and the need to build an effective incentives mechanism; and (*b*) the 'bureaucratization' of economic life and the need to severely curtail the scope for central interference in operational economic decision making. It was clear that in the late 1960s no incentive mechanism worth the name actually operated in Polish conditions. So long as the authorities felt it necessary to depress consumption to bolster lagging growth rates there could be no role for a vigorous incentives mechanism. In the context of wages growth being held down, the variable part of wages (linked to results) became viewed more or less as a necessity by most Polish workers, while managers, seeking to tread as safely as possible the dangerous path between the faithful execution of central command and the desire not to stir up a hornets' nest of labour force discontent, found ways of paying workers their bonuses whether or not premium tasks were in fact successfully completed.

A crude indicator of the growth of economic centralization is given in the number of mandatory tasks passed down to enterprises from higher authorities. Before 1956 and the reform of that year the number of such directives was not regulated in any way. The decision of the 1956 reform was that this number should be reduced to only eight. However, by as early as May 1957 new indicators had been added to the list until by mid-1959 their number officially reached nineteen.[11] A study of four centrally-planned industrial enterprises in 1968 showed that they received between sixty-two and ninety-four plan targets and an additional forty bonus tasks.[12] Another attempt to count the directives received by enterprises indicated that the figure typical in 1972 was about 117.[13] The Economic Director of the Machine Tools Association believed that this was an under-estimate and the 1972 figure should really be close to 160.[14] When one bears in mind that the enterprise directorate is also bombarded by an inherently uncountable number of informal targets often communicated by telephone it becomes clear that the opportunities for central inter-ference were large and, judging from evidence above, had probably grown throughout the 1960s.

However, the paradoxical result of the proliferation of directive tasks is that central control is probably weakened rather than strengthened since a point is quickly reached where there are too many directives competing for the undivided attention of management, some are likely to be in contradiction with others, and the net result is that upon some criterion (perhaps relative size of premium or ranking in importance of the senders of commands) choice has often to be exercised between directives: some will be executed while others will not. Strong pressures also arise to feign the achievement of plan targets. The consequence is unhealthy for all concerned: for the central planners who are 'cheated'; and for the enter-prises management who are encouraged to 'cheat'. Central control is weakened (but not because of a sensible and considered growth in enter-prise decision making), and performance deteriorates all round. This then, was the economic environment enterprises were condemned to inhabit in the early seventies and one consequence was the understandable demand from management that the enterprise plan be reduced to a single sheet of paper.[15]

The Sixth Party Congress confirmed that the evolving official view on the appropriate direction of economic reform reflected the wider social discussion. A resolution was adopted at the Congress which asserted the need to 'increase the effectiveness of central-planning and economic management' while simultaneously increasing 'independence and initiative in the work of associations, combines and plants'.[16] A formula was being suggested where central authorities would concentrate on strategic and developmental economic tasks leaving day-to-day decision making in the hands of managers in the factories. Immediate steps should be taken to

Figure 6.3 Polish Industrial Organization

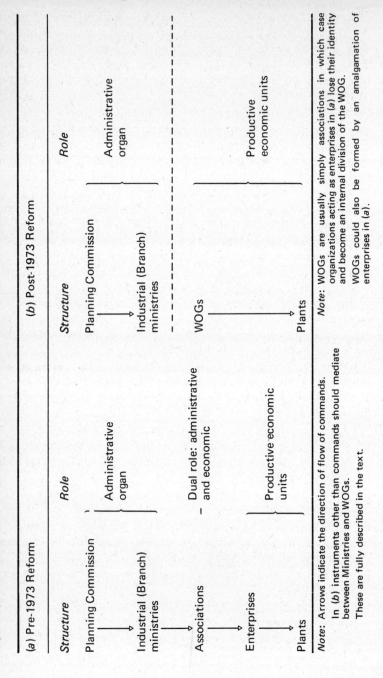

(a) Pre-1973 Reform

Structure	Role
Planning Commission	Administrative organ
Industrial (Branch) ministries	
Associations	– Dual role: administrative and economic
Enterprises	Productive economic units
Plants	

(b) Post-1973 Reform

Structure	Role
Planning Commission	Administrative organ
Industrial (Branch) ministries	
WOGs	
Plants	Productive economic units

Note: Arrows indicate the direction of flow of commands. In (*b*) instruments other than commands should mediate between Ministries and WOGs.

These are fully described in the text.

Note: WOGs are usually simply associations in which case organizations acting as enterprises in (*a*) lose their identity and become an internal division of the WOG.

WOGs could also be formed by an amalgamation of enterprises in (*a*).

'debureaucratize' economic life by sharply reducing the permissible numbers of individual central commands being addressed to lower economic units even before any thorough reform was properly introduced. The Congress noted that profitability should be further developed as a yardstick against which enterprise decision could be independently made and lastly, but with profound implications, large economic organizations (Wiełkie Organizacje Gospodarcze or WOGs) should form the basic economic unit in any new management system (see Table 6.3).

In the new spirit of enthusiasm of the immediate post-Gomułka months, change occurred quickly. Only a few weeks after the Sixth Congress closed the Council of Ministers accepted a resolution increasing the authority of enterprise directors on matters relating to wages and premiums. This was speedily followed by another resolution granting managers even wider powers and curtailing the number of central directives.[17] Meanwhile the Party–Governmental Commission on Reform made a final report to the Central Committee in April 1972. In June a group was set up to see to the implementation of the reform – the 'New Economic and Financial System' – to be formally launched on the 1st January 1973.

Poland is a country that has had a relatively long experience of economic reform, or at least of 'economic experiment'. This might be thought to cause some embarrassment with each wave of reform measures and the implicit (and sometimes explicit) notion that previous reforms had somehow failed to live up to expectations. During the discussions of 1971 people wanted to know why past reform attempts had failed so dismally. The Central Committee in its report to the Sixth Congress listed the following factors:[18]

(a) the lack of a link between reform and general socio-economic policy (most evident recently in the inconsistencies between wage policy and the strategy of intensive development);

(b) the lack of any general reform conception which generated inadequate reforms of a 'partial' sort;

(c) too rapid introduction of reform elements with insufficient preparation to accommodate reform in the national economy and in national economic policy making and planning;

(d) the lack of clarity in how main economic mechanisms would function in the future;

(e) the contradiction inherent in attempts to maintain the traditional form of economic management (commands) while trying to make greater use of economic instruments;

(f) the lack of co-ordinated work on reform and the failure to fix responsibility for reform somewhere in central government. In the past highly placed individuals had made decisions on reform in the absence of widespread discussions.

Table 6.4 The Growing Impact of the New Economic and Financial System

	1973	1974	1975
Number of industrial WOGs	24	62	110
Share in total industrial employment %	18	39	61
Share in total industrial sales %	25	45	65

Source: Blazyca, *Economic Reform in Polish Industry: The Experience of the 1970s.*

It was hoped that the 1970s reform effort would benefit from the experience of errors, and in some ways this happened. Thus the Party-Government Commission was set up to organize a reform *discussion* with a relatively large group of experts (around 120) which would contribute to the notion of developing a comprehensive or complex reform and ensure the abandonment of the previous partial approach to reform. In some other ways the Gierek reform discussion shared the characteristics of earlier reform debates both in Poland and elsewhere in Eastern Europe. For example, the 1973 reform was to be of the experimental type well known in the 1960s in Poland. The 'New Economic and Financial System' was to embrace only a small number of specially selected but extremely large economic organizations (WOGs) in 1973. Results would be carefully monitored, adjustments made if necessary to the new system, and then in 1974, further organizations would join the system until the process of 'creeping-reform' could be said to dominate economic decision making. The actual course of reform implementations is charged in Table 6.4.

Again, like all other East European reforms (apart from the Yugoslav) the Polish discussion in the early seventies could be said to possess a managerial or technocratic character. It was certainly a reform that would, and did, appeal to enterprise directors and was distinguished by completely overlooking any planning role for workers or organs of workers' self-management. While top level managers appeared to approve the direction of reform and eagerly awaited the increased power and status that this would bring, at the same time it is very difficult to find in the contemporary Polish press indications of great enthusiasm for reform on the part of lower-level management, say, at the level of the factory or plant.[19]

The following points are worth noting in relation to the new Giant Organizations (WOGs):

(i) WOGs are huge organizations, the average size in terms of employment of the first twenty-four to join the new system in 1973 was around 33,500. The very largest WOGs were the first to join the reform. By 1975 average size by employment had dropped but still reached a staggering 26,200;[20]

(ii) the reasons for the choice of giant organizations as the basic unit of of a new, modernized Polish industry were never thoroughly argued in public though there was allusion to the idea that scale fosters technological progress;[21]

(iii) the WOG as 'the fundamental link in the management system' was to be considered as the enterprise in Polish industrial organization and this involved a tacit departure from the position that had existed since the early fifties when the single-plant unit was recognized as *the* enterprise in Polish industry.

Following the frequent changes in Polish industrial organization can be confusing.[22] It is sufficient for our purposes to note simply that in the early 1970s 'gigantomania' gripped and dominated the imagination of the leadership to such an extent that judicious warnings that great scale can bring great dangers were simply ignored.[23] In passing, it is interesting to speculate whether given some of the other changes which we know to have taken place in Polish economic policy in the seventies (the 'opening' to the West) this excitement with large economic organizations may not also have been a production of envious glances at the seemingly irrepressible dynamic of giant capitalist corporations.

Economic reforms usually come with two elements: (*a*) the organizational, which we have discussed and (*b*) with proposals for altering in a fundamental way the sphere of economic decision making, or the manner of that decision making, at various levels of the economic hierarchy. The 'New Economic and Financial System' was no exception and carried with it radically new procedures for enterprise (WOG) decision making.

First of all if the WOGs were coming up in the world and were to be the units to benefit from the commitment to greater enterprise freedom then the central planners in the Planning Commission and the men from the Ministries would have to lose some powers to accommodate the new role of the WOGs. How then should the choices open to the enterprise be regulated in the absence of traditional directives? This was where the reformers showed their inclination to experiment with new mechanisms which could be 'tuned' by the Centre and for which activity the Centre would be equipped with a range of new instruments. These mechanisms would, however, be largely self-regulating. Once set by the authorities in Warsaw, the enterprise would be aware of the rules of the game, a new game played unlike traditional planning. So long as the rules were respected all the Centre had to do was make fine adjustments to the (as it turned out) delicate reformed economic mechanisms. It also had to ensure that there should be no cheating: that economic agents would not offend the social interest.

It may be most helpful to examine the new economic mechanisms that were to be introduced alongside the traditional solutions that existed and to do this in turn for the following economic categories: output; wages and labour; investment; and foreign trade.

Apart from only six broad areas where directives could still be issued, enterprises would no longer receive detailed output targets as in previous annual plans. Instead of a high achievement/plan ratio as success indicator enterprises would be judged according to value added and profit growth from year to year. Any such growth would carry some reward and the extent of the reward would be automatically generated by new mechanisms described below. The proposal may seem uninspired but this interpretation would ignore the fact that implementation of the above measures would mark a fundamental turning away from the traditional central-planning system.

Most attention both within Poland and further afield has concentrated on the new incentive system proposed for WOGs. A simple formula captures the essence of the new mechanism. It reads:[24]

$$F_n = F_0 \left(1 + R \cdot \Delta P_d\right)$$

and it contains the proposal that given an enterprise wage fund for some base year (F_0), this is carried forward from year to year and supplemented by some proportion (R) of growth in enterprise value added (ΔP_d). Growth in value added or net output which can be achieved through greater value of sales or lower costs leads also to a larger wage fund which is solely at the disposal of the enterprise either for employment growth or wage growth. Where previously in traditional planning both these variables had been controlled by strict limits imposed from on high, now the enterprise would have to decide itself how best to distribute its scarce wage resources between, in essence, more employment or greater incentives. Central control over wages and employment policy would be achieved not by directives but by allocation of the norm 'R' and, initially, by defining the size of the base wage fund and base value-added. The authorities were obviously concerned that wages should be amenable to control, and that it should be possible to define a wage policy. In the solution mentioned, the Reform Commission had come up with an ingenious new instrument to achieve that end. It is worth adding that a managerial bonus fund was also to be set up in this case linked to profits growth. This premium fund would grow in proportion to profits mediated by another coefficient fixed by the central authorities – the norm N. So the new system in fact contained two success indicators – value-added and profits. The reasoning behind this decision was seldom made clear.

Investment decisions were to be in part decentralized and in part dealt with through an enlarged role for the banking system. First of all an enterprise fund, in other words, a decentralized investment fund, was set up as the residual of net profits once all other commitments had been satisfied. The aim of this was to provide modest resources at the disposal of the enterprise to enable it to carry out fairly small investment of the modernization type and to finance its working capital needs. Again the aim was to impose the discipline on the firm of being forced to choose between competing ends under conditions of scarcity – either to have more working capital or more modernization from the scarce resources available. This of course required the Centre to ensure that the enterprise fund would not become too big. To this end the central authorities defined the particular rules to be followed in setting up the fund, that, for example, this fund should not exceed 4 per cent of the value of the enterprise's working and fixed capital. Any excess was drained off to the State Budget via steep taxes and administrative rules. For more substantial investment the enterprise should be forced to turn to the Bank where credits bearing an interest rate usually of 8 per cent (it was raised from 3 per cent as part of the reform) could be obtained, provided the Bank was satisfied with the viability of projects. Interest on bank credit would be costed against value added, limiting the possibilities of wage fund growth, and so by this device both long-run and short-run economic decisions could be integrated in one economic account. The enterprises should be encouraged by this to consider more carefully the profitability of investment. All of this seemed a great stride forward on the strict limitations on use of investment which were characteristic of traditional planning and which time and again proved to be so extremely wasteful and generated huge and insatiable investment demands.

Foreign trade was also to be brought into the overall enterprise accounting system through a system of transaction prices (foreign trade coefficients) which would translate foreign trade prices to złoty and which would be centrally fixed. In addition, growth of exports should contribute to the growth of foreign exchange resources available to the firm. Again a centrally determined norm, D, would define the proportion of export earnings to fuel the foreign exchange fund. The system would therefore, it was hoped, encourage export activity. Once more, all of this represented immense progress in a system where minimum exports tasks and maximum permissible imports were simply targets and limits handed down by central organs.

Four general features are worth noting about this reform conception. First, the reform, its mechanisms and instruments, focused on the relationship between the Centre and enterprises understood as giant concerns (WOGs). It did not concern itself with the style of management within WOGs. Secondly, the reform clearly aimed to restructure decision-making spheres and to clarify something that often became muddied in traditional planning (areas of responsibility and authority at various points in the economic management hierarchy) but again it avoided doing this *within* the firm. Third, flexibility in economic life was to be encouraged through devising mechanisms and instruments of a wider variety than traditional planning permitted — norms *R, N, D,* tax rates and interest rates. Fourth, and perhaps most important the new economic and financial system aimed to replace arbitrariness in economic affairs by clear and easy to follow procedures.

In the immediate post-December days the need to devise a new economic policy favouring consumption was a necessity for survival of the new leadership. Economic reform was expected by sections of society especially by professional economists and senior industrial management. It was also noted that steps had to be taken to ensure a harmony between policy and reform measures — at least this was pointed to at the Sixth Party Congress as a critical condition for reform success. As time passed a seemingly more coherent set of policy measures were evolved in which reform appeared also to have a secure place.

Other 'errors' of the Gomułka period were highlighted. It seemed at the time that almost simultaneously with the change of leadership in 1970 went a radical shift in attitude to foreign trade. The change was quite appropriate. A more active involvement in international economic relationships could easily be justified within the broad aim of fostering efficiency growth throughout the economy. Alongside the distinction between extensive and intensive growth one could also distinguish the concept of the 'closed' and 'open' economy, or, as a Polish economist has recently put it:[25]

The new strategy of socioeconomic development, assuming a transition from extensive to intensive development, needs also to rest on the idea of the open economy. That idea required, in turn, a fundamental change in the function of foreign trade — and namely that trade should fulfil an active rather than a passive role. Active foreign trade should encourage, above all, improved economic effectiveness through a more rational shaping of the productive structure of the economy.

This represented a fundamental change over traditional command planning. Where previously investment decisions had been made in blissful but costly ignorance of the international economy, now active participation in foreign trade would help determine the Polish pattern of industrial specialization.

Poland ended up then, in 1972-73, with a new economic package in which every element was directed to the hitherto elusive goal of intensive development. Productivity growth would be favoured by consumption growth. Consumption was no longer to be treated as simply a residual in national income once more important commitments had been met. Agricultural development was also to receive greater emphasis than had been the case in the Gomułka period. This was particularly important given the large proportion of family expenditure on foodstuffs and the high income elasticity of demand for meat. Modernization and greater specialization of industry would also play a key part in fostering productivity growth and, in turn, this would be facilitated by an opening of the economy in trading relationships particularly with the industrialized West. The status of foreign trade, like consumption, would also be elevated from residual to key economic magnitude. Meanwhile a profound economic reform would ensure that the quality of economic decision making throughout the system would be thoroughly improved.

4. Economic Performance 1971-75 – Incipient Economic Crisis

A superficial glance at economic results for 1971-75 indicates a marked improvement in performance over the previous five years. Where Gomułka had failed to arrest falling growth rates Gierek succeeded. Incomes grew at a much more rapid rate as did consumption and, in particular, private as opposed to social consumption. The 'economic miracle' as it became known is captured in the data shown in Table 6.5. The Sixth Party Congress had promised immediate improvements in consumption and there can be no doubt that these were provided. Partly the improvement was due to a sudden growth of imports of consumers goods but good agricultural results, aided by favourable weather, also facilitated a significant growth in meat consumption of some 32 per cent between 1970 and 1975 compared to only 7.7 per cent over the previous five years.[26]

The rosy impression generated by the data given is hardly impaired when one notices that employment growth over 1971-75 was only marginally higher than in the previous five years at 3.5 per cent compared to 3.3 per cent per annum. The productivity improvement in the economy as a whole was therefore substantial at an average rate of 5.7 per cent compared to 2.6 per cent per annum in the previous five years. It would seem that the goal of intensive economic growth had in fact been achieved and the Gierek policy, treating consumption as a growth factor, thoroughly vindicated. Partly though, this labour productivity growth was due to a growth in capital per man of 2.2 per cent compared to 1.3 per cent per annum over 1966-70.

Table 6.5 Polish Economic Performance in the Early Seventies (Average Annual Percentage of Growth Rates)

Net Material Product	1966-70	1971-75
(*a*) Produced	6.0	9.4
(*b*) Distributed	5.9	11.3
Gross industrial production	8.6	10.5
Gross agricultural output	1.8	3.7
Private consumption	5.1	8.6
Social consumption	8.5	10.5
Nominal monthly wages	3.7	9.8
Consumer prices	1.6	2.4
Real wages	2.1	7.2

Source: CMEA Data 1979, Vienna, Wiener Institut für internationale Wirtschaftsvergleiche, 1979.

In socialized industry labour productivity growth accelerated to an annual average rate of 7.5 per cent in 1971-75 from 5.2 per cent in 1966-70 and again a growth in capital per man from 4.3 per cent to 7.2 per cent per annum was partly responsible for this. In addition to the greater utilization of fixed capital, productivity was probably also promoted through the tapping of some of the reserves (better utilization of hoarded capital and labour) built up in industry in the Gomułka years. The general enthusiasm which gripped Polish society in 1972 and 1973 and the huge fund of goodwill towards Gierek probably also, for a short while at least, aided the productivity drive.

The favourable summary of economic performance given above can be seriously challenged when one moves on to consider issues related to economic balance and stability. Fast growth may be desirable but a rate of growth that is uncontrolled, that outstrips the capacity of an economy to adjust to higher growth is unwelcome. The problem in Poland over 1971–75 was that economic balances were being upset by the growth policy chosen and these disequilibria eventually posed problems of economic adjustment. It is worth noting that a major source of controversy in Polish economic debate in 1981 is precisely the difficulty in agreeing on a stabilization plan to correct the imbalances which can be traced back to the early seventies.

To return to those imbalances, we may start by considering the wages-productivity relationship which had been so carefully and strictly controlled by Gomułka and control of which is essential to anti-inflation policy. Over the 1960s in socialized industry wages grew at 70 per cent of the rate of productivity growth. In 1972 this ratio was also maintained at 70 per cent. By 1973 however it had crept up to 100 per cent then to a peak in 1975 of 163 per cent before falling to 146 per cent in 1975. Incomes policy had been thrown to the wind. This growth of purchasing power in excess of output growth was bound to sow the seeds of inflationary pressure. A critical feature of the early seventies was the huge jump in the rate of growth of investment in the economy as a whole from 8.1 per cent per annum in the late sixties to 18.4 per cent over 1971–75. In industry the acceleration was even more marked from 7.7 to 21.9 per cent per annum. From the viewpoint of any incomes–output balance this gigantic investment effort could only make things worse as incomes were generated without any hope of extra output for some time at least, and, as it actually turned out in some cases, there would never be an output contribution from some of the wilder early seventies investment projects.[27]

When economic proportions are considered it is clear that following policy decisions of the early seventies three key economic balances were being put at risk. First, wages growth outstripped output growth as became clear when the first lengthy queues began to appear in 1974. Despite large increases in agricultural output, good grain harvests, and growth in livestock herds, the growing demand for meat could not be satisfied. Second, investment growth exceeded the physical capability of the economy to accommodate investment projects as lengthening gestation periods, and a widening investment front testified. The share of investment in national income grew very suddenly from 25 per cent in 1970 to a peak of 36 per cent in 1974. Third, the parallel growth of consumption and investment facilitated by Western credits and revealed in a growing trade imbalance with a growing debt burden, also by 1975 began to cause concern. One thing above all else was clear, and it was clear to many Polish economists: the economy would have to adjust to these imbalances and it would be better to have a controlled programme to manage this adjustment rather than to court economic collapse by allowing queuing and other forms of informal rationing to intensify.

Talk of programmes leads naturally to a consideration of plans. The Polish economy was supposed to be directed through some kind of planning whether it be traditional or reformed central planning. One of the main functions of planning is surely to avoid such imbalance that is likely to lead to economic crisis. Why was Polish planning so unsuccessful in the early seventies that all these disequilibria could so easily emerge?

The fact is that it is exceedingly hard to imagine what the function of the plan was in Poland in the early seventies. All major targets were grossly overfulfilled. The December 1971 Party Congress anticipated a growth of investment on average of 7.7 per cent per annum up to 1975. The result was a growth rate of 18.4 per cent per annum. Real wages were supposed to increase by 17-18 per cent and actually increased by 41 per cent. The cumulative trade deficit with capitalist economies was twenty times above that planned for 1971-75.[28] Every key economic variable seemed to be out of control.

How could such a state of affairs come about? The story as it has unfolded in the 1980-81 Polish economic discussion and which we have no reason to dispute goes something like this: the Gierek leadership, overjoyed with good economic results in 1972 and believing that the 'economic miracle' could be sustained through consumption growth and ease of access to foreign credits, decided to favour continued rapid economic expansion – plans were regularly revised upwards. The problem was that no matter the size of the upward revision actual results in the critical wages and investment areas still exceeded targets. The phrase 'open-planning' was coined to justify every above-plan result. Before being relieved of his position as Chairman of the planning commission in September 1980, Tadeusz Wrzaszczyk admitted, 'open-planning was, in 1971-75, a screen behind which economic planning was replaced by voluntarism in decision making and a lack of any discipline in implementation of decisions'.[29] Perhaps the best way of explaining the demise of central planning is to resort to the strong competing pressures playing on central decision makers. It seems to be generally accepted that branch interests exploited the shifts in policy to their own advantage. The Gierek leadership was too weak to act as arbiter of the social interest. It was too concerned with wages and the dangers in slowing the rate of growth of wages that it effectively gave up all other responsibilities in the economic sphere. It was easier to believe in the efficiency of 'over-planning', and the 'propaganda of success' which insisted that every above-plan result was spectacularly in the interests of society. Of course there was also the advice of the 'court economists', as Mieszczańkowski has put it, which urged continuation of headlong expension.[30] This was more palatable advice than the warnings of some economists that the only destination on this route would be economic disaster, and that to avoid economic chaos, consumption, investment and foreign trade should be more carefully controlled.[31]

The central authorities must carry the blame, if blame be attached, for creating an economic environment in which all things seemed possible without particular strain or tension. The initial impetus to wages growth was through a central reform of basic rates in 1972 and this fed through the 'New Economic and Financial System' to be reproduced, with something over, from year to year. The encouragement of rapid investment growth and the apparently unlimited possibilities in obtaining foreign credits infected all firms with an even stronger than usual investment appetite. Investment decisions were no longer properly accounted for. Bad decisions were made both at central level and at lower levels of the management system. The steel mill 'Huty Katowice' is often pointed to as an example of the sort of error committed by the Gierek leadership but there were countless other smaller mistakes spurred on by the general atmosphere. Many firms took the view, for example, that if difficulties with supplies emerged why not take out a hard currency credit and find a foreign supplier? 'Hooking on to the investment plan' ('zaczępić się o plan') always a concern of socialist enterprises became even more important because it was so easy to do in the boom conditions of the early seventies. The interdependencies in the economy which should have been respected in well-considered investment policy were completely ignored leading to uncoordinated decisions and a huge waste of investment resources. One meets complaints in the Polish press that Western machinery and equipment was often simply left to rust in packing cases exposed on construction sites. Further testimony to the investment chaos of the seventies is also given by Polish offers of uninstalled capital goods for resale in 1981. The plan simply ceased to function. As Brus put it at the time, 'It is a bitterly paradoxical fact that the economy defended in the name of planning against the introduction of elements of self-management, perhaps of the Hungarian type, appears increasingly strongly to be drifting under the influence of anarchic processes, controlled neither by market nor plan.'[32]

The economic reform was at first eclipsed by wider policy changes and then all but completely obliterated. By 1974, after little more than one year of operation, the new mechanisms, were more or less completely

Table 6.6 Wages and Productivity Growth

Annual percentage growth of:	Initiating units		All industry	
	1973	1974	1973	1974
1. Average wages	8.8	11.6	9.2	13.0
2. Productivity	11.6	11.6	9.2	9.6
3. 1:2	0.76	1.0	1.0	1.35

Source: Z. Wit, 'Jednostki inicjujące nowy system ekonomiczno finansowy w planie na 1975 rok', *Gospodarka Planowa*, No. 4 (1975).

suspended. The authorities were in 1974 beginning to show more concern that wages growth should be moderated. They noticed with some trepidation large wage funds being accumulated by the new WOGs funds that could under the rules of the reformed system be placed on the market at any time. Despite the fact that the wages–productivity ratio was actually healthier in WOGs than in industry as a whole, action was taken to disable the capacity of the WOGs to utilize their free wage resources (see Table 6.6).

The manner in which the authorities acted against the reformed system was not to suspend it formally but to create new reserve wage funds that would need to be deposited with the organization's supervising ministry. It also appears that the norm, R, supposed to remain constant for a number of years, was revised downwards. The pharmaceutical concern, POLFA, complained for example that in 1977 their R was equal to a mere 0.1.[33] Next, a new norm to regulate the wages–productivity relationship was introduced, the norm O. In 1975 for similar reasons the large sums lying in the enterprise funds of the WOG, funds that might further disrupt already strained investment activity, caused concern to the authorities. Investment funds were also substantially recentralized. The management of the WOGs found themselves playing a new economic game in the reformed system with a rule book that kept changing. By the end of 1975 the reform had effectively been suspended.[34]

There is little doubt that inflationary pressure and growing disequilibrium was the gravedigger of the 'New Economic and Financial System', but that would not be to tell the story completely faithfully, since there must be some doubt as to the sincerity of the authorities in introducing reform. At the Sixth Party congress discussions about previous reform failure, it was emphasized that an important factor had been the inconsistency between the direction of reform and the direction of economic policy.

Yet there could hardly be a recipe more suited to destruction of the WOG system than to place the delicate mechanisms constructed, mechanisms aimed to encourage choice under conditions of scarcity, in the maelstrom of a frantic expansion where scarcity was the last thing on the mind of enterprise directors. Furthermore. it seems that many initiating units, when they joined the new system, were not properly attired in that they often had to wait months before being allocated the particular value of their norms R, N, and D. In fact the norm D for foreign trade, was hardly ever introduced, and ministries regressed too readily into a pre-reform relationship with WOGs, that is, one regulated by formal or informal command. Of course it may be argued that it was hard for the ministry to inhabit two worlds: one where it received a traditional type of plan, directives and all, from the Planning Commission, and the other where this plan had to be translated into a language understood by the people in WOGs where directives were more or less formally prescribed.

To summarize, difficulties in the technical design of reform, together with an ambiguous attitude to reform on the part of the highest political leadership, and its overwhelming affection for a huge economic expansion, combined effectively to demolish the early 1970s' economic reform.

5. The Economic Manoeuvre

The Gierek boom came to be seen as an enormous bubble. After good economic results in 1972 and also in 1973 shortages began to be noticed on a growing scale in 1974 and 1975. Much of the reported gains in output growth turned out to be spurious reflecting simply the possibilities for monopolistic industry to improve results through price increases. Any trace of incomes policy completely vanished. The construction sector of the economy became hopelessly overcommitted to a growing number of new investment projects. The trade deficit soared, particularly in exchanges in hard currency. The economy was characterized by menacing disequilibria in many spheres.

The 'propaganda of success' made change difficult to embrace and when steps were taken to ease inflationary pressures, for example through price increases in 1976, the best that can be said is that the measures were ill-considered. The watershed in policy making in the Gierek years came at the end of 1976 when it was tacitly admitted in the Fifth Party Plenum in early December that errors had been made in past policy, not least in the June attempt to raise prices without social approval. There would have to be belt-tightening. The dash for intensive growth would have to be moderated. Economic balance had to be restored. A package to provide this was outlined at that December meeting: the time of 'Economic Manoeuvre' had arrived.

The 'Manoeuvre' comprised a set of measures aimed at restoring economic equilibrium in the three key areas of wages and output, investment and construction capacity, exports and imports. The mechanism by which

Table 6.7 Shifts in Economic Policy, 1976-80

| | Average annual percentage growth rates | |
	1971-75 Actual	1976-80 Plan
National income	9.4	7.1
Industrial production	10.5	8.2
Agricultural production	3.7	3.0
Nominal wages	9.8	5.0
Real wages	7.0	3.0
Imports	23.6	4.7
Exports	19.2	11.8
Investment	18.4	8.0

Source: CMEA Data 1979, and Polish press.

this was to be achieved was simply a reassertion of central control and direct command over economic life. Great emphasis was laid on the need for economic agents to respect plan targets for the appropriate wages growth-productivity growth indicator. Investment was to be cut across the board by administrative fiat. Imports were also cut and steps were taken to encourage rapid export growth especially to capitalist economies. A less frenzied and more balanced growth pattern was the goal as the figures in Table 6.7 indicate.

The 'Manoeuvre' would seem to have had some success if success be judged by an examination of investment or import growth over the years of the later seventies. While investment grew at 18.4 per cent per annum on average over 1971-75, in 1976 its growth was a mere 2.2 per cent. In 1977 investment growth was slightly higher at 4.3 per cent but 1978 saw virtually no growth and 1979 and 1980 witnessed very sharp investment cutbacks.[35]

The same trend is evident in the decline of import growth from an average annual rate of 23.6 per cent over 1971-75, to 10.6 per cent in

1976 then 5.4 per cent in 1977. In constant prices the decline was from 15.3 per cent in the earlier five-year period to an average of only 2.4 per cent per annum over 1976-79. Total exports, meanwhile, had their growth rate reduced from 10.7 per cent over 1971-75 to 6.2 per cent per annum over 1976-79. The real impact of the trade manoeuvre is however only seen if the geographical structure of trade is considered. The data in Table 6.8 clearly indicates that over 1976-79 an important trade shift was being

Table 6.8 Shifts in Polish Trade Structure, 1976-79

	Average annual percentage growth rates in constant prices			
	Exports to		Imports from	
Years	Socialist economies	Capitalist economies	Socialist economies	Capitalist economies
1976	−3.0	12.3	7.6	11.4
1977	10.6	4.1	12.1	−10.5
1978	7.5	2.8	4.7	−1.2
1979	9.6	2.1	1.7	3.9
1976-79	6.8	5.3	6.3	−1.4
1971-75	12.0	8.4	8.3	26.4

Source: Wieslaw Rydygier, 'Zludzenia i rzeczywistosc', *Zycie Gospodarcze*, No. 41 (1980).

engineered away from a too heavy reliance on capitalist economies and in favour of East European partners. This is certainly the picture as far as imports are concerned where there has probably been, where possible, some substitution of socialist for capitalist imported inputs (imports from East European countries grew by 6.3 per cent per annum in real terms while imports from the West declined by an average of 1.4 per cent each year). Where substitution has not been possible there is evidence of growing disruption of Polish industry as inputs upon which industry came to rely in the credit boom of the early 1970s were simply cut off. The data also indicates that exports to the West have proved increasingly difficult to achieve.

In spite of strenuous efforts, wages proved much more difficult to bring under control. Greater emphasis was given to the need to respect strictly the wages–productivity indicator set in annual plans. Press campaigns were launched to explore the possibilities of tapping the undoubtedly huge labour and productivity reserves hidden in the enterprise.

In 1977 the earlier reform of 1973, the 'new Economic and Financial System', was revitalized and reintroduced as the 'Modified Economic and Financial System', The main changes however seemed to reinforce a central, rather than an enterprise control over key economic magnitudes and wages in particular. Yet attempts to assert strong central control over wages, to build a new incomes policy, failed completely. Central wages policy, for enterprise managers, had to compete with irresistible demands from the work force for higher wages. Ways could easily be found of meeting these demands whether by paying bonuses for spurious fulfilment of any of the many premium tasks (the proliferation of which was also a consequence of attempts to regain a strong central control over the economy); or by fudging workers' qualifications to place individuals at higher than appropriate points on the wages scale; or by finding ways to increase sickness benefits or holiday pay.

The overall judgement that commands wide Polish support is that the 'Manoeuvre' failed because it was too little too late. Action should have been taken to combat growing disequilibria much earlier than 1977, or better still, the decisions taken in 1972-73 to proceed with the highest possible rate of growth should never have been taken. The impression of successful manoeuvre given by real investment and import cutbacks is in any case mistaken since these were in fact very harmful for the economy. Viewed in this way as a much needed process for adjustment the 'Manoeuvre' acted with a suddenness in 1976 (first major investment cuts) and in 1977 (imports from the West severely cut back) that was simply disruptive to an economy that had become used to growth easily secured by seemingly unlimited investment resources and credits for Western imports. In particular it was not properly understood just how much the Polish economy had come to depend upon imports from capitalist economies not, as many believed, for technological innovation but simply to fuel the current production needs of Polish industry. Rydygier, for example, takes the view that around 66 per cent of credits obtained in the 1970s were used to buy the material supplies needed for current production.[36] Of the remaining credits he believes that around 14 per cent were used for grain, and 20 per cent for machinery and equipment. The result was a steady deceleration in output (National Income) growth over the years from 7.1 per cent in 1976, 5.6 per cent in 1977, 2.8 per cent in 1978 and then a sharp contraction in 1979 of −2 per cent and the slump of 1980 of −6 per cent.

Weakness in agricultural policy became more apparent. The stock of pigs had, for example, increased from 13.4 million in 1970 to 21.5 million in 1975, but then stagnated to reach only 21.7 million in 1978. What is of interest is that between 1975 and 1978 there was an increase in the State sector's pig stock of 2.5 million, while the private sector's stock was reduced by 2.3 million.[37] This structural change reflected the leadership's basic hostility to private farming and was the natural outcome of obstructing the access of private farmers to industrial inputs, especially fertilizer, and to imported animal foodstuffs. Grain imports grew rapidly in the face of poor harvests (due to bad weather) and the thirsty demands generated by the leadership's preference for the building up of giant livestock herds on State farms. Private farms, although more efficient than State farms, were denied resources and were also denied the possibility of becoming even more efficient through limitations on private land purchase.

The 'Manoeuvre' was also an extremely crude device with which to attempt to restore economic balance relying as it did on a proliferation of central directives that met countervailing pressures elsewhere in the economic hierarchy. That is to say, it failed to come to terms with both a very strong wage-push from below, and the vested interests of economic branches in securing even from a globally smaller investment total their 'rightful' share of resources. The 'Manoeuvre' could try to curb the broad profligate growth of investment or imports, but as was made evident, it failed completely to restructure those magnitudes in favour of productivity growth. The period of 'Economic Manoeuvre' was the period, as is now generally admitted, when economic decisions came even more to be taken in a voluntarist manner, unguided by any objective economic necessities or by the plan. The 'Manoeuvre' could not by its very nature instil a pro-effectiveness style of decision making throughout the economy. Yet restructuring in favour of more rapid productivity growth was its aim. To actually achieve that objective would require deep changes to decision-making spheres and procedures, i.e. economic reform.

As this conclusion became increasingly unavoidable reform began to be more seriously discussed. At various times in more recent years the Gierek leadership was said to be courting economic reform,[38] yet the Eighth Party Congress of December 1980 proved disappointing from the viewpoint of any ceremonial unveiling of such reform. Indeed, as far as economic measures are concerned the Congress seemed to argue for a continuation of the 'Manoeuvre' with particular emphasis on overcoming the deepening (despite earlier remedial steps) of the balance of payments disequilibrium. In this spirit a reform of one aspect of the economic system -- the foreign trade sector -- was discussed and ratified by the Council of Ministers in May 1980.[39] It was a modest affair and, to many, disheartening in that it focused exclusively on one area of economic decision making to the detriment of a more comprehensive approach which might attempt to improve the quality of decision making throughout the economy. Against the lessons of all previous reform attempts the proposals were thoroughly 'partial' rather than 'complex' in nature.

6. Conclusion

Poland in 1971 enjoyed a new leadership promising an abandonment of the traditional goals of growth for its own sake and their replacement by the idea that growth should be aimed directly at providing higher living standards, to satisfy the consumption needs of society. Yet in June 1981 a Polish journalist could ask his Finance Minister to comment on the view that Poland would go into history as 'the first country which has borrowed over $25 bn. to introduce a system of rationing and worsen living standards'.[40] How could such dramatic failure come about?

It seems to us that the Polish crisis of 1980–81 is due to the interaction of four major factors. First, the political leadership has proved to be extremely weak and unable to resist strong but narrow demands. Second, a steady source of pressure on governmental economic decision making has come from the large branch ministries interested simply in self-aggrandisement. Third, wage demands have been continuous, strong and irresistible. Fourth, the interaction of the first three factors produced an economic deterioration to which alternatives could not audibly be put due to a lack of respect on the part of the leadership for channels of communication of popular opinion.

Throughout the seventies Poland's major economic needs have been for a shift of agricultural policy to one that responds to opportunities for efficiency gains and for a profound reform of industrial decision-making procedures involving enough decentralization to favour the growth of productivity in the plant on a continuous basis. The import of Western technology proved no substitute for this reform.

One can safely say that this is still the most essential need of the Polish economy even if now, unlike 1971, immediate economic conditions are unsuitable and would not permit such a reform to function. In this case some stabilization programme which would naturally lead to reform is more appropriate. The basic difficulty in attempts to devise this programme is that society, having lost faith in the Gierek leadership, is not prepared to place its trust in Kania. The Ninth Party Congress of July 1981 may be a positive step in restoring trust and laying the basis upon which strong, but socially acceptable, political leadership can be built. With the enormous influence of the new trade unions and the rights won by them to have a voice in economic affiars the previous resistance to opening economic problems up to wide discussion can also be overcome. Perhaps also in the course of social discussion wage demands will be moderated in return for a veto over the direction of economic policy, a veto that in any case surely exists today. In addition, the consensus to emerge may be so powerful as to permit the reorganization of the central apparatus of economic administration and in particular to overcome the destructive particularism of the vested interests, of industrial branches. The four factors that led to the present Polish crisis would then have been satisfactorily dealt with and a solid foundation for economic reform would exist.

As the debate during 1980–81 has shown, this reform would be quite unlike the 1973 version. The major difference would be that rather than being a reform focused on the most senior managers located in the head offices of the largest firms in the country, the reform would be centred on workers in the plant and rest crucially on some form of workers' self-management. Where the WOG system was to be steered in a technocratic manner through central manipulation of price and tax parameters and the norms R, N, and D, reform in the 1980s will be guided by some system which brings together workers' plans and so a democratic style of economic decision making is likely to be its main feature. This is not to deny that many difficulties will still have to be met in attempts to marry social and local interests, and that economic restructuring will pose severe problems for a socialist society aiming to guarantee basic rights such as the right to a job. None the less, the greatest hope that those issues will be sensibly tackled comes in the fact that these problems are now openly discussed, unlike in the Gierek years, and that this discussion is likely to become better organized in the months after the extraordinary Ninth Party Congress of July 1981, a meeting which many hope will become known as the first Congress in 'renewed' Polish socialism.

Notes and References

1 J. G. Zieliński, *Economic Reforms in Polish Industry*, Oxford, OUP, 1973, p. 10.
2 See Władysław Baka, 'Rozwoj systemu planowania i zarzadzania w Polsce Ludowej', *Gospodarka Planowa*, No. 6 (1979).
3 Female participation rates (%) changed as follows: Poland: 1960, 40.2; 1970, 46.4; Czechoslovakia: 1963, 38.9; 1970, 42.3; GDR; 1960, 36.9; 1970, 42.3; Hungary: 1960, 33.2; 1970, 38.6; UK: 1961, 29.3; 1970, 32.2; USA: 1960, 24.6; 1971, 30.9 (Teresa Mantorska, 'Ludnosc czynna zawodowo w Polsce na tle wybranych krajow', *Wiadomosci Statystyczne*, No. 2 (1975), p. 9.
4 *The European Economy, 1950s to 1970s*, UNECE, 1974, p. 16.
5 M. Nasilowski, *Analiza czynnikow rozwoju gospodarczego PRL*, Warszawa, P.W.E., 1974, p. 65.

6 Wages grew on average by 3.6 per cent per annum, productivity by 5.2 per cent per annum, *CMEA Data, 1979*, (Vienna, Wiener Institut für Internationale Wirtschaftsvergleiche, 1979, p. 155 and p. 206.
7 Reform proposals in the 1960s were of the piecemeal and undramatic experimental sort as we have already commented. The most innovatory measure apart from reform policy was the unsuccessful attempt to restructure industry through the idea of 'selective development' of certain branches, a policy that was overturned by the resistance of the industrial branches that would not have been favoured for development. On this see Zieliński, *Economic Reforms in Polish Industry*, p. 90, or J. Staniszkis, 'On Some Contradictions of Socialist Society: The Case of Poland', *Soviet Studies*, 31 (1979), 167-87, p. 171.
8 'Krajowy zjazd ekonomistow', *Życie Gospodarcze*, No. 3 (1971).
9 See for example Jan Mujzel writing in February 1971, 'Wiodace ogniwo – systemu funkcjonowania', *Życie Gospodarcze*, No. 7 (1971); or Mieczyslaw Mieszczankowski, who wrote in June 1971, 'the previous system of wages and incentives was the main brake on economic growth and a barrier to the efficient functioning of the economy', in 'Rozwazania nad reforma', *Życie Gospodarcze*, No. 24 (1971).
10 Piotr Jaroszewicz, 'Wezlowe problemy spoleczno-gospodarczego rozwoju kraju w latach 1971-75', *X Plenum PZPR*, Warsawa, KiW, 1971, p. 11. Centrally authorized wage increases were approved through Resolution No. 222 passed by the Council of Ministers on 11 August 1972.
11 J. M. Montias, *Central-Planning in Poland*, New Haven, Yale University Press, 1962, p. 305.
12 Zielińksi, *Economic Reforms in Polish Industry*, p. 118.
13 J. Dzieciolowski, 'W sieci wskaznikiw', *Życie Gospodarcze*, No. 13 (1972).
14 J. Marzec, in a discussion organized by *Życie Gospodarcze* and reported under the title 'Zmieniac przez dzialanie', No. 21 (1972). In the same discussion the Economic Director of the pharmaceutical firm, POLFA, was moved to ask, 'Are the methods of planning in a socialist economy integrally linked with the institution of indicators and guidelines?' At another meeting another Economic Director of a large firm complained that 'the number of these measures increases from year to year which means that planning is more complicated and there are fewer people in enterprises who can make their way through them ... The number of formulae used in planning, which it is necessary to abide by at present, would fill a whole book.' See 'Mechanizm sluzacy postepowi', *Życie Gospodarcze*, No. 35 (1971).
15 W. Bilut a member of the directorate of the large enterprise, PONAR-KOMO, ibid.
16 'O dalszy socjalistyczny rozwoj PRL w latach 1971-75', *VI Zjazd PZPR*, Warszawa, KiW, 1972, pp. 584-9.
17 Resolutions No. 23 and No. 49 passed by the Council of Ministers on 28 January 1972 and 18 February 1972 respectively, see *Monitor Polski*, No. 11 (1972), para. 80 and No. 13 (1972), para. 90.
18 'Sprawozdzenie komitetu centralnego Polskiego Zjednoczonej Partii Robotniczej za okres miedzy V a VI zjazdem', *VI Zjazd PZPR*, pp. 30-2.
19 This is the impression gained by the author from a survey of the Polish economic literature in the early seventies, see G. Blazyca, *Economic Reform in Polish Industry: the Experience of the 1970s*, University of Sussex, doctoral dissertation 1978, unpublished, pp. 64-5.
20 Calculated from Table 6.4 and industrial employment figures from *CMEA Data 1979*.
21 As Pajestka put it, 'Resting the organizational structure on giant concerns is above all linked with the particular need of organizing modern economic processes and

the need to link R & D with production which it is often very difficult, and sometimes impossible to do except on a large scale.' J. Pajestka, 'Doskonalenie gospodarowania w organizacjach wprowodzajacych nowe zasady ekonomiczno-finansowego', *Nowe Drogi*, No. 10 (1973), p. 52. See also Baka, op. cit., p. 306.

22 A more detailed account of these changes can be found in G. Blazyca, 'Industrial Structure and the Economic Problems of Industry in a Centrally Planned Economy: The Polish Case', *Journal of Industrial Economics*, 28 (1980), 313–26, where it is argued that large economic organizations were favoured by the planners because of the ease with which it was thought that this would provide a means of guaranteeing for the centre its ability to control economic events.

23 A well-known Polish economist who was also actively involved in implementation of the reform attacked the view which saw the WOGs as synonymous with the New Economic and Financial System. This 'can have, and probably already has had, a negative influence on many small industrial units which understand that WOGs will ruin their future': see B. Glinski, 'Jak interpretowac haslo WOG', *Życie Gospodarcze*, No. 10 (1973). Earlier criticisms of the failings of industrial associations (large groupings of many firms, usually all the firms in a given branch of industry, many of which simply became WOGs after 1973) were also available but seemed to get overlooked in the reform discussion. See for example S. Jakubowicz, 'Organizacja to nie schematy', *Życie Gospodarcze*, No. 20 (1971).

24 Detailed English language accounts of this and other mechanisms introduced in the reform can be found in any of: D. M. Nuti, 'Large Corporations and the Reform of Polish Industry', *Jahrbuch des Wirtschafts Ost-Europa*, 7 (1976), 345–405; Blazyca, *Economic Reform in Polish Industry*; P. T. Wanless, 'Economic Reform in Poland 1973–79', *Soviet Studies*, 32 (1980), 28–57.

25 J. Monkiewicz, 'Handel zagraniczny w rozwoju spoleczno-gospodarczym Polski', *Gospodarka Planowa*, No. 1 (1980), p. 32.

26 The following data is of interest:

Average annual percentage growth rates (current prices) of:	1966–70	1971	1972	1973	1974	1975
1. Imports of industrial consumer goods	7.7	25.9	33.2	4.5	20.5	13.2
2. Total imports	9.0	11.9	21.4	33.1	33.4	19.6
Elasticity of growth of consumer goods to total imports 1:2	0.86	2.18	1.55	0.14	0.61	0.67

Source: CMEA Data 1979, p. 359. Meat consumption data is also from *CMEA Data 1979*, p. 287. Unless otherwise stated the data given in Section 4 is from the same source.

27 Apart from the vast resources expended to so little beneficial effect at Huty Katowice problems have cropped up with almost every major investment or modernization project. Tractor production, for example, which was supposed to have been aided by a licence from Massey-Ferguson only reached 54,200 units in 1979 against a planned figure of 87,000, *Życie Gospodarcze*, No. 10 (1980). When the decision was made in 1975 or 1976 to press ahead with a scheme for colour television production using a Ferguson licence it was anticipated that output would reach 300,000 sets per annum in 1980. Actual production that year was about 60,000 sets. See Andrzej Nalecz-Jawecki, 'Rozsynchronizowanie koloru', *Życie Gospodarcze*, No. 41 (1980).

28 Tadeusz Wrzaszczyk, Chairman of the Planning Commission 1975–80, in discussion at the Sixth Plenum of the Party in September 1980, see *Nowe Drogi*, Nos. 10–11 (1980), p. 100.

29 Wrzaszczyk, op. cit., p. 97.

30 M. Mieszczańkowski, 'Kryzys w gospodarcze-przyczyny i drogi wyjscia', *Nowe Drogi*, No. 12 (1980). It is worth noting Wrzaszczyk, op. cit., on 'open-planning': 'Returning to performance over the whole decade I would like to say that although I guided the Planning Commission after the first five years, I am convinced, that even in 1971–75 there were not sufficient resources to maintain the plan, and, at different levels it had to give. It is clear that when the highest level is not taking decisions located in the plan then in resorts (Ministries) and regions the same practice will be generalized. And as a result of this one will get wild investment ('dzikie inwestycje'). That is just what happened. Remember comrades how it was announced: we built illegal roads, plants, stadiums, And the response: very good, we thank you.'

31 As the economic crisis deepened in Poland an impressive body of unofficial and independent economic criticisms began to appear, which unfortunately, has received little attention in the West. An overview of the major critiques to appear is given by W. Brus in 'Problemy gospodarcze Polski', *Kultura*, July–August (1979). One of the most important pieces of independent economic analysis is, *Uwagi o sytuacji gospodarczej kraju*, published by NOWA in Warsaw in March 1978 and reprinted in *Aneks* (London), No. 20 (1979). Another concise overview of this and other unofficial economic discussions is provided by Edward Szczepanik, *Ksztaltowanie sie pogladow Polskiego Rucha Oporu na polityke gospodarcza*, London, IBZK, 1979.

32 Brus, ibid., p. 207.

33 'W Sejmie: Adaptacja Systemu', *Życie Gospodarcze*, No. 50 (1977).

34 Full details of the recentralization procedure can be found in Blazyca, *Economic Reform in Polish Industry*.

35 All data presented in this section is from *CMEA Data 1979*, and from a reading of *Życie Gospodarcze* over the relevant years.

36 See the discussion, 'Czy jestesmy skazani na zadluzenie', *Życie Gospodarcze*, No. 50 (1980).

37 Mieszczańkowski, op. cit., *Nowe Drogi*, No. 12 (1980).

38 See J. G. Zieliński, 'New Polish Reform Proposals', *Soviet Studies*, 32 (1980).

39 See A. Lubowski, 'Przywileje dla eksportu', *Życie Gospodarcze*, No. 20 (1980); and W. Rydygier, 'Nie tylko dla wybranych', *Życie Gospodarcze*, No. 42 (1980).

40 *Trybuna Ludu*, 4 June 1981.

7 Employee Self-management and Socialist Trade Unionism

GEORGE KOLANKIEWICZ

Trade unions ought particularly to participate in working on laws concerning socialist economic organizations and worker's self-management. Economic reform ought to be based on fundamentally widened enterprise autonomy and on the real participation of worker's self-management in management.[1]

In the heady atmosphere surrounding the emergence of NSZZ 'Solidarność', the question of participation in and responsibility for economic management was submerged beneath the oppositional struggle surrounding the birth of the independent trade unions. Added to this was the legacy of disillusionment inherited from the travesty of employee participation which had characterized the Conference of Workers' Self-management (KSR) and the abolition of the last platform for a worker's voice — the Workers' Councils (RR). It is necessary to examine briefly the course of events surrounding the repeated appearance of self-management structures in order to understand not just the emergence of Solidarity itself, but also the determined push for genuine factory self-management which came to the surface in early 1981. Thus it was no semantic coincidence that Solidarity included the term 'self-managing' (or self-directing) in its declarative title since the ethos that underlay it had a direct line of descendance from the spirit of events in Poland in 1956 and 1970. Likewise the search for historical veracity which accompanied the critical scrutiny of Poland's recent and not so recent past, inevitably brought into focus the key industrial democratic institutions: the factory councils of 1945,[2] the workers' councils of 1956,[3] and the Workers' Commissions of 1970. Their demise provided a series of pointers to Solidarity which were incorporated into their programme. That there had to be factory-based organizations other than simply trade unions, was forcefully put by the Wałesa-figure of 1956, the Warsaw party activist Lech Gozdzik, who when asked what advice he would give to the new union replied, 'Return to our idea of worker's councils. The new unions must defend and not manage. You cannot do both at the same time; production must also be in the hands of the workers.'[4] The startling similarity of demands, such as the abolition of the newly created industrial associations (*zjednoczenia*) as representatives of a stiflingly parasitic bureaucracy; and the attacks on symbols of senseless extravagance (i.e. the 'Lenin' and 'Katowice' Steelworks in 1956 and 1981) were all too obvious. There were also sufficient veterans of the 1956 workers' council movement available who were prepared to draw the appropriate conclusions and provide a physical rather than simply ideological continuity.[5] Whilst the consensus was that little progress had been made since 1956 and that the legislation on workers' councils from that year could act as the basis for more advanced formulations, the very existence of Solidarity provided an institutional guarantee which was not present then.

1. Self-management and crisis

The name and the activity of workers' councils goes back to post-1918 Polish independence, and factory self-management is inextricably tied to moments of crisis and hope in Polish affairs. The rights of control accorded to Factory Councils in February of 1945 and to Workers' Councils in November of 1956, although shortlived, concerned for example, the limitation of managerial prerogative, control of wage funds and premium distribution, and powers of internal control. The absence of external vertical or horizontal links between these councils inevitably isolated them, and their spontaneous nature left them within an institutional structure which gradually whittled away their internal sovereignty. To this extent Solidarity saw the need to combine legislation on self-management and the enterprise (where this was separate in 1956) with wider economic reforms aimed at radically decentralizing the economy in a 'market' and 'profit-oriented' direction. This in turn implied considerable structural innovations, particularly in labour allocation between sectors and in administrative concentration at the ministerial and intermediate levels. Therefore, whilst employee self-management councils began to appear in advance of the much-delayed legislation, Solidarity never allowed the 'practice' of self-management to distract it from the wider context of reform. Indeed, industrial self-management whilst being the cornerstone of Solidarity's aim of a 'self-managed society' was only one part of a wider scenario, which was to include regional democracy and ultimately the re-emergence of parliamentary democracy, over all of which Solidarity sought to cast its protective mantle.[6]

The process of emasculation of the workers' councils which began with the Ninth Plenum of May 1957 and the transfer of policy making (as opposed to daily management tasks) to the trade unions, was concluded in the December 1958 legislation on the Conference of Workers' Self-Management (KSR). Herein the rights of the Workers' Councils were handed over to the KSR which now included party and trade-union representation and gave the party apparatus effective control. The lesson for the future was that any employee self-management body must consist of directly elected representatives of the whole workforce with no ex officio members from socio-political organizations.

In due course, by the time of the Second National Council of KSR representatives held in December 1959, the workers' councils, rather than defending the interests of employees were relegated to the major task of ensuring work mobilization, work discipline and raising productivity. There followed a gradual fusion of party, union and workers' council activists, with the KSR working in the interests of management both in terms of internal labour relations as well as in the redistribution of residual premiums and bonuses.

In 1963 the membership of the KSR was broadened still further to include co-opted representatives of technical and youth organizations. By now the KSR was an ally of management in the process of plan negotiation with higher adminsitrative levels, the workers' council, as the weakest link in a discredited line-up, had lost all authority.[7] What is significant is that the erosion of the workers' councils' powers (save for the 1958 legislation) was carried out solely by *directives* of the Central Council of the Trade Unions, its plenum, praesidium or executive committee and not by legal enactment.[8] Understandably in 1980 Solidarity demanded that the direct supervision of self-management be carried out by the Sejm or, better still, by a newly constituted second chamber grouping all self-managing entities in society.

This institutional incarceration of the workers' councils, which in terms of the 1958 legislation were to be constituted of at least two-thirds manual workers, witnessed the disappearance of the last genuine organizational platform for a working-class voice and contributed in this way to the birth of Solidarity. However, as if the above-mentioned destruction of the workers' councils were not sufficient, the aftermath of the crisis of 1970–71 saw a growth in managerial power. Rather than heed the lessons of Gdańsk and Szczecin, the Gierek regime, whilst paying lip-service to self-management at the Sixth Contress, gave the pseudo-technocratic forces the lead with only the party being envisaged as a counterbalance. From 1975 onwards the workers' councils physically began to disappear, and the KSR became a management discussion club. The hoped-for economic decentralization collapsed, and workplace democracy disappeared under the looming economic crisis.

A brief respite was granted after the 1976 riots, and the Second National Conference of the PZPR decided to re-activate the KSRs to head-off further working-class discontent. A resolution of the Politburo of the PZPR decreed that there should be KSRs in all enterprises, and that one-third of their members must be workers engaged directly in production. At the same time representatives of the KSRs should be allowed a voice at the level of the association (*zjednoczenie*) and to constitute a special group concerned with self-management at the KW level of the party, chaired by the first secretary himself. A circular was sent from the President of the Council of Ministers dated 5 February 1978, to ministers, association directors and enterprises, reminding them of their 'obligations to the self-management organs'.

The injection of workers into the KSR briefly enlivened the debates, but these workers were rapidly disenchanted by their lack of impact and by the fact that their term of office was limited to one year; but in due course they were pacified by procedural changes. Since there were now so few workers' councils remaining there was no organizational base for the young activists to develop a common position *vis à vis* management.[9] The trade unions were of little help since their powers had been drastically curtailed despite, or perhaps because of, their internal re-activation in the aftermath of 1976, with the birth of the workers' opposition forming around KOR at first and later around the embryonic independent trade-union movement. Nevertheless, these workers (some 280,000 of them elected by secret and direct elections from the factory department level) provided an excellent training ground for disillusioned activists.[10]

However, the proceedings of the Second and Third National Conference of Self-Management representatives held in July 1978 and June 1979 respectively, focused exclusively on *production* matters, giving support to those who saw all such self-management initiatives as purely cosmetic, serving to channel workers' dissatisfaction.

By December 1978 only some 536 workers' councils remained; a tenth of the number which existed twenty-one years earlier, in spite of the growth in the number of enterprises and factories during that time. In 1980 even the famous FSO factory in Warsaw, which was associated with the workers' councils of 1956, did not elect a workers' council, and in total only six were reputed to remain. This *de facto* abolition of the workers' councils was followed a few weeks later by the July strikes culminating in the birth of Solidarity.[11] These strikes should not have surprised anyone, least of all the Polish leadership, since even routine sociological research had indicated just how great was the disparity between the perceived and the desired role of workers' councils and trade unions in representing workers' interests.[12] Other disquieting results revealed that 76 per cent of workers employed in the largest industrial enterprises (the 'core' working class) perceived certain social groups to be exploiting the work of others, and some 43 per cent saw these groups as earning more than they were entitled to. In 1974, when this study was carried out, most workers saw no difference between the workers' councils and the trade unions, and considered that the former had no better chance of fulfilling workers' demands than a direct appeal to management. By 1978 the party's own research showed that most workers believed that the KSR was totally under management influence.[13] KSRs had become production conferences, where only the voice of management was heard, and where an agenda was imposed that rarely discussed the economic and welfare interests of workers. These answers were elicited from the subsample consisting of those respondents who were not totally ignorant of the KSR's functioning.[14]

2. A New Working Class Needs New Self Management

The level of accurate knowledge concerning the working class in Poland appears to have been inversely proportional to the amount of research expended upon it. Whilst some researchers indicated that the working class of the seventies was better educated, younger, more demanding, and more self-assured, the dissolution of the traditional stereotype of the 'worker' still came as something of a schock. The working class had been consistently 'under-estimated' by social scientists and the authorities alike. There remained an ingrained fear amongst the latter of those dark, emotive massses manipulated by anti-socialist elements. The manual/ non-manual divide was perceived by some 60 per cent of worker respondents in 1975 as highly visible,[15] despite the fact that the educational qualifications of manual workers had increased rapidly. For example, in 1960-61 there were only some 78,400 graduates of elementary technical vocational schools — the major source of semi-skilled and skilled workers in the economy: for 1977-78 the figure was 366,500. Between 1970 and 1977 there had been a 63 per cent growth in the total number of elementary vocational school graduates employed in the economy of whom three-quarters went into industry, construction and transport.[16] It was therefore shortsighted of the authorities to withdraw participatory organizations from the working class or, worse still, to be seen to be cynically providing superficial palliatives. Likewise even the specious arguments used against working-class demands for self-management, such as their immaturity, lack of education etc. were less tenable than they were in 1956.[17]

The other side of the coin indicates that management 'qualifications', both at the factory and higher level, left much to be desired. 'Autocratic' management had been perceived by workers as the major source of divison within the workforce.[18] Managers had to some extent become better educated, but had in the process lost contact with the working class either through social origins or occupational career.[19] Buttressed by the new Labour Code passed by the Sejm in July 1974 giving managers wide-reaching powers, particularly in the area of dismissals (e.g. the infamous Article 52) 'managerialism' became the hallmark of the 1970s. However the overall lack of qualifications both of enterprise directors and their administrative supervisors made them cling to the centralized directive form of management. Of the 111 *zjednoczenia*, 68 *zjednoczenia* directors had less than complete secondary education, and nearly 10,000 enterprise directors had not completed secondary education. Some 104,000 so-called 'specialists' did not have complete secondary education and 53,000 had only elementary education. This 'underqualification' was brought about through 'negative selection', a *nomenklatura* policy of promoting those stupider than yourself.[20] The block on the upward career mobility of young educated cadres which resulted from this policy may also have had three other consequences:

(i) First, the administrative apparatus suppressed the 'specialist intelligentsia' through bureaucratization and multiplication of 'managerial' positions. In this way its lack of qualifications was not highlighted as it might have been;

(ii) Secondly, the administrative apparatus preferred to import foreign technological know-how rather than develop its own educational capital, since the latter would have required the formation of 'partnership' relations with professional groups involving a diminution in directive power;[21]

(iii) Thirdly, any form of economic decentralization or self-management would have threatened this 'quasi-bureaucracy' and thus was to be opposed.

It was not, for example, rule by technocrats or specialists that was seen as at fault, but that in response to demands for professional skills, some careerist elements within the bureaucracy manufactured academic titles, and forced economic centralization for the advancement of a 'mafia of interest'. These two factors when combined gave none of the genuine benefits of centralization but all of its disadvantages.[22] It was to be this bureaucratic opposition spawned during the period of imposed modernization in the 1970s which was to be the major opposition to the self-management movement.

3. Management or Participation in Management?

Article 13 of the Polish Constitution states that 'employees participate in management'. It was introduced in the 1976 amendment of the constitution ostensibly to enshrine self-management, but was to prove to be a powerful weapon in the hands of the bureaucratic opposition to genuine self-management. To indicate how regressive this formulation was, the law of 1956 accorded workers' councils the right to 'manage the enterprise, which is part of national property in the name of the employees'. It was little wonder then that considerable pressure emerged to reinstate the 1956 law. Initially, however, the old KSR format, revived by the incorporation of Solidarity activists, was seen as the likely way forward. It had been the arbitrary centralized rule of the CRZZ, so the argument went, which had condemned the KSRs.[23] The new unions (independent, branch and autonomous) could be given one-third of the KSR representation and the right to veto KSR decisions, which was in effect seen as the right to strike.[24]

Solidarity, however, did not wish to be drawn *directly* into self-management since this would make it into an arm of production-management and undermine its defensive posture. Also the fact that the factory party first secretary was generally chairman of the KSR did nothing to encourage Solidarity. However, the spontaneous formation of self-management councils was forcing Solidarity's hand whilst it was also becoming increasingly clear that the KSR was far too compromised to survive as a viable model.[25]

Whatever the form of management that would evolve and whatever the composition of the 'council', a key question was the nature of the relationship between the employees and the means of production. This in turn raised the thorny question of 'property rights'. State, group (collective), individual, and personal property were the traditional categories, but the ground between genuine collective ownership of the means of production and state ownership (with centralized control) provided the main field of manoeuvre. Neither the constitutional definitions of basic types of property rights, nor the 3 January 1946 Nationalization Law which took over all enterprises capable of employing more than fifty employees per shift provided guidance on the nature of the enterprise–State–nation relationships let alone the vexed question of a 'self-managed' enterprise in a State-run economic system.[26] Lange, whose work was to be used liberally by all sides in the ensuing debate, saw the State economy as one where socialist enterprises hold national property in trust, but which are self-managed within the limits of the national economic plan and general directives of State economic policy. Relations between such enterprises should be based in principle on a system of 'direct contracts', which would replace a system of distribution from above: the latter being confined to exceptional cases where, for example, access to deficit goods, particularly raw materials, could not be resolved by a price policy.[27] Control of self-managed enterprises would be carried out by a second chamber of the Sejm — a suggestion which he withdrew, however, in 1961. In contrast the 1980 debate demanded greater scope for dismembering, amalgamating, or even selling-off the means of production where they were uneconomical to the enterprise. Here even the notion of 'usufruct' fell short of the desired prerogatives.

In the post-August period the principle of management–worker relations espoused by Solidarity was one of the collective contract. Either the contract could be enacted between the self-management organs and the director (in which case the latter was outside of self-management) or between self-managed enterprises, which included the director as an employee of the employees' council, and the State.[28] In some enterprises the pressure of events had left a vacuum which had to be filled. The party, engaged in its pre-Congress 'renewal' withdrew from chairmanship of the KSRs. Solidarity for its part was delayed in its Factory Commission elections, and management were left with no one to speak to. Grass-roots projects thus emerged, often encouraged by management and based upon the 1956 workers' councils legislation with appropriate modifications.[29] Controversy raged over whether party and union executives should be guaranteed a place on the self-management organ — since, as they claimed, they were democratically elected by their own constituents. The weight of opinion was that such organizations could have an advisory role, unless their members were directly elected. What if the party first secretary was elected to the praesidium of the employees council? Could certain office holders be denied passive election rights? Furthermore, should there be a system whereby all departments in an enterprise were represented, or should there be no 'election key' as such, either for sociopolitical organizations or for departments? The issue of the *nomenklatura* was quickly seen to be the root of all future problems. If the party had to base its influence within the self-managing council solely upon the confidence of the workforce in individual party members, then party control, for the sake of which Gomułka had so brutally cut back the workers' councils, would be at best haphazard and highly unpredictable. If however they could control the appointment of the enterprise director, through their right of affirmation (and informal nomination) then, given that day-to-day management would remain largely unchanged, the party would retain a powerful foothold within the enterprise.

A more roundabout tactic for retaining State control was provided in the form of the so-called 'supervisory council' as opposed to 'employee council'. The former would be comprised (apart from employee representatives who could be in a small majority) of representatives of the central authorities, local authorities, suppliers and clients, banks, consumer and ecological organizations. Understood thus, employee self-management would be replaced by 'economic self-management'.[30] Clearly the principle of direct election, and therefore direct accountability, would be undermined by such a proposal; the manager–managed distinction would be maintained (a key principle of self-management being its eventual abolition) and finally, given that there would be 10,000 or so enterprises, where would all the supervisory nominees be drawn from? The more radical proposals at this stage were clear that some voice must be given to the political authorities within the enterprise, but this would be more in the form of interpellation rather than decision making.[31]

4. The Route to Reform

Group Ten of the Government Economic Reform Commission had already worked out the general outlines to the self-management project by mid-December 1980 and then commenced, as it claimed, to tap the opinion of the 'unions'. In the initial formulation, the employees' council (Rada Załogi)[32] was granted the right of veto over the nomination and dismissal of the enterprise director. However, whereas the key theses of the self-management project were ready by early January, they were not published until mid-March, and only became more widely available in April of 1981. In the intervening period, factories such as Ursus, FSC Starachowice, and the Cellulose plant in Swiecie had developed and put into practice their own versions of self-management.

These differed from the broad guide-lines published in mid-February by *Trybuna Ludu*, the Central Committee organ. Apart from matters relating to the constitution of the self-managing body, it was stressed that self-management had to show clearly the 'connection between work and pay at all levels once the plan had been decided'. Whilst squarely confronting the problems of factory over-employment, the self-management bodies also demanded a cut in the number of ministries and a fundamental change in the role of the *zjednoczenia*, away from management co-ordination. In fact, voluntary associations (*zrzeszenia*) were being formed in some industries in anticipation of the implementation of reform.[33]

Although much less spontaneous than the growth of workers' councils in 1956, self-management in practice began to outpace legislation. The proposers of the reform theses provided several possible solutions to such questions as who could vote (i.e. whether pensioners formerly employed in the factory could be included), who could be elected; and the competence of self-management (and including the nomination and selection of the enterprise director, as well as the legal 'immunity' and 'liability' of members of the self-management body). Whatever criticisms were immediately addressed to the reformers, their stock reply was that they were limited by Article 13 of the constitution which states that employees 'participate in management' not that they or their representatives actually manage. To this the retort was, does 'participation' imply 1 per cent or 99 per cent participation?

As a foretaste of the eventual course of events, a practical self-management project initiated by the 'Elana' textile factory in Toruń, which was by no means as radical as some wished it to be, was already doing the rounds of those factories looking for a viable model acceptable to the workforce (which the government proposals clearly were not). The projects had to be seen to have been 'spontaneously' generated; the mark of authenticity during days when concern with 'manipulation' had reached levels of collective paranoia.[34] However, there were those who repeated that in addition to controlling management appointments, plan formulation, work and safety, self-management had to go beyond the individual enterprise, in order to ensure the achievement of the 'social interest' and to mobilize the bureaucracy. The building of the 'Fiat 650' may have been in the social interest as perceived by the centre, but for those confined to the miseries of a wretchedly under-invested public transport system, it was clearly a case of victory of a 'sectional interest'.[35]

Whilst the government experts claimed that Solidarity had been consulted at all stages of the process, either directly or indirectly through their representation on the working party, Solidarity for its part retorted that it had nowhere been able to make public the objections of its experts.[36] In purely logistical terms, once Solidarity had completed its elections to factory commissions its attention would inevitably have to shift to self-management. Factories and enterprises were experiencing severe difficulties such as in raw materials' supply, and a lack of management initiative, due largely to the general inertia which gripped all government and party bureaucracies prior to the Extraordinary Ninth Congress of the PSPR in mid-July.

5. The 'Network'

Solidarity's initiative was born out of the almost accidental formation of a 'horizontal association' of seventeen (initially fifteen) key factories, one from each area, corresponding to the pre-1974 regional divisions. These factories had in general been the headquarters of the MKZs during the general strike alert in the aftermath of 'Bydgoszcz', With the Warski (Szczecin) and Lenin (Gdansk) shipyards taking the initiative, the first meeting of the 'Network' (Sieć Wiodących Zakładów Pracy), took place on 14/15 April at the Gdansk shipyard, devoted primarily to the issue of self-management. Coincidentally this was the date of that other well-known meeting of the party 'horizontal association' in Torun. In a similar way they stressed that they were not official bodies issuing resolutions, but would simply formulate proposals. From the outset, the Network rejected the idea of 'participation' in management and stipulated that the self-management organ must appoint the director. Self-management would allow Solidarity to take a more constructive part in economic 'renewal' without accepting the responsibility for macro-economic decisions in which they had no say. Union strike action could counter bad government discussions but it could not provide the basis for the positive initiatives increasingly being demanded of Solidarity.

Time, however, was of the essence, since the government project was ready to be published and would then go to the Sejm, where new proposals could not be added. There was clearly some opposition from within Solidarity, lest its participation in self-management 'blunt its cutting-edge'. It could also provide an alternative source of authority to the union's hierarchy and become a whip to beat them with. Finally, a question of timing arose. Should self-management be introduced ahead of the wider government economic reforms and thus be constrained by the latter, or should they all proceed in unison? At the end of April[37] a compromise was agreed, whereby Founding Committees for Self-management were to be set up in enterprises (very much in the way the trade unions were introduced), whose task was to produce individually tailored self-management statutes and election regulations (within the bounds of the project to be proposed later by the Network). The propagation of the idea of self-management by these committees would ensure a 'homogeneous' approach to the question and this would in turn pre-empt management manipulation. The Network sent its 'Theses concerning the statute on employee self-management' to Group Ten of the Reform Commission in mid-May. By then the issue was beginning to arouse general interest and more concerted opposition. At a meeting held in June the National Consultative Committee of Solidarity formally attacked the government proposals on self-management and insisted that its research centre present alternative proposals by mid-July.[38]

The prime objection presented by Solidarity to the government proposals was the separation of the two issues of (*a*) enterprise autonomy and (*b*) self-management prerogatives. This was not only reminiscent of the 1956 reforms, but was also indicative of the piecemeal nature of the whole reform exercise. Solidarity combined the two issues in its project on the 'social enterprise'. It was clear by early June that whereas the appointment and dismissal of enterprise directors would be the acid test for any self-management proposals, employee self-management as such would be the issue around which the future shape of wider economic reform would be moulded.[39] It was clear that Solidarity's proposal would give the employees' council considerable rights not just over cadre policy, but also in deciding the general direction of economic activity, organizational structure, income division, co-operation with other enterprises, and internal information control as well as social welfare matters.[40]

6. Social Enterprise vs. State Enterprise

It is possible to juxtapose the government's[41] and Solidarity's[42] proposals on certain key issues, although judging the distance between the two positions depends very much on the political position of the observer. For some, Solidarity's project was a mixture of 'anarcho-syndicalism and Christian democratic solidarism', for others the State's proposals were a blatant defence of 'bureaucratic centralism'. The two key issues are the property status of the enterprise and the appointment and rights of its director.

(*a*) Group Property

The Network proposals envisaged the enterprise as being *managed* by the self-management organs, whereby the enterprise itself rules (władać) over a part of the national wealth *transferred* to it by the founding organ (the State). The exclusive disposer (*dysponent*) of enterprise property are the employees acting through their self-management organs. The government proposals for their part simply stated that the enterprise 'husbands (*gospodaruje*) the national property apportioned to it' on the basis of 'independent economic activity in accordance with the goals of the national socioeconomic plan'. The Network project makes no mention of the plan and only refers to achieving 'the desired economic and social goals through the rational exploitation of resources', to which end the enterprise is 'accorded all rights to the property apportioned to it.'[43]

Little wonder that First Secretary Kania at the opening of the Extraordinary Ninth Congress of the PZPR, was prepared to initiate the ensuing attack on this shift from 'societal' to 'group property'. The cry went up that Solidarity, under the guise of employee self-management was actually appropriating national property. It was the banner under which the whole of Solidarity's proposals were attacked. *Our* 'mines, shipyards and steel-works' were to be taken over and owned by employees. The 'socialization' of state property, it was argued did not entail such far-reaching formulations. It was soon clear, however, that this was a 'false' debate, focusing on the nature of ownership, rather than on the level of influence employees had over the functioning of the enterprise, the 'relations of production', and the division of the surplus product.[44]

Whilst this was indeed the case, the whole question of 'property relations' in Polish society was in a complete state of disarray, and the introduction of terms such as 'communal' (territorial), State (in the government project), and 'collective' ownership as well as participation in ownership or 'mixed' forms (share purchase) only further confused the situation.[45] It appears that during the passage from Reform Commission to the Sejm certain of the more radical proposals were anonymously deleted, but the Network carried out its own 'auto-correction' by replacing the word '*władać*' (rule or possess) by '*dysponuje*' (disposes over) . . . 'that part of the national wealth apportioned to it'. Whilst this quietened political criticism, doubts were still raised, given the power of disposal over resources that Solidarity desired, as to whether monopolistic enterprises, largely unaccountable and uncontrollable by the fiscal measures left to the State, would emerge.

Given the different starting points for 'self-managing, self-financing and independent[46] enterprises', it was likely that differentiation between and within sectors of the economy would increase, and that particularistic interests would dominate the 'general societal interest'. Likewise in a scarcity economy, particularly as regards raw materials, full self-accounting might penalize some enterprises unjustly. The utopian perception of the 'market' and profit-orientation of these social enterprises overlooked certain problems such as who should pick up the pieces in terms of redundancy and unemployment if an enterprise should fail; what would happen if enterprises in their search for profit go only for 'up-market' products; and how could it be ensured that such areas as cultural consumption and health and welfare do not suffer further under-investment.[47]

The general tenor was that enterprises could not be subsumed under a single all-embracing piece of legislation since they faced widely differing economic social and political problems. Solidarity however insisted that the legal system and the Sejm would provide sufficient scope for admin-istrative–ministerial and social control respectively. The usual instruments of parametric control such as prices, taxes, credit, customs dues, as well as the five-year plan enacted by the Sejm would be quite sufficient.[48] Similarly profit orientation was the only basis for self-accounting within a decentralized system and would also ensure better contract discipline between enterprises; the reduction of bureaucratic superstructures and most importantly, would provide a measure of what was received from society (capital goods) and the wealth produced by the enterprise employees.[49] The 'social enterprise' could not, it was claimed, alienate the property at its disposal although the draft project gave the employees' council the right to 'purchase and dispose of' capital equipment to other (private?) enterprises in the interest of profitability and reorganization. Likewise they could amalgamate or disperse as organizations, provided monopolistic practice was avoided.[50] Clearly some conditions over the disposal of societal property had to be included since the search for a quick profit may be too tempting. It was suggested that there be an obligation to re-invest or pass to the state income gained from the sale of capital goods. Likewise, interest payment on the net value of capital property should be exacted to symbolize the nature of the 'lease' relationship.[51]

(b) The Enterprise Director: Whose Employee?

The discussion around property rights was a 'false' debate in another sense, namely that de facto managerial power rested with whoever appointed the enterprise director (given the principle of 'one-man management', which concentrated authority and responsibility in the person of the director and a socialist management cadre). The Network proposal stated almost laconically that the right to appoint and dismiss the enterprise director and to provide opinions on the candidates for positions of deputy director and chief accountant belonged to the employees' council. The government proposal clearly stated that the 'founding organ' (ministry or local government authority) appointed and dismissed the director with the agreement of the employees' council. In certain cases, the latter could appoint directors but these also required confirmation by the founding organ. As elsewhere, the government sought to reduce most of the powers of the employees' councils to presenting opinions, approval, and evaluation, with very few actual powers of decision making. It was left to the Council of Ministers to determine those circumstances where candidates could emerge through open competition, whereas the Network project clearly stated that public competition was the only basis for appointment of a director. Furthermore the Network proposed that the director could be removed either by a referendum of the employees or by his failure to obtain the annual approval (*absolutorium*) of the employee's council.

The crisis in the Polish Airlines LOT was seen as a trial run for this element of employee power. Whilst this specific instance was a case of a long-running battle between the airline enterprise and the ministerial bureaucracy, the issues it raised, such as the role of the *nomenklatura*, the autonomy of enterprises dealing in an international market (i.e. control over foreign earnings), as well as the position of 'strategic' enterprises in the self-management reform, were all crucial. A compromise solution was achieved after the personal intervention of the Prime Minister which all agreed could have been offered before the crisis broke. It was indicative of how much of a staged confrontation this was, taking place as it did during the Party Congress.[52]

Solidarity saw management appointments as crucial, if self-management was not again 'to be reduced to the role of watering flowers in the director's office'.[53] The enterprise director had to be made accountable to the employees, otherwise he would be forever looking upwards to his superiors. To imagine that he could serve two masters – the employees and the State – was to consign the director to continuous schizophrenia. State influence, Solidarity argued, would not be removed, but simply re-directed into more appropriate channels of control.[54] The director would remain in day-to-day control, represent the external face of the enterprise, and could halt an employees' council resolution should it be against the law. Government proposals had certain obvious loopholes with directors vetoing employees' wishes should they 'seriously undermine the social interest', however the latter was to be defined. It was clear that such rights would, in tandem with the above prerogatives of self-management, break the political control of the centre which had been maintained through the succession of crises. It would begin to dismantle the *nomenklatura* system which had fallen into such disrepute during the 1970s. This fight with the *nomenklatura* had the support of many rank-and-file party members who had often seen their own reputations marred by totally unacceptable appointments. Solidarity and party organizations had indeed initiated many competitions (*konkursy*) for management positions throughout the country. Here it was reiterated that simply accepting or rejecting nominations proposed from above was likely to produce 'tame' nominations, whereas a system was required which would produce the best possible nominees.[55]

On the basis of the LOT experience, the State reformers argued that there had to be differentiation of enterprises according to their strategic and economic positions, and that full self-management rights could only be accorded to peripheral consumer-oriented industries. In the first sign of nascent independence, the Sejm sub-commission required the government to specify clearly what the criteria for such a group of enterprises might be so that *ad hoc* inclusions could not be made. As to selection by competition, then clear guidelines for the constitution of such a commission had also to be provided in advance.[56]

Solidarity, in supporting the maximum subordination of the enterprise director to the enterprise rather than to the State administration, stressed that compromise solutions were not possible, since directors could not be expected to combine the societal and individual interests as the conflict between the two could not be resolved at the enterprise level, where it would inevitably lead to greater conflict.

7. Conclusion: Compromise and Mutual Veto

And yet, all the indications were that a compromise would emerge largely due to the role of the Sejm. Whereas the intransigent tone of the resolutions of the Third Plenum of the Central Committee (devoted to the question of employee self-management) appeared to set the stage for a further confrontation, the actual plenary debate displayed considerable internal opposition to the 'hardline' stance over appointments procedures. In fact, the 'horizontal reform movement' within the party had shifted its attention from intra-party problems to self-management.[57] Accepting the need for some form of social control over key, long-term decisions taken by self-management (e.g. changes in direction of production, long-term investment, etc.) the party rank and file also saw a need to 'reform' the existing system of the *nomenklatura*. For their part, management appointments would depend on the significance that the enterprise had for (*a*) the functioning of other enterprises, (*b*) its provision of public services, (*c*) the national defence, (*d*) its 'monopolistic' tendencies and (*e*) the functioning of the region as a whole.[58] Whatever the internal limitations for each enterprise, the eventual designation of the successful candidate from amongst the contesting nominees would require the consent of both the State administration and self-management, i.e. some form of mutual veto powers. Furthermore, wherever the State was granted supervisory rights over a particular enterprise then these would be based on legislation not generalized interference.[59] All in all, despite the aggressive resolution of Solidarity's Congress delegates demanding a national referendum (something which may have been taken as an affront by a Sejm working under considerable pressures), a position had emerged where wide-ranging powers of appointment and policy were granted to self-management with the possibility of certain exceptions in particular instances to be decided upon by the mutual agreement of both sides.[60] Despite Politburo insistence, the Sejm, in what may prove to have been an historic declaration of legislative independence, passed a law that, whilst not acceptable to the Solidarity radicals, will be a solid cornerstone to future economic reform.[61]

Notes and References

1 Point 6, 'Protokol Porozumienia', *Głos Wybrzeża*, 1 September 1981.
2 J. Gołębiowski, 'Problemy nacjonalizacji przemysłu' in *Uprzemysłowienie żiem Polskich w XIX i XX wieku*, Warsaw, Ossolineum, 1970.
3 G. Kolankiewicz, 'The Working Class' in D. Lane and G. Kolankiewicz (eds), *Social Groups in Polish Society*, London, Macmillan, 1973.
4 H. Krall, 'Słowa na trzy dni', *Polityka*, 6 December 1980; S. Lipiński, 'Losy', *Życie Gospodarcze*, 21–8 December 1980.
5 W. Słonimski, 'FSO, Styczień, 1957', *Życie Warszawy*, 5 March 1981.
6 S. Kurowski, 'Inspiracje i żródła programu:, *Tygodnik Solidarność*, 24 April 1981.
7 T. Żukowski, 'Chylenie się ku upadkowi, *Polityka*, 18 July 1981.
8 Wytyczne Komitetu Wykonawczego CRZZ, 9 January 1959; Uchwała II Plenum CRZŻ, 12 February 1963; Wytyczne KW CRZZ, 10 April 1963; Wytyczne Praesidium i KW CRZZ, 20 October 1964.
9 'Wzmocniony głos', *Polityka*, 23 February 1980.
10 Z. Żieliński, 'Aktualne problemy funkcjonowania i rozwoju samorządu robotniczego', *Gospodarka Planowa*, 2 (1979), pp. 57–60.
11 T. Żukowski, 'Ostatnie Mohikanie', *Polityka*, 8 August 1981.
12 L. Gilejko (ed.), *Obraz świadomości robotników wielkoprzemysłowych w Polsce*, Warsaw, Instytut Wydawniczy CRZZ, 1980, p. 104.
13 A. Owieczko, 'Aktywność samorządu robotniczego i efektywność zarządzania gospodarką', *Idologia i Polityka*, No. 12 (1980).
14 W. Stelmach, 'Udział robotników w procesach zarządzania socjalistycznynmi zakładami pracy', in A. Wajda (ed.), *Klasa Robotnicza w Społeczenstwie Socjalistycznym*, Warsaw, IPPMil, 1979.
15 M. Wojciechowska, *Kultura*, 4 January 1981.
16 Owiecko, 'Aktywność . . .', loc. cit., p. 62. The number of industrial workers with elementary vocational education had almost doubled between 1970 and 1979 from 879,300 to 1,421,800; cf. *Rocznik Statystyczny*, 1980, p. 153.
17 S. Chelstowski and K. Szwarc, 'Robotnicza Samorządoność', *Życie Gospodarcze*, 31 August 1981.
18 W. Bielicki and S. Widerszpil, 'Z Problematyki przemian społecznych w Polsce Ludowej' *Nowe Drogi*, No. 7, (1979).
19 J. Wasilewski, 'Społeczne mechanizmy selekcji na wyzsze stanowiska kierownicze', *Studia Socjologiczne*, No. 2 (1978).
20 S. Karas, 'Kwalifikacje a awans', *Życie Warszawy*, 16 April 1981.
21 K. Kloc, 'Nie straszmy sie samorządem', *Przegląd Techniczny*, Nos. 33-34 (1981) pp. 10-13.
22 S. Maciejewski, 'Demagogia technokratow', *Gazeta Krakowska*, 23 January 1981.
23 L. Bar, 'Jaki samorząd', *Trybuna Ludu*, 17 November 1980.
24 T. Bartosziewicz, 'Wymogi praktyki a wymogi społeczne', *Trybuna Ludu*, 14 November 1980.
25 'Zawierzyc załogom', *Życie Gospodarcze*, 30 November 1980.
26 For a foretaste of this debate but in the context of the 'internationalization' of state enterprises within Comecon see A. Nasilkowski, 'Rozwój własnośći panstwowej w PRL i jej związki z własnością innych panstw socjalistycznych' in A. Łopatka and J. Szewczyk (eds), *Prezmian stosunków własnościowych w PRI*, Warsaw, IPPMiL, 1977.

27 O. Lange, 'Jak sobie wyobrazam polski model gospodarczy', *Socjalism*, Vol. 2, Warsaw, 1956.

28 B. Słotwiński, 'Samodzielność dla przedsiębiorstwa', *Prawo i Życie*, 7 December, 1980; J. Gajda, 'Samorząd poza przedsiebiorstwem', *Życie Gospodarcze*, 7 December 1980.

29 'Samorząd – tak, ale skuteczny', *Nowości*, 29 December 1980.

30 S. Jakubowicz, 'Nadzorcze czy robotnicze', *Polityka*, 24 January 1981.

31 Cf. 'Nie KSR, a samorząd pracowniczy', *Gazeta Pomorska*, 15 January 1981.

32 *Podstawowe założenia reformy gospodarczy – Projekt*, KiW, April 1981.

33 'Samorząd-Już', *Życie i Nowczesność*, 12 March 1981; M. Szczuka, 'Samorząd w nowym wydania', *Gazeta Toruńska*, 11 March 1981.

34 *Express Wieczorny*, 2 March 1981.

35 A. Matałowska, 'Samorząd wyobrażony', *Polityka*, 18 April, 1981.

36 'Dlaczego Stworzono KSR-y', *Agencja Prasowa*, A.S., No. 6.

37 J. Poprzeko, 'Zanim reforma nas uszcęsliwi', *Życie i Nowoczesność*, 21 May 1981; J. Szczepański, 'Sieć zakładów wiodących', *Tygodnik Solidarność*, 12 June 1981.

38 'Uchwała Prezydium KKP NSZZ "Solidarnosc" w sprawie projektu ustawy o samorządzie pracowniczym', *Tygodnik Solidarność*, 26 June 1981.

39 H. Chadzyński, 'Podmiot czy uczestnik'?, *Życie Warszawy*, 26 May 1981.

40 For the government projects on trade-union law, the state enterprise and employee self-management see *Głos Pracy*, 30 June 1981, 1 July 1981 and 2 July 1981 respectively.

41 'Projekt ustawy o przedsiębiorstwie społecznym', *Życie i Nowoczesność*, 9 July 1981.

42 W. Marianski, 'Socjalizm czy syndykalizm', *Trybuna Ludu*, 13 July 1981.

43 *Trybuna Ludu*, 15 July 1981.

44 J. Krol, 'W ramach dyskusji o przedsiębiorstwie', *Słowo Powszechne*, 29 July 1981.

45 For an attempt to extract some substantive legal content from this morass see 'O samorządzie bez nerwów', *Życie i Nowoczesność*, 23 August 1981.

46 A Lezczyński, 'Drugie spotkanie w sprawie samorządów pracowniczych', *Trybuna Ludu*, 8–9 August 1981.

47 R. Malinowski, 'Przedsiębiorstwo społeczne (1) and (2) Teoria i Realia', *Życie Warszawy*, 21–2 July 1981, 24 July 1981.

48 A. Fornalczyk, 'Społeczna własność a samorząd pracowniczy', *Tygodnik Solidarność*, 31 July 1981.

49 J. Wiszniewski, 'Nie porozumienia wokoł przedsiębiorstwa', *Polityka*, 8 August 1981.

50 'W sprawie ustawy o przedsiebiorstwie i samorządzie pracowniczym' *Tygodnik Solidarnosc*, 28 August 1981.

51 Z. Fedorowicz, 'Samorazad-przedsiębiorstow – administracja', *Polityka*, 22 July 1981.

52 A. Kozmiński, 'LOT nie ma dyrektora', *Trybuna Ludu*, 3 July 1981; J. Maziarski, 'To nie był zamach stana', *Kultura*, 5 July 1981; 'Lataj LOT-em', *Tygodnik Solidarność*, 17 July 1981.

53 W. Kuczyński, 'Ataki na Sieć, *Tygodnik Solidarność*, 17 July 1981.

54 S. Jakubowicz, 'Spor o samorząd', *Tygodnik Solidarność*, 10 July 1981.

55 J. Stankiewicz, 'Ustawa o samorządzie i słabe punkty', *Tygodnik Solidarność*, 31 July 1981.

56 I. Dryll, 'Ile komu samorzadu', *Trybuna Ludu*, 18 August 1981.

57 'Uchwała, III Plenum Konitetu Centralnego PZPR w sprawie zadań partii w kształtowaniu pozycji samorządu załogi socjalistycznych przedsiębiorstw w warunkach reformy gospodarczej', *Trybuna Ludu*, 4 September 1981.

58 'Stanowisko VIII Sesji poznańskiego forum myśli politcznego', *Życie i Nowoczesność*, 27 August 1981.

59 A. Łopatka, 'O upowszechnieniu samorządu', *Słowo Powszechne*, 31 August 1981.

60 'Uchwała I Krajowego Zjazdu Delegatów NSZZ Solidarność, *Tygodnik Solidarność*, 11 September 1981.

61 C. Bobinski, 'Poland's MPs force a climbdown', *Financial Times*, 25 September 1981.

8 Educational Policy and Educational Reform in the 1970s

JANUSZ J. TOMIAK

The decade 1970–80, seen in retrospect, was a period of increasing difficulty and mounting tension at all levels of education. Clearly, many problems were deeply rooted in the trends and tendencies discernible in the earlier decades; many could be said to have their origin in the decisions taken in the 1960s, or even in the 1950s and in the policies pursued over a long period of time. It was, however, only in the late 1970s that attitudes highly critical of the prevailing policies began to gain a wider circulation and only in the summer of 1980 that open demands were made which were a clear and unmistakable sign that fundamental issues were really at stake.

One of the first and, by far, the most important persons to clearly identify the system of education as a crucial instrument in the struggle for a better future for Poland at the beginning of the last decade was Jan Szczepański, an outstanding Polish sociologist, the author of numerous works in the field, and president of the International Sociological Association in the years 1966–70. In his *Rozważania o Rzeczypospolitej* (*Thoughts Concerning the (Polish) Republic*), published in 1971, he argued that it was education which was deciding the future of all nations in the twentieth century:

> it is (the work in) the scientific laboratories and the universities which to a large extent determines in our times the fate of states and social systems . . . The governments and the nations which do not understand this, which do not secure for their citizens the quality of learning that corresponds to the demands of modern times and which do not demand from them the highest possible qualifications are doomed; doomed irrevocably. Contemporary civilization is a scientific civilization and those who are unable to adjust to it, will go to the wall.[1]

In Szczepański's opinion, both scientific progress and the quality of education in Poland left much to be desired. The crucial decisions were in the hands of political leaders, who often were lacking in professional competence and administrative and organizational ability; there was too much waste of human talent as well as physical resources; not enough expertise in directing scientific and technological research; and little incentive to maximize individual and collective effort. Schools were not succeeding in producing highly disciplined, responsible and hard-working individuals; not enough importance was attached to moral education, civic education and character-training (as a result of which there was widespread corruption and lack of respect for public property). In sum, the opportunities of the 1960s had not been properly taken advantage of in Poland in contrast to the other countries of the socialist camp.[2]

In another book of his, *Refleksje nad oświatą* (*Thoughts on Education*), published in 1973, Szczepański considered the role of education in determining the cultural, social, political and economic profile of the country. Accepting its paramount importance, he argued that the fundamental weaknesses of the Polish system of education were rooted in the lack of a precise relationship between the school system as such and the society as a whole, that is, between the different kinds of educational establishments on the one hand and the totality of institutions, groups and processes shaping the character and behaviour of the individual citizens, on the other. To overcome the existing deficiencies, he advocated positive action in the shape of educational reform, in order to enable all young people to continue studying right up to the level to which their abilities and aptitudes entitled them (the principle of universality); to make transfer from one type of school to another possible (the principle of diversification); to ensure the fulfilment of individual potential, and in particular, to provide the appropriate opportunities for both the highly talented and the slow learners (the principle of flexibility). He also suggested the introduction of facilities for educational and vocational guidance of pupils (the principle of scholastic and professional orientation); and the creation of abundant opportunities for each individual to keep up with scientific and technological advances in the area of his/her specialization and to improve his/her professional qualifications (the principle of lifelong education).[3] Szczepański, together with a small group of other critically inclined writers and publicists, represented at the beginning of the last decade a scientific outlook, based upon careful observation and rigorous analysis of complex social, political and economic phenomena. The conclusions he drew, led him to utter serious warnings that behind the ostensibly solid facade there were grave weaknesses in the socio-political and economic order of the country which warranted action, but which first of all required official recognition.

Unfortunately, the political leadership, bound to the principle of 'democratic centralism', became increasingly deluded by a wholly unrealistic vision of a 'Second Poland', happily sailing on towards increased prosperity, guaranteeing equality of opportunity and personal happiness to all and sundry within a 'developed socialist society'. There, dogmatic pronouncements replaced critical discussions, demagogy and rhetoric took the place of analysis, and slogans and shallow catch-phrases replaced a real effort. Undeniable achievements of hard-working individuals went unrecognized, while a virtual avalanche of distinctions and decorations was bestowed on the growing ranks of conformists and opportunists. When early in 1980 the sudden realization of the impending crisis came, the full extent of the real weaknesses was revealed to all. Educational shortcomings became more apparent, critical comments increased.

1. Education and the Economy: Human Capital

To be quite fair, it must be admitted that some positive features of the educational system could not be dismissed out of hand. The level of educational attainment of the labour force had improved quite considerably over the last two decades, reflecting both the explosion of aspirations among young people as well as the effort by the State to extend the opportunities for study at all levels of education. Whereas in the year 1960/1 there were some 350,000 students aged 18 to 24 in full-time post-secondary establishments (including higher education), in 1974/75 the number reached 750,000. Improved qualifications should have a positive effect upon industrial output and all-round labour productivity, provided, however, that there is at the same time an improvement in the supply and quality of capital equipment under conditions of full employment. The late 1970s in Poland, however, instead of showing a growth in human aspirations as well as promising a high return to investment, witnessed a rapidly growing gap between the two. This was due, above all, to poor judgement and a frequent lack of competence among the top decision makers, but in no small measure also, to the intensifying international competition and deepening world recession. The complete lack of appreciation of the catastrophic dimensions of the Polish predicament in the late 1970s on the part of Polish experts, can best be seen by contrasting any of the speeches made by Mr Stanisław Kania or General Jaruzelski at the Ninth Extraordinary Party Congress in July 1981 with the statements made by the experts in economics of education and educational planning from the prestigious Institute of Science Policy, Technical Progress and Higher Education in Warsaw. Their *Report on Graduate Employment and Planning of Higher Education in Poland*, published by the International Institute for Educational Planning in Paris in 1978 declared that the country 'with the average GNP value per head in the range of US $2,000-2,200, belonged to the group of ten most developed European countries, and twenty most developed countries in the world'[4] and, naïvely predicted that the 1980s would be characterized by 'a continuation of the fast growth strategy of the 1970s, with a radical shift to intensive technological development'.[5]

This kind of forecast, based upon pious hopes rather than properly tested empirical evidence, is in itself proof of the existence of an enormous gulf between the rhetoric characteristic of a system perennially prone to present the existing state of affairs in grossly over-optimistic terms and the true conditions. The latter have now been revealed over the last few months through more open and honest reporting, much more courageous criticism, special investigations and inquiries. Set against the failure of long-term policy measures which were unable to solve a whole range of problems, they provide the key to a proper understanding of the real nature of the 'Polish crisis'.

2. Educational Opportunity: Social Structure and the Urban–Rural Divide

In accordance with its Marxist principles the Gierek administration in the 1970s tried to speed up social and economic development in the rural areas in the hope of acquiring staunch political support. The urban–rural gap proved, however, to be much too big to be meaningfully reduced. In educational terms the last decade could not bring easy success where the earlier decades had largely failed. The evidence given in the recent *Report Concerning the Life and Work Opportunities of Youth (Raport o warunkach startu życiowego i zawodowego młodzieży)* confirms that life in rural areas is difficult and that children and young people living there are still at a considerable disadvantage in comparison with those who live in urban areas. The implications of this issue can be appreciated from the fact that some four million children and young people under 18 live there; 700,000 more than in towns. Well over half a million children living in the villages have far to travel each day to their elementary schools; almost as many do this in order to attend vocational schools. This requires the child, or more frequently an adolescent, to spend ten to thirteen hours per day away from home. Village schools lack thousands of fully qualified teachers and, understandably enough, the level of education of an average teacher in the towns is twice as high (if measured by years of training) as that of the teachers in the rural areas. Apparently, some 30,000 to 80,000 youngsters in the countryside do not complete their basic education every year. Among the 120,000 or so young people starting work on the land every year, 2 per cent have complete secondary general education, 22 per cent have attended agricultural vocational schools, while the rest have either completed, or left prematurely without finishing, the basic eight-year school.[6]

The average size of the family in the countryside is much bigger than in the towns. This has direct socio-cultural implications. Family expenditure on books, periodicals and newspapers varies enormously, depending upon its size: a childless couple spend 334 złotys per year per person; a family with one child — 114 złotys; a family with four children — 7 złotys. Even when one translates these figures into expenditure per family per year, the differences are fundamental.[7] Social expenditure directed specifically towards helping the rural population in the form of a network of cultural centres, libraries, cinemas, sport facilities, etc., is inadequate, while the specialists working there often have not completed secondary education (and occasionally even basic education).[8] The rural–urban dichotomy is a permanent feature of many countries and cannot be eliminated in the short run. However, real weaknesses of Polish agriculture, such as a low degree of mechanization and automation, perpetual problems with the maintenance of agricultural equipment and the virtual impossibility of obtaining spare parts for it, indicate the nature of the predicament.

Basic primary/lower secondary education was restructured after the Second World War with the purpose of providing comprehensive general education for all children aged seven to fifteen throughout the country (see Figure 8.1). The formal equalization of access to the same kind of school could not, however, bring about a genuine equalization of educational opportunity in a country so highly differentiated in terms of social and economic background. As the latter could not be easily eliminated, strong tendencies towards uniformity clearly showed themselves in the organization of schools and control over the curriculum.

3. Curriculum Content: Preparation for Life and Preparation for Work

The school programmes which operate in Polish education are, as in all of the continental European countries, fixed and rigid. All the teaching syllabuses are prepared by officially appointed theoreticians and practically experienced experts, who are directed by the *Institute of School Programmes* (*Instytut Programów Szkolnych*). All the syllabuses must be approved by the Minister of Education and, subsequently, they must be fully implemented by the practising teachers in all individual schools. Changes in the content of learning can only be made with the explicit consent of the Minister. While a rich, encyclopaedic concept of the curriculum prevails, containing no less than fifteen subjects (plus three options)

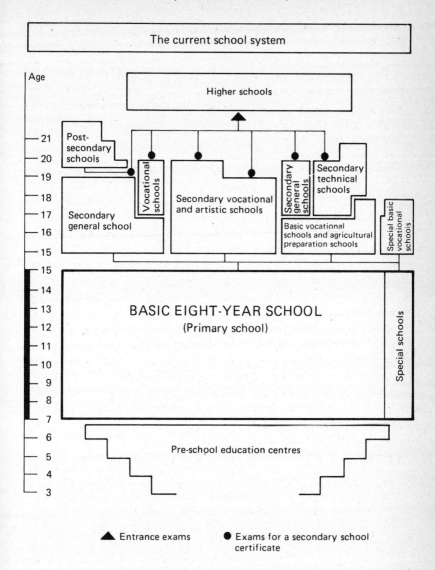

Figure 8.1 The current system of education. *Source:* Ministry of Education in Polish People's Republic, The Development of Education in Polish People's Republic 1974–1976, A Report for IBE, Geneva; Warsaw, 1977, p. 60.

for the children in grades five to eight in the basic school and as many as eighteen subjects (plus four possible options) in the four grades of secondary general school, certain subjects possess a special significance, or rather ought to possess a special significance, according to the prevailing philosophy of education.

Preparation for life and preparation for work, inculcating into each pupil and into each student respect for physical effort and acquainting the young with the foundations of modern science and technology, have always been very important principles in any secular system of education and, particularly, in a socialist system of education. The Polish schools, however, have avoided – rather unexpectedly – the term *polytechnical education* and have instead included in the curriculum of general education for schools *practical-technical training* and *technical education*. Yet, the difference between the two from the conceptual point of view is fundamental: polytechnical education is seen in the Marxist–Leninist theory of education as a basic, fundamental and indispensable dimension in learning, opening up the way for a deeper understanding and appreciation of the significance of the scientific-technological perspectives in modern life in general; technical or practical-technical education deals with specific tools and the ways of handling them. The latter do not constitute a distinctive perspective, do not permeate the teaching of all subjects, but rather resemble the teaching of woodwork or metalwork. Certainly, linking theory and practice in this respect provides a real challenge. There is, however, an acceptance of the fact that 'the concept of practical work integrally linked with theoretical instruction in order to introduce students into the world of productive work and teach them its rules, has proved difficult to elaborate'.[9] What is even more fundamental is the general tenor of instruction in preparing the pupils for life and work in a way which truly reflects the realities of adult life: its toughness, its complexity and its highly competitive character. It appears that an undue pride and simple glorification of 'socialist achievements' may do more harm than good by presenting too rosy a picture of socialist reality in Poland. In the words of Jan Szczepański:

> The internal conflict of school upbringing is, that in its desire to mould the pupil according to his own best standards and to prepare him for future life, an environment is created which is remote from real conditions, imparts an idealistic concept of life and working conditions, so that when the pupil goes out into the real world, he finds that what the school has taught him is of very limited application, and that he is even less prepared for fitting into community life.[10]

Religious Education

Religious education for the younger as well as the older child has, in accordance with the tenets of Marxism-Leninism, long since been banned from the schools. The expected weakening of religous belief has not, however, taken place. Rather the reverse has occurred. The teaching of the Catholic religion goes on with the same rigour and vigour as in the older times, but this takes place outside the school in church halls. The timetable for the different age groups is worked out with a precision characteristic of an efficient business organization and attendance is almost universal. This certainly provides a great contrast with most of the other European countries, East or West for that matter, but it is a characteristic which has its deeper significance. Rooted in the past, but particularly in the times of the partitions, when the country constituted parts of alien state administrations and the Polish nation had to face outright hostility and brutal repression, religion provided the shield behind which both the Polish language and the national cultural heritage could be passed on from generation to generation. Principled behaviour and high moral standards — frequently disregarded in practice — have always been taught by the Church. Similarly principled behaviour and high moral standards have always been taught — though finding their legitimation in an entirely different philosophy of life — by the Marxist-Leninist regime. For a time both coexisted and accepted each other's right to exist, and even each other's integrity. However, when the scandal of a both overtly and covertly corrupt party leadership broke in the summer of 1980 and the former leaders were ignominiously expelled from the Polish United Workers' Party in July 1981, this came to be seen as a demonstrative proof of the hypocritical nature not only of individuals, but of the system as a whole. To restore the system's respectability and credibility in the eyes of the population as a whole, including the younger generation, will now require a truly gargantuan effort.

4. The Explosion of Educational Research Institutes: The Report on the State of Education

Critical comments could not go totally unheeded. Early in the 1970s the decision was taken to provide a lasting research basis for continuous educational progress. A whole number of specialized scientific research institutes were created in 1972, which were designed to increase empirical knowledge of the educational process and to promote a rigorous analysis of the existing form and content of education, so that the functioning of the different levels and sectors of the Polish educational system could be improved. These were the Institute for the Study of Youth (Instytut Badań nad Młodziżą, IBM), the Institute of Pedagogy reorganized as the Institute of Pedagogical Research (Instytut Badań Pedagogicznych, IBP), the 'Institute for Teacher Training' (Instytut Kształcenia Nauczycieli, IKN), the Institute for Vocational Education (Instytut Kształcenia Zawodowego, IKZ), the Institute for School Curricula (Instytut Programów Szkolnych, IPS) and finally, a year later, the Institute for Science Policy and Higher Education (Instytut Polityki Naukowej i Szkolnictwa Wyższego, IPNiSW). They researched into many aspects of education from child development to curriculum design, teacher training, vocational education, higher education and scientific progress, and the relation of the whole educational system to social and economic policy. Outstanding educational experts with prolonged experience in their respective fields were given the task of directing research work of the Institutes and their divisions: Professor Wincenty Okoń (IBP), Professor Tadeusz Nowacki (IKS), Professor Jan Kluczyński (IPNiSW), Professor Stanisław Krawcewicz (IKN). Professor M. Maciaszek (IPS), Professor S. Mika (IBM). All of these institutes have been doing useful and, indeed, valuable work by pursuing research projects and special investigations, and by publishing important reports on a wide range of subjects. All the same, they have experienced financial and personnel constraints, seen able leaders replaced by politically inspired appointees, and had to face the fact that many of their suggestions and proposals for action were not implemented because of the lack of funds or politically motivated opposition.

Quite independently of the work undertaken by the research institutes, an attempt was made in the early 1970s to scrutinize the whole field of educational endeavour in the country. In January 1971 Henryk Jabłoński, at that time Minister of Education and Higher Learning, nominated a Committee of Experts to prepare a *Report Concerning the State of Education in the Polish People's Republic.* At its head stood Professor Jan Szczepański, while the members of the Praesidium included professional educationalists of long standing and experience: Michał Godlewski, Zofia Kietlińska, Czesław Kupisiewicz, Jan Kluczyński, Wincenty Okoń, Antoni Rajkiewicz, Kazimierz Secomski and Bogdan Suchodolski. The Committee was given the double task of analysing the present school system as well as alternative forms of education. It was charged with defining the aims and elaborating the future model of Polish education in the context of envisaged social, cultural and technological change.

The *Report* came out in an abridged version in March 1973 and in a full version two months later. It was a thorough analysis of the Polish educational system, comprising 480 pages. The experts considered carefully the role of education and child rearing in a modern society; the demographic, social, political and economic influences upon education; the different kinds of schools and educational establishments, and the contents and methods of learning. The place of the family and of various other institutions and organizations in the education of youth; possible alternative models of the educational system; as well as the planning and financial aspects of education were also considered. The analysis of the different features and aspects of education was more successfully accomplished in the *Report* than any clear specification of reform proposals.[11] While the comments and observations appeared to be sound and valid, the criticism of the prevailing shortcomings was muted and the ultimate outcome of such a concentrated and protracted effort of a group of expert educationalists was, in practical terms, very limited, largely due to the lack of financial resources and a lack of determination by the government to effect more substantial changes and improvements.

The second half of the 1970s produced a temporary decrease in the number of 7 to 16 year old children, but the problems of better equipment for schools, improved educational attainment, more efficient transport facilities for children living further away from their school, and greater opportunities for the children from rural areas to attend vocational schools and secondary schools tended to crop up quite regularly in the daily press as feature articles, short comments and letters to the editor. Most disturbing though was the way in which young pupils were conditioned into an acceptance of the predetermined objectives, by bureaucratically minded teachers, backed up by ministerial directives. The negative character of such a crypto-authoritarian teacher-pupil relationship has been recognized, but it has not been easy to do very much about it. As the principal exponent of modern educational thought in Poland, Professor Wincenty Okoń has stressed that, in educational terms the essence of work in a modern school must be a very close rapport between the teachers and pupils. However difficult it may be to achieve in practice, in a large and inadequately equipped school,

> the true value of education consists, above all, in the active input into the process of learning by the pupils themselves, that is the degree of active involvement and (the capacity for) independent learning, the sequence and the speed in mastering the required material as well as the effectiveness with which this is accomplished.[12]

To help the individual teacher in the classroom, Polish educational psychologists and pedagogues have recently produced an extensive collection of specialized professional texts. Yet overworked and underpaid teachers have been finding it increasingly difficult to cope with the growing pressures of classroom teaching.

5. Higher Education

Priority for Reform

The central issues in higher education in the 1970s were university autonomy; the principles of selection for higher education; balance in the content of study; the questions of student welfare, students' organizations
and student participation in decision making; and students' perceptions
of the negative and positive features of their own education and job-
placement. Systems based upon bureaucratic centralism have to guard
themselves all the time against the unwarranted reformatory zeal of the
central administrative authorities. The counter-productive nature of this
certainly seems to have been the case in the PRL, where, according to the
research undertaken in the matter, in the period 1945–67, no less than 211
different official ministerial decrees were issued altering the organization
and activities in higher education establishments working the field of
economics. They introduced 55 organizational changes in higher institutions of this kind, 66 changes in departmental organization, 98 changes
in the different sections, 535 in the faculties, 82 in the institutes, 91
in the regulations for correspondence studies, etc.[13] There is little wonder
that faced with such a flood of directives, the system as such began to
suffer from a real handicap and the teaching and research personnel could
not operate effectively under conditions which lacked both stability and
continuity.

Universities: Autonomy and Appointments

The question of university autonomy became an important issue in connection with the increasing rigours of manpower planning and the considerable organizational changes in the late 1960s, when the traditional
faculty structures based upon individual chairs (*struktura katedralna*)
were modified to include the different kinds of institutes: departmental,
inter-departmental and complex scientific-industrial establishments (*struktura instytutów*). The intention was to link teaching and research with
the actual problems of production and to attain a higher measure of integration between the two fields. In practice this has resulted in excessive
diversification, fragmentation and bureaucratization and has brought
about internal resistance against governmental direction and what was
considered to be an undue interference with university autonomy.

Equally important was the question of key university appointments.
Nominees of the Minister of Higher Education and Technology to the post
of University Rector have been thought to be unwilling to respond to the
faculty and students' demands for change. Pressure from below did, indeed

recently, remove those who were considered to be hardliners; e.g. Professor Zygmunt Rybicki, Rector of the largest Polish university (the University of Warsaw) for more than a decade, was replaced by Professor Henryk Samsonowicz, formerly Dean of the History Department of the University, in the autumn of 1980. Professor Samsonowicz, chosen by the University Senate, wasted no time in making a clear statement in which he declared that an institution of higher education should first and foremost be concerned with developing the personalities of the students and that the institutions of academic democracy should be based upon a well-defined model of a community of those who teach and those who are taught. This community should be guided by the principle of joint decision making in matters of research, internal organization and teaching, so that the content and methods of learning are de facto decided by the *Universitas Studiorum*. The new legislation in the field of higher education expected in the autumn of 1981 is now confidently expected to be based upon such principles.[14]

Universities: Student Selection and Welfare

The regulations concerning selection for higher education have for a long time been a source of controversy in Poland. Preferential treatment of applicants coming from working-class and peasant backgrounds, introduced in 1963-64 and reinforced in 1967 aimed at an increased student recruitment from these sectors of population. Although there was such an improvement in the period immediately following the reforms, a reverse tendency later began to manifest itself. There also was a pronounced dissatisfaction with the actual mechanics of awarding points for social origin in admission to higher educational establishments. This concerned a rather simplistic notion of the occupation of the parents, inadequate weight attached to family income and other criteria, and resulted in help being extended to those who did not really need it, and in not being received when clearly it was justified. There was also rather disturbing evidence of premature drop-out among students admitted to a course of education on a preferential basis. While only some people seem to have suggested the actual abandonment of the system of preferential treatment of certain social categories of students, many voices have clamoured for a drastic revision of the existing procedures. In the end the balance of the argument swung towards those who advocated a straightforward competition for entry, only marginally influenced by other, i.e. social, considerations. The situation as it is, still represents a dilemma for all who are concerned about the equality of educational opportunity. Admitting students through an assessment of their performance in a competitive examination is justified in a society which has established a reasonably uniform life style for all of its citizens, but that seems to be far from the case of Poland today. Sociological investigations confirm that access to higher education as well as the students' performance is very much the function of the students' social origin, parental educational background, parental aspirations, family size and the character of place of residence.

The question of the general welfare of and state assistance to students has been the subject of countless discussions, articles in the press and letters to the editors of local and national newspapers and periodicals. With the explosion of numbers of full-time students in the 1950s and 1960s, the pressure for places in student hostels and student homes began to mount, despite additional buildings becoming available for that purpose. The quality of accommodation, meals and services in general has generally tended to decline with time. *The Report on the State of Education in the Polish People's Republic* accepted that in 1971 at least 20 per cent of young people studying full-time in higher education failed to find vacancies in student hostels, while there was about the same proportion of students who were not receiving State scholarships, even though their material circumstances really warranted it.[15]

The Sensitive Subjects of the Higher Education Curriculum

The actual balance between different subjects in the content of higher education has also provoked a keen exchange of arguments. The point at issue has been the place and character of the socio-political group of subjects, embracing Marxism–Leninism and Dialectical Materialism, which analyse political developments and current affairs from the Marxist point of view. This has always been a compulsory element in all courses of higher education without exception since the end of the Second World War. It was taught and examined in every establishment of higher education, even if the majority of the students displayed little enthusiasm for it and often considered it to be not only an unnecessary distraction from the proper field of study, but simply quite superfluous. The authorities nevertheless have, invariably and consistently, insisted upon its inclusion in the programmes of study. The students striking in the Universities of Warsaw and Łódz early in 1981 included in the list of their demands the request to make the socio-political subjects non-compulsory. The issue seems to be, however, of a more fundamental character and reaching a compromise over it may be more difficult than meeting some of the other demands of the students such as the abolition of censorship restrictions for students and the provision of free access to archive materials and sources so far unobtainable (even to research students) without special permits.

The teaching of national history has always been an important issue in People's Poland. The official syllabuses and teachers' instructions at the level of secondary education and the teaching of the subject in higher education establishments invariably made a special point of interpreting the Polish past in such a way that those whose views of influence seemed to indicate religious or nationalistic tendencies appeared in a negative light. Frequent assertions were made that the teaching of recent Polish history was decisively biased and many important events and occurrences were deliberately omitted or grossly distorted. These gaps or tendentious comments have, traditionally, been filled or corrected at home by the parents or grandparents, but the need for a more detailed and formal approach resulted in Polish history courses being offered by the Flying University. This first had to operate as a clandestine organization, but in the autumn of 1980 it began to operate quasi-officially and in 1981 quite openly, attracting large numbers of not only university students, but also older teenagers, keen on finding out for themselves 'what really had been the case'.

Student Organizations: Resistance to Enforced Integration

Student organizations went through a process of far-reaching integration in the early 1970s away from the diversity of youth and student organizations that had been characteristic of the later 1950s and the 1960s. There were then separate and distinct organizations in existence: the Polish Scouts Union (Związek Harcerstwa Polskiego, ZHP), with its splendid tradition of over sixty years of service to the nation and the country and a distinguished record of activities against the occupying German forces during the War and in the Warsaw Rising of 1944; the Socialist Union of Polish Students (Socjalistyczny Związek Studentów Polskich, SZSP), established in 1957 under the aegis of the Polish United Workers' Party; a million strong Union of Rural Youth (Związek Młodzieży Wiejskiej, ZMW), also established in 1957 and operating under the joint patronage of the PUWP (PZPR) and ZSL (United Peasants' Party). In 1973 the Federation of Socialist Unions of Polish Youth (Federacja Socjalistycznych Związków Młodzieży Polskiej, FSZMP), came into being, bringing together all the above mentioned organizations as well as the Socialist Union of Young Servicemen (Socjalistyczny Związek Młodzieży Wojskowej, SZMW). The integration of these hitherto separate units was far from receiving popular support from their rank and file and seemed necessary only to the political leadership, aiming at greater cohesion and more effective control over the younger generation as a whole. Yet, instead of strengthening the youth movement as such, it brought about a growing criticism of existing arrangements, weakened its constituent parts and turned thousands of young people towards a search for an alternative form of participation through an involvement in a more genuine grass-root movement. In the end the Federation of Socialist Unions of Polish Youth was dissolved due to the increasing friction and growing disagreements among the representatives of the constituent organizations. Meanwhile, the Third Extraordinary Congress of the Socialist Union of Polish Youth (Związek Socjalistyczny Młodzieży Polskiej, ZSMP, formerly ZMS), held its meeting in Warsaw in May 1981. It is interesting to note that to the participants themselves it appeared to be 'the first congress which was not subject to manipulation'[16] and in which 'genuine discussions took place'.[17] The new statute of the Union omits the clause concerning the leading role of the PZPR, even though it clearly states that there are close ideological links and common objectives. It appears that even the ZSMP has managed to attain a not inconsiderable degree of independence.[18]

The students' criticism of the principal features of their lives and studies and their dissatisfaction with the existing state of affairs resulted in an attempt to organize a nation-wide students' strike in February 1981. Pressing for an immediate recognition of their independent union, the students set up strike committees in several Polish universities and, in the highly loaded atmosphere of direct political confrontation with the government, began to occupy the buildings belonging to all the major universities. The most active seemed to be the students of the University of Łódź, who set up the Inter-University Co-ordinating Committee where they organized a month-long sit-in support of their demands. After a long series of meetings and talks, an agreement was signed between the Minister of Higher Education, Janusz Górski and the representatives of the Committee on 18 February, giving the students the permission to set up their own free union, the Independent Students' Association (Niezależny Związek Studentów, NZS).

The other concessions, wrestled from the government were of two kinds. Most concerned matters directly relating to students' work and activities. Among them were: allowing the universities autonomy to decide upon what socio-political courses were to be taught and on what basis (compulsory or not); permitting the students the full freedom of choosing what foreign language to study in their course programmes; declaring the ending of compulsory pre-university work practice for all students; barring police forces from entering the university precincts; promising the revision of history textbooks and the appointment of teaching staff on merit and not on political grounds; allowing the students' organizations to hold commemorative meetings on their own initiative. The other points concerned more general issues: the length of military service for students and the right of each person to obtain a passport without undue delay. The students, on the other hand, agreed to acknowledge in their constitution that the Polish United Workers' Party was the leading force in society and to defer for further consideration the points concerning the release of political detainees (in particular the members of the illegal Confederation of Independent Poland) and the relaxation of general censorship rules. In fact, the delays in releasing the political detainees led the Independent Students' Association to plan protest marches in all Polish university cities on 25 May 1981. In the face of a mounting pressure from all directions, including the Church, the party and the Solidarity movement itself, as well as the university Senates, the students finally decided to cancel most of the protest meetings. The exceptions were in Warsaw, where it took a much less spectacular appearance than had actually been planned, and in Poznań, where it was limited to the university precinct only.

6. Manpower Policy

Matching Graduate Education and Employment

A very special aspect of higher education in Poland represents the problem of transition from study to employment. The planned graduate employment system came into force in the PRL not under Edward Gierek, but under Władysław Gomułka, with the Act of 25 February 1964. This provided, however, the basis upon which the whole system of planned entry into employment came to rest in the 1970s. According to the provisions of the Act, it is compulsory for students upon graduation to accept employment for a specified period, usually for three years, in a state or co-operative enterprise authorized to employ students. This concerns all specializations in polytechnics, medical academies, institutes of economics, institutes of agriculture (except horticulture and dairying), teacher training academies and in the following types of study in the universities: law, mathematics, physics, geo-physics, chemistry, economics and English, German and Russian philology. This means that some 80 per cent of graduates finishing full-time courses are subject to the provisions of the Act and planned employment procedures. The main responsibility for planning the allocation of graduates to different kinds of jobs rests with the Minister of Employment, Salaries and Social Affairs. The records available reveal that the provisions of the Act are quite rigorously observed: in the period 1964–75 some 315,000 students completed full-time education courses in higher education establishments and about 245,000 of them were subject to the planned employment provisions of the Act. Jobs were allocated to 221,000 (i.e. about 90 per cent of those affected) through the planning channels of the Ministry. The remaining 10 per cent were either the students who were exempted for special reasons (e.g. took positions in higher education establishments, were called up for military service or were disabled) or obtained official permission to postpone allocation for a time for strictly defined reasons.[19] In comparison with the simple direction to employment, operating in Poland in the early 1950s, the present set-up is a less rigorous form of planned job placement. It appears that the employing organizations and units of production would like to see it become more flexible rather than keep it in its present form, while about a quarter of them think that it does not perform its role and ought to be replaced by yet another planned system or, simply, by a free labour market.[20] It is more difficult to say what the students themselves think about it, in the absence of open inquiries, but it is frequently asserted that many of them would prefer to choose their jobs freely.

Teacher Training and the Revival of Professional Tradition

It is the teachers who fundamentally determine the quality of education and the degree to which the younger generation identifies with the national traditions and ensure the cultural continuity of a nation. The Polish teachers, as a distinctive group, tempered in their defence of the Polish language and the national historical heritage in the long years of foreign domination; in their struggle for a higher professional status and better working conditions and higher pay in the inter-war years; in their fight for survival in the course of the Second World War during which they had never ceased to teach the young in clandestine classes secretly held in Nazi-occupied Poland (containing in their decimated ranks numerous radical leaders, talented thinkers and able organizers); have always been a sort of an avant-garde. The Union of Polish Teachers, now more than fifty years old and over half a million strong, has seldom lacked the courage to resist what it thought to be wrong and to defend the professional integrity and interests of its members.

One of the earlier attempts of Edward Gierek's administration to establish a lasting foundation for a strengthened and more confident teaching profession was to formulate and solemnly proclaim a Charter which was to serve as a complete code of ethics and, at the same time, to provide a legal and administrative framework for the employment of teachers of all ranks by the State. The Charter of Teachers' Rights and Obligations was proclaimed on 27 April 1972. In its preamble it stressed that the Polish People's Republic took particular care of the teachers in whose hands was the education of the whole nation. In defining the role and tasks of all teachers working in schools and higher education establishments, it expressed the most noble sentiments by stating that each teacher should educate his or her pupils and students in the spirit of socialist morality and according to socialist principles of inter-personal co-operation, love for the Motherland, peace, social justice and fraternal feelings for the working people of all countries. Each teacher should instil love and respect for work, a sense of personal responsibility and social discipline; pass on the foundations of general and specialized knowledge, take good care of his pupils' abilities, awaken in them different kinds of interests as well as the capacity for independent thought, and promote in them the willingness to participate actively in the process of developing the national economy, culture and social life. In its subsequent articles it declared that the teachers were duty bound constantly to improve their theoretical and practical knowledge and their professional qualifications through self-education, and regularly to attend courses organized for this purpose by the educational authorities. Conditions of service were closely specified (improved scales of pay, the compulsory number of contact hours per week for teachers in all kinds of schools, the awards, special premiums and honorary titles which could be granted to the teachers; entitlement to leave and the right to certain kinds of social assistance in matters of health and accommodation in rural areas; the formalities connected with contractual professional obligations and the granting of retirement pensions). Attached to it all was the decree of the Council of Ministers, introducing new scales of pay for the different categories of teachers, heads of schools, professors and lecturers teaching in the universities and other kinds of higher education establishments, with effect as from 1 May 1972.[21]

The Charter was designed as an instrument for raising the general status and esteem of the teacher in the eyes of society as a whole. It came shortly before the whole country celebrated the bicentenary of the establishment of the Polish Education Commission in October 1773, which through its efforts as the first Ministry of Education in the world, organized a national system of education, defined the rights and duties of teachers and published modern school textbooks generally building the foundations for a national cultural revival in the closing years of the eighteenth century. Linking the new Charter with the approaching anniversary was in itself an important move and created, for a time, a positive sentiment among the teachers and in the nation as a whole. Its practical significance was, however, overshadowed rather quickly by the lack of evidence of a real improvement in the working conditions of teachers. Mounting difficulties in securing a better material basis for the schools and other educational establishments and a growing disenchantment with the absence of any appreciable improvement in the living standards of the population as a whole, were only made worse through ill-conceived and irritating speeches by the political leadership who were unable to discern the real nature of the difficulties which were being encountered.

The gulf between the excessive verbalism and empty rhetoric in which the members of the government and the leading party cadres in the 1970s excelled on the one hand and the harsh nature of the reality of daily life on the other, was ostensibly widening in the course of the last decade. The Seventh Congress of the Polish United Workers' Party, held on 8-11 December 1975, formulated a very promising programme of action in respect of the needs of the teachers:

> The teaching profession should receive particular attention and care. It is necessary to care for the improvement of the living and working conditions of teachers, raise their professional and ideological qualifications, create an atmosphere of friendliness, confidence, gain the help of society and increase the social importance of the teaching profession.[22]

Proposals of this kind, heralding action, raised teachers' expectations in the short run. However, they were doomed to result in increased bitterness and accusations of dishonest dealings on the part of the government, once it had become obvious that in reality very little was being done to improve the teachers' conditions.

Faced with growing difficulties in executing their work and performing their duties, the teachers in many localities began to unite themselves in November 1980, to demand a fair deal from the educational authorities. In Gdańsk, where the movement for the liberalization of the system began, the teachers associated in the NSZZ Solidarity Committee for Workers in Education opened up a dialogue with the Ministry of Education Departmental Commission, which — as the teachers' representatives themselves claimed soon afterwards — rapidly degenerated into a monologue. The teachers' demands focused on three main issues:

(1) the material basis of education, i.e. the share of education in the national income of the country, which they argued was too low, especially in respect of basic general education;

(2) the teachers' work, which they claimed had reached totally unacceptable levels of ten hours per day, taking into account the teaching, preparatory and extra-curricular obligations;

(3) the reform of the whole system of education and in particular the envisaged structural changes, the need for an improvement in the school programmes and better textbooks and other learning aids.[23]

Other local teachers' committees also began to demand the right to discuss the above issues and the Minister of Education, Krzysztof Kruszewski found himself under a vigorous and concerted attack from many quarters. In fact this was so great that after a few weeks' heated exchanges with the teachers, he was forced to resign and was replaced by a new man, Bolesław Faron. The latter made a solemn promise to consider the teachers' demands carefully and, particularly, to reduce the heavy work load of teachers in schools and to improve their material conditions. Both requests were very difficult to meet under the circumstances.

7. Education as a Cultural Concern

Meanwhile came the evidence that other interest groups were beginning to show concern for educational reform and had decided to make their demands explicit. In December 1980 the Executive Committee of the Polish Writers' Association decided to formulate on behalf of its members its own views concerning the future of education in the country. A group of writers worked for six months under the leadership of the novelist Leszek Prorok and formulated the Association's postulates on the subject, which were submitted as a memorandum to the Minister of Education in the middle of July 1981. These included the following requests: that a National Education Council should be brought into existence in order to keep continuously under review the educational developments in the country; that its members should include the representatives of the different branches of learning, well experienced pedagogues, representatives of the trade unions as well as of professional, cultural and religious organizations and associations and, in due course, also the representatives of the associations of parents. The memorandum stressed further the need for increasing the budgetary expenditure on education, so that in the end it would attain the average level of expenditure of other European countries. The passing of a new statute for higher education establishments, which — in the writers' view — ought to have the right of independently formulating their own programmes of study and research and of commanding enough resources to properly fulfil the tasks expected of them, was seen as particularly urgent. In addition, the writers expressed their satisfaction that the reform of official curricular programmes and of school syllabuses in Polish language and literature, history and civic education in particular, was under way and that there was every hope that the necessary changes would be introduced at the beginning of the school year 1982-83. The Polish Writers' Association declared its paramount interest in the teaching of Polish language and literature and stressed that the aim in teaching them should be to acquaint the young generation not only with the wealth of Polish literary achievements, but also to make quite explicit its intimate connections with the best examples of the European cultural tradition as a whole.[24]

8. Conclusion

Many things have been changing in the People's Republic of Poland in recent months. All in all, a general consensus seems to prevail that education, if it is to be a positive force in society must contribute to social harmony, genuine political participation and economic progress in the land and also offer to everybody an opportunity to share actively in a common cultural heritage. If education cannot do this, it must be reformed and the pressures for reform have recently manifested themselves in Poland in an unmistakable way. Obviously, a system of education seldom deteriorates to the extent that it becomes totally inadequate and unacceptable. The Polish system as it is, still possesses some strengths as well as very definite shortcomings. The high quality of Polish education is generally accepted and the achievements of Polish academics are universally recognized. The thirst for knowledge and the determination to move on in the world are as characteristic of Polish youth today, as they were of earlier generations. None the less, the problems are grave enough, and the multidimensional character as well as the depth of the present crisis makes their solution extremely difficult. The material constraints will, no doubt, constitute a barrier to a speedy improvement, but there is still a hope that the determination of the masses to insist upon the relaxation of ideological constraints will enable the educational system to acquire enough impetus of its own to overcome the existing inertia and rigidity and that the ongoing 'renewal' will produce in the end the results that people have set out to attain.

Perhaps there is more than just hope. In recent months serious Polish periodicals such as *Polityka* and *Kultura* began to publish articles in which honest and straightforward words were used and honest and straightforward arguments were made. Commenting on education in Poland today, Stanisław Bortnowski wrote recently in *Polityka*:

The Polish educational system serves the richer [section of the population] and degrades those who are worse off. This degradation — as can be judged from the analysis of syllabuses in Polish language for the basic vocational schools — is reinforced further by the subordination of the content of study to an ill-conceived ideology which destroys art, destroys reflective thought, destroys all deeper emotions and simply reduces everything to indoctrination.[25]

These are courageous words which have not been heard in Poland for the past forty-odd years. One must respect a person who uses language of this kind. It is a language of an open society. Far from doing harm, it does a lot of good. It helps to establish a foundation upon which a real renewal and a real progress can be based.

Notes and References

1 J. Szczepański, *Rozważania o Rzeczypospolitej*, Warszawa, Polski Instytut Wydawniczy, 1971, p. 29.

2 Ibid., p. 88.

3 Szczepański, *Refleksje nad oświatą*, Warszawa, Polski Instytut Wydawniczy, 1973, p. 188; also pp. 112–17.

4 B. C. Sanyal and A. Józefowicz (eds), *Graduate Employment and Planning of Higher Education in Poland*, a case study prepared in collaboration with The Institute of Science Policy, Technical Progress and Higher Education of Poland, Paris, International Institute for Educational Planning, 1978, p. 243.

5 Ibid., p. 82.

6 B. Biskupska, 'Dzieci drugiej kategorii', in *Kulisy, Express Wieczorny*, 31 May 1981, p. 7.

7 Ibid., p. 7.

8 Ibid., p. 7.

9 Sanyal and Józefowicz, *Graduate Employment and Planning of Higher Education in Poland*, p. 171.

10 Ibid., p. 170.

11 Cf. Komitet Ekspertów, *Raport o stanie oświaty w PRL*, Warszawa, Państwowe Wydawnictwo Naukowe, 1973.

12 W. Okoń, *Zarys dydaktyki ogólnej*, Warszawa, Państwowe Wydawnictwo Naukowe, 1965, p. 10.

13 Szczepański, *Refleksje*, p. 106.

14 'What should a university be like?' in *Poland*, No. 5 (1981), p. 48. Cf. also 'W poszukiwaniu modelu', in *Kultura*, No. 15, Vol. 19, p. 1 and p. 4.

15 Komitet Ekspertów, *Raport*, p. 149.

16 J. Jaskiernia, 'To była lekcja demokracji', in *Kulisy, Express Wieczorny*, 10 May 1981, p. 1.

17 Ibid., p. 1.

18 Ibid., p. 6.

19 Sanyal, and Józefowicz, *Graduate Employment and Planning of Higher Education in Poland*, p. 186 and p. 193.

20 Ibid., p. 203.

21 'Karta praw i obowiązków nauczyciela', in *Głos Nauczycielski*, 14 May 1972, pp. 1–12.

22 Ministry of Education in Polish People's Republic, *The Development of Education in Polish People's Republic, 1974–1976*, a report for the International Bureau of

Education in Geneva, Warszawa, Wydawnictwa Szkolne i Pedagogiczne, 1977, p. 25.
23 *Trybuna Ludu*, 12 November 1980, p. 1.
24 *Trybuna Ludu*, 11/12 July 1981, p. 1.
25 S. Bortnowski, 'Szkoła potakiwania', in *Polityka*, 4 April 1981, p. 10.

9 Health Policy and Health Service Reforms in the 1970s*

CHRIS RUSSELL HODGSON

During the current crisis in Poland, the health service has been the subject of a great deal of criticism. In fact there has been an open, if limited, debate about the state of the health system for the whole of the past decade. This was fired by the crisis of December 1970, and culminated in specific demands appended to the Gdańsk Agreement in September 1980.[1] In the early 1970s the new government, in response to mounting pressure over the previous decade, toyed with the problems of social policy; Gierek realized that a coherent approach to social policy was needed, and health policy featured prominently in this new strategy. This emphasis marked a qualitative change in the thinking of the regime and hopes were duly raised as, of course, they were raised in other branches of the economy. Yet however well-intentioned these policies may have been, little changed in practice. By the end of the 1970s the state of the health service was once again regarded as critical. In June 1980 the Third Plenum of the Central Committee of the Polish United Workers' Party (PZPR) devoted the whole session to the problems of health; the fact that health was the sole focus for discussion indicates the gravity of the situation. Stanisław Kania, who was soon to succeed Gierek as party leader, outlined the problems of the health service in some detail.[2] Sadly, the problems were identical to those discussed so earnestly in 1971: shortages of drugs, equipment and personnel, low morale among health service workers, poor organization, and a lack of integration — all the old problems persisted.

There seem to be three main reasons for the failure of the policies of the 1970s to remove the problems that had dogged the health service for so long. In the first place there are obstacles within the health service itself. In particular, there are conflicting systems of priority, incompatible principles of health care organization and an emphasis on curative, specialist, hospital-based medicine. Secondly, hindrances exist within the socialist system of decision making. Decisions about health care are 'input-based', with quantitative indicators used to the exclusion of any real assessment

*This chapter is adapted from a paper presented at the Thirteenth Annual Conference of the Centre for Russian and East European Studies (University of Birmingham), Windsor, 26–8 July 1981; it forms part of a doctoral thesis under preparation.

of health needs and standards of care. Thirdly, there are intractable problems within the Polish economy; funds are not easily diverted from the productive sector of the economy, and even when they are, there is no guarantee that the money will be translated into useful resources. These fundamental problems are not likely to be tackled as a result of the current crisis. The question 'what next?' invites a pessimistic response in view of the gloomy economic forecast.

1. Health Policy – Its Reappearance in the 1970s

An important consequence of the 1970 crisis was the revival of social policy, including health policy, which in turn paved the way to health service reform. Social policy as a subject for debate and deliberation in a public, political sense scarcely existed in the 1950s and 1960s. There had been a lively debate on all aspects of social policy in the early years of the regime – from 1944 until 1949, when the 'hardliners' won and the Socialist Party was absorbed into the PUWP.[3] Following this, social policy debate was effectively crushed by Socialist dogma: increased production would lead to improvement in all spheres, including that of health. Since 1970 social policy has once again emerged as a legitimate issue for debate at both public and governmental levels. The impetus for the re-emergence of social policy was the party's declaration on the 'importance of the family', a declaration which followed the 1970 crisis; the 'family' and 'national pride' are always regarded as hallmarks of stability in the aftermath of a crisis. Not only was a new type of policy being talked of, but the mechanism of policy making was itself influenced in an important way by the crisis: public opinion and the opinion of interest groups became a significant input to the policy-making process.[4] For instance, after the December crisis, the new government conducted special 'consultations' in about one hundred large industrial enterprises to determine workers' preferences as to how best to use the additional resources being made available to raise the standard of living. The role of experts became more pronounced also; Jan Szczepański's Expert Committee on Educational Reform is the best-known example, with the Expert Committee who devised the 'Health Service Development Programme to 1990' following close behind.[5]

That the new emphasis on social policy, including health policy, marked a qualitative change in official thinking is made clear by the prominent Polish medical sociologist Magdalena Sokołowska in an article in 1974; 'Such terms as "social policy" or "social planning" entered the official vocabulary only after December 1970 when the new leadership came to

Table 9.1 Indicative Changes in the Polish Health Service 1960-1970-1979

	1960	1970	1979
A. Personnel			
Doctors	28,708	49,283	66,702
– of whom female (%)	38.4	47.6	51.1
Dentists	9,316	13,611	17,956
– of whom female (%)	78.0	81.3	81.7
Nurses	61,907	102,838	163,693
– of whom fully qualified (%)	64.0	79.2	92.0
Midwives	9,199	12,171	16,780
Doctors per 10,000 population	9.6	15.1	18.8
Nurses per 10,000 population	20.7	31.5	46.2
B. Outpatient Facilities			
Urban polyclinics	4,625	5,566	5,803
– of which industrial health centres (%)	47.5	42.2	43.4
private/cooperative centres (%)	4.1	7.7	6.9
Rural health centres	1,394	2,508	3,205
Consultations			
In urban polyclinics	119,873	176,322	235,544
– in industrial health centres (%)	19.2	19.3	21.2
– in primary care centres serving local population (%)	79.5	76.6	74.5
– others*	1.3	4.1	4.3
In rural health centres	12,703	25,935	39,685
C. Inpatient Facilities			
Hospitals	653	673	677
– of which psychiatric	27	31	39
TB sanatoria	86	66	32
Hospitals beds (per 10,000 population)	55.4	62.9	66.8
– of which psychiatric (per 10,000 population)	10.1	11.1	10.5
TB sanatoria (per 10,000 population)	8.0	5.8	2.6
No. of patients treated (per 10,000 population)	867.7	994.5	1,199.2

* 'Others' includes consultations in student health centres and private/co-operative health centres. In 1979 the latter accounted for three times the former.

power. Previously, the word policy was synonymous with "economic policy" and planning with "economic planning".[6] The new government's concern with social policy came to the fore at the Sixth Party Congress in December 1971, when the improvement of health care was counted as a priority issue. Gierek stated that 'a matter of special importance is that of a marked progress in health care and, in particular, better and more adequate utilization of resources. The expenditure for this purpose will be 86 per cent higher than in the previous five-year period'. Health policy was regarded as a worthy subject for investigation from this point on, and several serious attempts were made to analyse health policy from a theoretical perspective.[7]

2. The Health Service in 1971[8]

Gierek committed his government to take a serious approach to health policy, and to develop the health service by a series of reforms. What were the problems to be faced? The latter years of the Gomułka era had been characterized by political intransigence and economic stagnation. Against this background the health service, in the tradition typical of Eastern European countries, was accorded little importance or status. Levels of pay were lower than anywhere else in the economy, morale was poor, attempts at reform in the 1960s had been of little consequence, and blame for poor health care tended to be placed at the feet of the hard-pressed health service employees. The official statistical tables show a steady improvement in health care and health status throughout the 1960s, but they do not show the gross distributional failings of the system. They overlook, in the first place, the fact that the elite were (and are) cared for by well-funded separate health services run by the Ministry of Defence and by the Ministry of the Interior. Meanwhile, in 1971, approximately one-fifth of the population − the private peasants and their families, who had resisted collectivization − were still excluded from the free State health service. Other rural dwellers, who *were* insured under the State scheme, were provided with scant and inadequate health facilities compared with the level of provision in towns. In urban areas standards varied greatly between one area and another, and between the industrial health service and the local health service.

As for the quality of care, this was the subject of embittered criticism, much of which appeared in the press after the 1970 crisis. In the following year, as the new Government struggled to formulate its policies, an open letter to the Minister of Health (then Jan Kostrzewski) appeared in *Polityka.*[9] The letter contained several specific criticisms, which echo other articles published at the time: integration between local districts (*rejon*) and hospitals, and between industrial and local outpatient clinics, was too weak; doctors were too bound up with bureaucracy and the pay structure was such that they usually worked in more than one post, resulting in poorer quality of care. Links between the local doctor (*lekarz rejonowy*) and his – or more likely her – patients were poor. In hospitals discipline among assistant staff was so poor that patients were often subject to the whims of nurses, cleaners (*salowa*) and even receptionists (*rejestrator*).[10] Medical equipment was not used effectively – equipment stood idle in some places, while in others there were huge queues. The pace of repairs, particularly in hospitals, was intolerably slow, so that in practice the number of beds was even lower than the statistical records showed. The letter stated emphatically that a lack of funds was not in itself sufficient cause for the worsening problems of the health service; the trouble was that the money was not used effectively.

The solution, then, was not merely to 'throw money at the problem'; unfortunately Gierek's formula did not take account of this.

3. Health Policy Reforms in the 1970s

Rural Health Policy

One of the major changes in policy in the 1970s was in connection with rural health care. On 1 January 1972 the State health service was extended to cover the private peasant-farmers and their families. This section of the Polish workforce had been excluded from the free State health service since the 1940s. The reform was a major breakthrough for the lobby which had been pressing for such reform since the 1950s.[11] The population group involved numbered over six million and they had previously paid for whatever health care they had received, whether from local private practitioners or the local State health facilities (where fees were lower but queues inevitably longer). Needless to say, their inclusion in the free public health sector brought a great strain to the local health facilities. The added burden was, in theory at least, taken care of by the provision of 3,300 rural health centres (*gminny ośrodek zdrowia* – GOZ). This plan had been prepared in the 1960s, and indeed by 1970 (i.e. before the legislation in question had been passed) there were already 2,000 in existence. But in order to cope with the added burden after 1972 the programme should have been drastically stepped up, not only to build more centres, but also to recruit more staff. In practice not enough GOZy were built (or converted), their equipment was inadequate and the staffing problems acute. Recognizing the need to step up the pace, the 'Programme of Development of the Health Service to 1990' adopted in 1973 proposed that the organization of the entire network of rural health centres be completed by 1975; details of means by which this was to be achieved were, however, somewhat lacking. Even by 1980 these problems remained unresolved, despite the fact that by then 3,200 of the proposed total had been built. Nine per cent of these GOZy did not even have their own doctor, which means that a further 9 per cent were sharing their precious staff resources. According to an official proposal in 1973, there should be three doctors per GOZ – a general practitioner, a paediatrician and a gynaecologist; this would have brought rural health facilities much closer to their urban counterparts. In fact, only 100 GOZy had a full staff quota in 1980, the 'normal' GOZ team now being limited to one doctor, one dentist and two nurses.[12]

The problems of attracting doctors to work in rural areas are seemingly intractable, but little or nothing has been done to remedy this at source – which is in the medical academies. The basic problem has always been that medical academies are too full of specialists to make a genuine appeal to the 'generalist' side of their students. Financial incentives have not worked either; in 1972-73 a rural doctor earned 2,000-3,000 zł. more than his urban counterpart, but since 1975 this disparity has been reduced and no longer exists. On the face of it, the policy was abandoned because it was not working, but a large part of the failure was due, it is claimed, to complaints by urban doctors. It is also said that there are problems associated with rural doctors having too much money to spend and too little to spend it on – the problem of alcoholism being the main one.

Paradoxically, those doctors who do choose to work in rural settings tend to rank high in the job satisfiaction stakes and to stay in their posts longer. They claim that rural practice gives them a greater degree of freedom and autonomy and they also undoubtedly like the 'tips' they customarily receive from patients; rural patients are not easily broken from the tradition of fee-paying, whether in cash or in kind. The problem is that, despite these attractions, the kind of doctor who prefers rural practice is rare.

A further paradox is that whilst the newly-included private peasantry fare worse than the urban population, the State-farm health centres are even worse. Here 20 per cent of the health centres are without a doctor. (There are only fifty-one State-farm health centres in total.) Attracting doctors to these health centres is extremely difficult: the workload, consisting largely of dull, repetitious prophylactic examination, is enormous; the salary is no better than elsewhere and there are no unofficial extras to soften the blow.

The achievement of the policy reform of 1972 in extending the coverage of the health service to a point where it is virtually universal is an important one; however, the attendant problems of rural health care have not been tackled adequately – the gap between town and country is still wide.

Table 9.2 Health Service Personnel: Overall Rate and Rural Rate in the 1970s

Rate per 10,000 population

		1970	1971	1972	1973	1974	1975	1976	1977	1978
Doctors	– all	14.2	14.7	15.0	15.4	15.8	15.9	16.2	16.6	16.9
	– rural	1.6	1.7	1.9	2.1	2.2	2.3	2.3	2.3	2.3
Dentists	– all	4.0	4.1	4.2	4.3	4.4	4.4	4.5	4.5	4.6
	– rural	1.2	1.3	1.4	1.6	–	1.7	1.6	1.6	–
Feldshers	– all	1.4	1.4	1.4	1.3	1.3	1.2	1.2	1.2	1.1
	– rural	0.6	0.6	0.6	0.6	–	0.6	0.6	0.5	–
Nurses	– all	30.2	31.3	32.5	33.7	35.1	35.9	37.3	38.6	40.4
	– rural	2.6	2.8	3.4	4.0	4.4	5.5	6.0	6.2	5.9
– fully qualified	– all	24.0	25.4	26.9	28.3	29.9	31.0	33.0	34.5	36.7
	– rural	2.0	2.2	2.8	3.4	–	4.7	5.3	5.6	–
Midwives	– all	3.5	3.6	3.7	3.8	3.9	3.9	4.0	4.0	4.1
	– rural	1.0	1.1	1.0	1.1	–	1.0	1.0	1.0	–

Note: Rural figures are outpatient sources only.

Source: Rocznik Statystyczny Ochrony Zdrowia – 1974, pp. 138, 139; 1976, pp. 171, 172; 1979, pp. 158, 159.

This disparity can be partly demonstrated with figures; for example, Table 9.2 shows the overall and rural rates of health service personnel. The increase from 1.6 country doctors per 10,000 population in 1970 to 2.3 in 1978 is not spectacular when compared with an overall (urban and rural) increase from 14.2 to 16.9.

Salary Reforms for Health Service Personnel

The health service has traditionally been the lowest paid branch of the economy. For a short time in the 1970s this position was changed, but the gains made in the heady first years of Gierek's rule were soon outstripped by gains in other sectors of the economy.

In October 1972 the first stage of a new pay structure for health workers was introduced; the second stage followed a year later. For the first time ever, workers in the non-productive sector were given increases that were relatively greater than in industry. Significant pay increases were accompanied by changes in the principles governing extra payments (for qualifications, length of service, 'quality of service' and so on). According to a summary by Marcinkowski (Deputy Minister for Health) in 1974, pay increases amounted overall to a net average of 34.2 per cent over 1971 salaries — an average of 685 zł. per month. The greatest increase in salary affected the middle-grade personnel — i.e. nurses — who received an overall increase of 43 per cent.[13] These figures do not fully coincide with those given in the statistical yearbooks however; from Table 9.3 it can be deduced that in 1973 doctors as well as nurses were receiving salaries showing a 43 per cent increase over the 1970 amounts. An analysis of the subsequent years of the decade shows clearly that doctors regained their position not only as chief earners, but as 'deserving' higher proportional increases than nurses.

In the second half of the decade, the health service lost its brief advantage over the other branches of the economy. At the beginning of 1981 an article in *Służba Zdrowia* detailed the failings of the salary reforms, and produced figures to illustrate the plight of health workers with regard to salaries in 1978.[14] These figures, reproduced in Table 9.4 show that the health service has a disproportionately high share of low-paid workers and this applies to non-manual workers to a high degree also. The reforms initiated in 1972 may have succeeded in ousting the cumbersome wage structure that had been in operation since 1967, but in real terms the health service has remained at the bottom of the pile.

Development Programme for Health and Social Welfare to 1990

Following resolutions concerning the health service which were made at

Table 9.3 Levels of Pay in the Health Service in the 1970s

Monthly salary in złoties – averaged

	1970	1972	1973	1974	1975*	1976	1977	1978
Doctors	3,466	3,700	4,954	5,569	(6088) 6443	6,595	6,888	7,191
Dentists	2,787	3,075	3,872	4,296	(4561) 4737	4,759	4,993	5,173
Medium-grade medical staff	1,629	1,815	2,314	2,633	(2749) 2904	2,911	3,043	3,212
Lower-grade medical staff	1,095	1,236	1,618	1,868	(1902) 2009	2,313	2,425	2,622
Technicians and administrators	1,967	2,136	2,627	3,009	(3307) 3479	3,623	3,841	4,010
Manual and service staff	1,409	1,590	1,942	2,250	(2386) 2531	2,705	2,891	3,093
All (health service)	1,753	1,953	2,460	2,805	(2971) 3142	3,252	3,418	3,615
National average (all employment)	2,235	2,509	2,798	3,185	3783	4,116	4,415	4,686
Health service as percentage of national average	78.4	77.8	88.0	88.0	(78.5) 83.0	79.0	77.4	77.1

*For 1975 the data in the two Roczniki (1976 and 1979) differ whereas for 1970 this does not happen. I include both figures, those given in brackets are from the earlier Rocznik. See *Rocznik Statystyczny Ochrony Zdrowia 1976*, p. 173, Table 5, and *Rocznik Statystyczny Ochrony Zdrowia 1979*, p. 160, Table 7.

Table 9.4 Proportion of Health Service Employees at Various Salary Levels: Comparison with Other Employees of the Nationalized Economy at the End of 1978

Percentage of employees earning given salaries (in złoties per month)

	Up to 2000	2001– 4000	4001– 6000	6001– 8000	8001 plus	Total
Employees in nationalized economy						
All	3.1	38.7	35.7	14.3	8.2	100.0
Health service and social welfare	8.9	66.4	17.1	5.3	2.3	100.0
Non Manual						
All	1.5	38.1	36.7	15.1	8.6	100.0
Science and technology	0.3	19.7	41.9	21.9	16.2	100.0
Education	0.6	33.8	43.7	9.6	2.3	100.0
Health and welfare	3.5	62.3	22.5	8.0	3.7	100.0

Source: Służba Zdrowia, 16 January 1981, p. 4.

the Sixth Party Congress, the government adopted, in February 1973, a development programme incorporating a scheme of health policy to be implemented by 1980. This cut into the five-year plan already in operation (1971–75), and the development was to be facilitated by a major injection of funds.

The notion of such a development programme was a novel one, and the experts who formulated it were clearly aware of the many problems facing the health service. The programme paid heed in the first instance to the areas stressed by the Sixth Congress resolution 'The Further Socialist Development of the Polish People's Republic'. Tasks included the material improvement of hospitals at all levels, improvement of psychiatric therapy, of public welfare institutions and of rural health centres; also the improvement of the functioning of the health service, with regard to smoother performance and greater attention to the quality of care. Special attention was to be paid to the needs of mothers and children, of industrial workers, agricultural workers, and the continuing problems of social diseases. Well-intentioned aims indeed, although the priority groups mentioned are almost the same as are found in the immediate post-war documentation on health care, with the notable exception, of course, of the agricultural workers. And once again, although verbal emphasis is on the need to develop outpatient care especially primary care, the quantitative emphasis is on hospital beds above all else.

The programme, which was finally approved in January 1973, set out a list of objectives entirely in keeping with the notion of 'developed Socialism'. The health care system was to extend to the entire population the benefits of the scientific-technological revolution, with the aim of approaching 'average European indices of health status, including infant mortality and life expectancy'. There was to be a real effort to reduce the disparity of service between urban and rural localities, and between different regions. Renewed emphasis was to be placed on the prevention and treatment of social diseases — tuberculosis and venereal diseases — and of diseases of civilization — circulatory diseases, cancers, occupational and psychiatric diseases.[15] The unwritten premise for this formula was that increased prosperity and technological invention would enable these aims to be achieved, and that the increase in the numbers of personnel and the material improvement of health facilities were the means to bring this about. Increases in staff levels by 1990 were to be as follows (in rates per 10,000 population): doctors, from 15.6 in 1971 to 20.0 in 1990; dentists, from 4.3 to 5.6; pharmacists, 3.9 to 5.6; nurses and mid-wives, from 36.5 to 59.0; other middle-grade or paramedical personnel, from 12.5 to 24.0. Moreover, emphasis was laid on the need to channel medical students into 'needy' areas, notably primary care (urban and rural), school health, the sanitary/epidemiological service, and psychiatry. Special mention was made of the need to rid doctors of time-wasting administrative and statistical chores — medical secretaries (one per 2–3 doctors) were to be introduced for this purpose. Meanwhile, improving the quality of medical care was to be tackled by a new system of postgraduate training, by 1974 centres for postgraduate training would be operating in all voivodships.

The programme was less original in its strategy for improving the material resources of the health service. Once again the simple formula was adopted: 'more money equals more hospital beds equals better health'. There was no clearcut proposal about improving the efficiency of resource utilization either by better allocation or by more effective back-up. Increased supplies of drugs and basic equipment such as syringes, catheters, dressings and so on are dealt with and particular reference is made to the need for more home production of these items, instead of relying on foreign imports (which are highly susceptible to hard currency problems). But basically the premise throughout the development pro-gramme is that more money will guarantee improvements.

Although it is not yet justifiable to list the failures of the development programme in its entirety — it is less than halfway through its course (1973-90) — a realistic appraisal of the situation to date indicates clearly that the goals of the programme will not be achieved. Specific tasks for the 1970s were not completed: rural health centres were short of their targets by 1975 when the entire network was supposed to be completed; the increase in hospital beds was also far less than anticipated — an article in *Trybuna Ludu* in March 1978 complained that the 1975-80 plan stood no chance of being fulfilled; of the planned 27,000 new beds, only 5,267 were added in the first two years of the plan, and given the deterioration of the economic situation, the second half of the plan was doomed to failure — twenty investment projects, involving over 8,000 beds were already threatened.[16] As to the easing of the bureaucratic burden on doctors, the 'medical secretaries' have never materialized. No radical re-distribution of personnel or resources has occurred which would level out the urban-rural and regional disparities. Further, the organizational changes which aimed at improving the integration and co-ordination of the health service (about which more later) have failed; this aspect of the programme has already been condemned and yet another reorganiz-ation is in the pipeline.

National Health Care Fund

In January 1973 Gierek announced a new idea for harnessing extra revenue for the health service: the National Health Care Fund (*Narodowy Fundusz Ochrony Zdrowia* — NFOZ). It was intended that the Fund should allow increased expenditure of 18-20 milliard złoty in the period up to 1980. The money was to be collected from various sources, the main one being via a system of regular 'voluntary pledges' (*świadczenie*) on the part of

Table 9.5 Income for First Year of NFOZ

Gifts pledged by state-employed workers	982.9 million zł
Gifts pledged by private farmers	209.1 million zł
Gifts pledged by co-operative workers	76.7 million zł
Gifts pledged by artisans (private)	22.0 million zł
Sales of postcards, calendars, etc.	30.1 million zł
Supplement on alcoholic drinks	909.6 million zł

Source: J. Kamiński, 'Narodowy Fundusz Ochrony Zdrowia: dotychczasowe wyniki i perspektywy', *Zdr. Publ.*, 85 (1974), 507-11.

industrial enterprises. The second main source of income was a supplement levied on alcoholic drinks – presumably this is voluntary also! A breakdown of income for the first year of the Fund (1973/74) is given in Table 9.5.

The Fund was launched with a target of at least 18 milliard złoty by 1980. According to figures quoted by Kania in his speech to the Third Plenum in June 1980, this target had been exceeded; the total being 23 milliard złoty. But despite its success as a money-spinner, and its value as a piece of propaganda – 'we care about our health' – the uses and abuses of the National Fund have come in for severe criticism. The KOR report[17] complains that the money collected is only partly spent, while the remainder 'sits in the bank succumbing to enormous inflation'; the reason being that the construction materials and medical equipment are simply not available to be bought (see Table 9.6).

Table 9.6 NFOZ Incomes and Expenditure 1973–77

Year	NFOZ income (million zł)	NFOZ expenditure (million zł)	Percentage not spent
1973	2,334	1,285	43
1974	2,672	1,182	56
1975	2,804	970	65.5
1976	2,985	940	68.5
1977	3,244	1,855	43

What has the NFOZ been used for? As usual, high priority seems to have gone to the provision of hospital beds. According to the most recent Statistical Yearbook for the Health Service, the Fund provided the following additions to health facilities over the period 1973/78: 1,170 hospital beds, 110 sanatoria beds, 628 places in homes for social welfare (geriatrics and disabled), 20 nurseries, 138 health centres, 29 specialist polyclinics and 658 places in nurses residences.[18] To put this in perspective, the annual health service budget now runs to well over 65 milliard złoty (64,107,000,000 zł. in 1978), while the NFOZ currently brings in about 4.5 milliard zł. each year. Even this figure pales when one considers the amount of money which was put into building the luxury hospital for the party and government elite at Anin; the cost was estimated to be 1.5 milliard złoty. There are also prevalent rumours to the effect the National Fund was probably used to finance the hospital. If this is so then the relevance of the Fund as a reflection of health policy for the general health service is brought into even more doubt.

Integration: the Introduction of the ZOZ system

One of the main components of the Development Programme to 1990 was the reorganization of the health service which took place in 1973.[19] The old 'closed' and 'open' systems (i.e. separate in-patient and out-patient systems) were replaced by a network of integrated units called ZOZy (Zespół Opieki Zorowotnej – health care complex or area health authority). Each province, or voivodship, was divided into a number of ZOZy, each of which comprised a general hospital, a number of specialist out-patient facilities and a number of local primary care centres. The medical director of the ZOZ was often the director of the hospital, but the hospital was not to be treated as a discrete unit anymore, but as part of the whole ZOZ, providing all levels of service for all patients. An official propaganda publication in 1974 outlined the intended benefits of the ZOZy:

> The most important objective of these changes is to strengthen primary health care and to use material and human resources better, which should result in wider availability and range of health services and improvement of their quality . . . The primary physician is the basic link in the new system. This fact ensures continuity of care for each patient, full and permanent information about his health and environmental and working conditions and make available preventive, therapeutic and rehabilitative services in the working places of the patient.[20]

The reality, however, has not lived up to these aims, and the most telling proof of this is the fact that the ZOZ system has been severely criticized and yet another reorganization is in the pipeline. The fact is that integration is not possible when primary care is split between industrial health centres, local health centres and co-operative health centres – some patients use all three. It appears, moreover, that integration is *less* today than ten years ago, because a number of enterprises are even financing their own hospitals. In any case, there are separate health services under the auspices of the Ministry of Communications, the Ministry of the Interior and the Ministry of Defence, so that integration at this level is not feasible. Emphasis on primary care which the ZOZ system was intended to provide is also largely an illusion; the fact that the ZOZ director is also likely to be the hospital director militates against this, and in any case, hospitals always take precedence. 'The government pays lip service to primary care', one informant told me, 'but hospitals have so many pressing problems that primary care is always left to one side.' This has been repeated by many doctors, and has been a common cause for complaint in letters and articles in the medical press.

One of the experts involved in the initial trial of the ZOZ programme has said that 'the ZOZ system would be a good system for the angels'.[21] The human factor has been ignored in practice, and in particular this applies to the need for senior doctors to be good and sensitive managers. The reform was rushed through, according to this informant, so that the trial was conducted for only three months before giving the go-ahead — he had recommended a trial period of three years. He strongly maintains that the ZOZ is too large a unit to be comprehensively managed; a population group of 40–50,000 would be manageable, but the ZOZ population may be much larger than that (over 250,000 in one extreme case, although the figures do vary widely). In terms of managing staff this is crucial as a ZOZ director cannot possibly have close enough contact with even the more senior personnel.[22]

Evaluation of some ZOZ programmes were made in the early years of the decade, and although it was still too early to judge whether the health service was more efficient as a result, these studies throw considerable light on the enormous problems of organization; the very fact of reorganization prevented an increase in efficiency in almost all the cases examined.[23] Now, after several more years have elapsed, the ZOZ idea has been subjected to much criticism, and yet another reorganization is under discussion.[24]

4. The Situation at the End of the Decade

The failures of the major reforms to tackle the problems facing the health service have been detailed in the preceding paragraphs.[25] The situation was exacerbated by the general economic deterioration which began in 1975/76. The health service had less money to cope with increased health demands — rates of occupational diseases, hospital-bred infection, alcoholism and venereal disease were all soaring. This had grave consequences for the quality of care. A comment on the situation is to be found in a twenty-two page document produced in 1979 by KOR.[26] This is a report on the state of the hospital system in Poland and was compiled by a group of medical specialists — hence its bias towards the hospital side of the service, and towards the medical profession as opposed to the other health personnel. The main contribution of the report lies in the detailing of the day-to-day horrors of the health service, and also the gross injustices of elite privilege — at least the report condemns the degree of privilege, if not privilege *per se*. The cost of one bed in a hospital for the elite (the party-government hospital at Anin) is 13 million złoty, while that for an ordinary citizen is only 1.2 million złoty. The health service is too low a priority, says the report, and if the top administrators and party policy makers have only been treated in the de luxe clinics barred to the ordinary citizen, it is not to be wondered at that they are blind to complaints about the service as a whole. In ordinary hospitals the shortage of beds is so serious that patients (or their families) frequently bribe the ward-chief (*ordynator*) to admit them to hospital; and in many cases patients are actually turned away. The 'official' bed includes six square metres of space per patient, but in reality only three or four square metres are allocated – so that there are three beds where there should be two. The corridors of provincial hospitals are so crowded with beds that it is difficult to move trolleys through.[27] Turnover of beds is difficult to increase because of bottlenecks in the diagnostic services, personnel shortages, poor organization and the increasing number of geriatric cases. There is a Polish joke that hospitals are increasingly full of geriatric cases because the patients have to wait so long for admission, and when they are admitted they have to wait so long for their illness to be diagnosed . . .

Hospitals, too, are old and repairs take months or years to complete. Equipment is old and often useless; it is said that only 6 per cent of beds in hospitals are in good condition. The problems of old buildings and equipment are exacerbated by the extremely low standards of hygiene. Given the very low status and pay for orderlies (*salowa*) this is not altogether surprising; these women are chosen by 'negative selection'; the job is of the very lowest order and motivation virtually nil.

Poor hygiene in turn compounds the problems of infection in hospitals: lack of sterilizing equipment, and particularly, lack of disposable hypodermic needles, leads to an alarming incidence of viral hepatitis according to the KOR report, and an article in *Zdrowie Publiczne* has cited an increasing incidence of hepatitis among hospital staff.[28] This starts the vicious circle of low staffing leading to a slackening of sterilization procedures leading to an increased risk of hepatitis . . . With an overall shortage of nurses – only 70 per cent of posts are filled – this situation is critical.

The supply of drugs is another area of great concern; foreign imports have been stopped on two occasions because of hard currency problems, on one of these occasions, in 1978, there were 'many' deaths attributable to the withdrawal of, among other drugs, insulin.[29] Meanwhile, home-produced drugs are of dubious quality and uncertain production. Drugs overall are in such short supply that hospital patients are on a daily 'drug ration' which forces doctors to keep on a number of patients who do not require drugs in order to increase the quota available for another patient.

These are some of the problems which daily aggravate the situation within the health service; none of them, it seems, have been significantly alleviated by measures taken during the 1970s. All of them are frequently

Table 9.7 Age-Specific Mortality Rates – 1960 to 1979

(per 100,000 population)

Age	1960	1965	1970	1975	1979*
All ages	755	738	813	873	
0-1**	54.8	41.4	33.4	25.1	
1-4	169	127	105	92	8(0)
5-9	55	46	46	43	4(0)
10-14	47	37	38	35	4(0)
15-19	85	67	72	72	7(0)
20-24	129	114	108	114	11(0)
25-29	154	132	124	124	15(0)
30-34	186	166	152	162	
35-39	233	222	217	226	31(0)
40-44	323	298	318	332	
45-49	489	445	473	429	69(0)
50-54	750	689	702	752	
55-59	1,182	1,004	1,132	1,112	1,22(0)
60-64	1,896	1,794	1,856	1,779	1,78(0)
65-69	3,017	3,010	2,978	2,857	2,80(0)
70-74	4,927	4,840	5,060	4,671	
75-79	7,625	7,702	8,051	7,768	7,61(0)
80-84	13,258	12,311	11,628	12,770	
85+	15,182	21,006	18,277	19,397	

* Figures available only to the nearest ten
** Infant mortality figures per 1,000 live births.
Source: Rocznik Demograficzny 1978, p. 94, Table 46.
Rocznik Statystyczny 1980, p. 47, Table 27.

referred to in both official and unofficial sources. But the issue to which official sources do not dare to refer to in public statements is the most important of all: age-specific mortality rates appear, for most age groups, to be rising, as Table 9.7 indicates, although this rise is partly in official tables by giving imprecise figures.[30] The fact that age-specific mortality rates are *not* included in the health service statistical yearbooks speaks volumes. The fact that they are unstable is indicative of the failure of the health service to cope with the demands placed on it.

5. Why the Policies Failed

There are three main reasons for the failure of the health policies of the 1970s. In the first place there are obstacles within the health service, which is based on various incompatible principles and directed towards conflicting goals. For example, although lip service is paid to the importance of primary care, the emphasis continues to be on specialist, hospital-based medicine. Even the critical KOR report in 1979 was concerned only with the hospital service, ignoring the whole issue of the place of hospital care within the health system as a whole. The answer of the experts seems to be that they cannot turn to the problems of primary care while there are so many problems in the hospital service. This attitude perpetuates the difficulties, for while primary care remains under-developed, the hospital service will be more and more overburdened with cases which could easily be dealt with by a more efficient primary care system. One example of this is the way in which patients refer themselves to specialists, rather than queue in crowded primary-care clinics; another is the fact that hospital doctors do not trust their primary-care colleagues' diagnoses — so diagnostic tests are repeated in hospital, thus increasing the time spent in hospital. The overall effect of this imbalance is that money allocated to the health service is swallowed up by an ever-increasing demand for specialist, hospital-based medicine; leaving little money to be spent on the primary-care part of the service, in which there is in any case too little interest.

Linked to the over-emphasis on specialist, hospital medicine is the problem of the over-emphasis on clinical curative medicine; prevention ('prophylaxis') is supposed to be one of the chief defining characteristics of Eastern European health systems, but in practice this counts for nothing.[31] Clearly doctors find clinical medicine more stimulating than routine preventive work; this problem is not peculiar to Poland, of course, but whereas government policy should attempt to rectify the situation, nothing is done in practice. On the contrary, government policy seems to be based on the unquestioning acceptance of the superior claims of preventive work, whilst medical practice merely continues to side-step it.

If 'primary care' and 'prevention' are under-emphasized in practice, the same is true for the other main catch-words of the policy-makers – 'integration' and 'co-ordination'. In this respect, the health service suffers from contradictory aims. On the one hand, the service is supposed to be moving to an integrated and co-ordinated whole, while on the other hand certain population groups are singled out to ensure that they, above all, receive adequate health care. The implication of this is in practice that these groups receive their health care in different sets of health facilities (industrial health care, party and government clinics, mother and child facilities and so on). This hardly makes for integration, particularly since patients do not necessarily attend the same sort of health facility each time. It is said that integration – which the ZOZy were intended to promote above all – has become, in fact, less attainable recently, because of the increasing number of industrial enterprises building their own health centres and even small in-patient clinics. In any case, the fact cannot be overlooked that there are already separate services for the army, the party/government elite and the transport network, each organized by its respective ministry; some small attempts have been made recently at ground level to share resources,[32] but nobody raises the issue of whether or not these separate health services should be left to exist as such at all, although their existence erodes the concept of integration and universal standards.

The second reason for the failure of reforms in the 1970s lies in the Socialist system of decision making. According to a Polish expert on health service organization, policy making is dogged by 'two conflicting tendencies of Socialism': on the one hand there is a tendency towards centralism, whereby all decisions progress upwards to the highest level of the decisional hierarchy, and on the other hand there is the tendency for pressure groups (especially the medical profession) to exert an influence on the process.[33] The continual bargaining between these two tendencies leads to what one might describe as 'Socialist inertia'. Other factors seem to be of equal importance, however, not the least being the emphasis on 'indices' rather than realities of any sort. The seemingly insatiable capacity to discuss the health service in terms of hospital beds is a good example of this; even the critical KOR report spends a lot of time debating the accuracy and adequacy of these bed ratios etc., without questioning the value of 'beds' as such. Improved indices of health facilities do not necessarily imply an improved health service. This is rather like assuming that educational systems can best be evaluated by counting the number of school desks. Health policy has little hope of tackling the 'real' problems – such as how to attract middle and lower grade staff, how to shift the emphasis onto preventive medicine and primary care, or how to ensure that competing 'priorities' receive a fair share – while plans and budgets are based solely on quantitative indices. Even if health policy were to be made on a more realistic basis, this would not solve the problem of the position of the health service *vis à vis* the rest of the economy; health policy is obviously limited by practical constraints and will never be given genuine high priority compared to the 'needs' of the productive economy. In this sense there has never really been a departure from the attitude that increased production would produce benefits in all spheres, health being but one.

Health care, then, is still seen as a spin-off, and the same is true of health policy. Health matters are considered as important when the party decides they are important, so health policies formulated by the experts who advise the Ministry are of little value until they coincide with the objectives of the party. One example of this is the report on the health of the private peasant-farmers submitted to the Central Committee in 1969 and 1970 was rebutted on both occasions – and dubbed the 'tears for the farmers' report; on the third occasion, in 1971, the same report was acclaimed, and became the basis of the legislation extending the health service. Another example can be found in a recent policy priority – alcoholism. The reason for the government's concern here is chiefly economic – in that the proportion of the national economy that is spent on alcoholic drink is more alarming to them than the increase in alcoholism with its attendant health risks.

The third reason why the health policies of the 1970s failed to remove the old problems is concerned with factors inherent in the Polish – or indeed any Socialist – economic system. The economy hinders the improvement of the health service in two ways. In the first place, since Gierek's economic reforms began to backfire in 1975, the economy slowed down and there was consequently less to share out among the various sectors, including health. In the second place there are always 'supply bottle-necks' in the system with regard to home-produced goods and foreign imports alike. Supplies of even life-saving drugs and equipment are subject to the vagaries of a resource allocation system which is inefficient, unequal and corrupt. Consequently, however much money is given to the health service, there is no guarantee that it will be converted into useful additional resources. In the immediate future, however, there is no need to dwell on the problems of spending extra money: since the crisis began in August 1980 there has been a continual diverting of funds to the productive sector of the economy. Material incentives are needed to stimulate production, the old argument goes, and so the health service is relatively worse off once again.

6. Conclusion – Prospects for the 1980s

Criticism of the health service, as was stated at the beginning of this chapter, is not new in Poland. In 1971, when new policies were being formulated, it seemed that the problems were being taken seriously. However, the solutions were aimed at the symptoms rather than the causes of the health service's problems. The reforms were badly and hurriedly implemented, and in retrospect it seems that optimism was based on Gierek's misguided maxim 'more wealth – better health'. Inadequacies of the economic and administrative systems subverted the reforms. Moreover, the ambitious capital expenditure plans were frustrated halfway through the decade by the failure of the expected funds to materialize and this contributed to a crisis in current expenditure on drugs, equipment and human resources. This in turn exposed the inefficient utilization of what few resources there were.

A decade of upheaval, reform and unfulfilled plans left the health service in the tragic position already outlined. Thus it was natural that the Gdańsk Agreement included demands for improvement in the health service. The sixteenth condition of the agreement reads as follows: 'To improve the working conditions in the health service and to ensure proper medical care for working people', to which was added an appendix listing specific health demands. Inevitably, the demands being made by NSZZ (Solidarity) are coloured by, and directed towards solving, the day-to-day problems of coping with an inefficient and corrupt health service. For obvious reasons, the major concern is with the working conditions of health personnel and the health conditions of workers. The real problems of elitism, resource allocation and manpower distribution are unlikely to be solved on this basis. Meanwhile these issues are being addressed by many health experts whose reports, commentaries and letters fill the pages of the press including the weekly health service newspaper *Służba Zdrowia*. A series of articles entitled 'The crisis – and then what?' focuses on the need to emphasize primary care 'the lynchpin of the health service';[34] lengthy debates examine the problems raised by the existence of private practice, the reorganization of the ZOZ system, and so on. Yet how much notice is taken of these critical reports and articles? In April 1981 an entire issue of *Życie i Nowoczesność*, the weekly supplement to *Życie Warszawy*, was devoted to a report compiled by a group of medical experts on 'The state of health and health care of the Polish population'.[35] It indicated clearly the tasks for the 1980s: reduction of mortality, particularly infant mortality; reduction of viral hepatitis, tuberculosis and hospital-bred infection; evaluation of the industrial health service; tackling the problems of alcoholism, amongst others. Two months later, when the Sejm was in the process of formulating two major policy documents, one of the authors of the report wrote a long article to the effect that no notice had been taken of it by the Ministry of Health.[36]

Health needs are going to be more pressing in the 1980s than they have been to date − a decline in living standards, quality of foodstuffs, availability of energy, and housing standards all have notorious consequences for health. This situation is exacerbated by the fact that the health service is the one area of social provision that relies heavily on technological resources, which were much encouraged in the 1970s. Cutting down on these resources and their maintenance can have disastrous consequences. Indeed this is already the case, for example it is reported that in some provincial hospitals premature babies are currently sharing incubators, two or three at a time.[37]

There is no hope of the situation improving in the foreseeable future in view of the severe economic crisis. The government has reverted to its traditional response 'we understand the problems, but we cannot afford to solve them'. This seems to be the beginning of a vicious downward spiral. Increasing demand will strain scarce resources even further and what little finance is available after coping with the most pressing day-to-day needs will be expended on short-term cosmetic remedies. With this in mind one might well ask for how long can Poland afford *not* to solve the real problems of its health service?

Notes and References

1 For a summary of the Gdańsk Agreement, see 'Protokół porozumienia . . .' *Polityka*, 6 September 1980, pp. 1, 3.
2 Kania's speech to the Third Plenum CC PUWP is reported in *Służba Zdrowia*, 4 July 1980, p. 2.
3 These debates are documented in the Polish Socialist Party Journal *Kuźnice* from 1944 to 1948.
4 This change in the policy-making process is discussed by the leading Polish sociologist Jerzy Wiatr, in: J. Wiatr and R. Rose, *Comparing Public Policies*, Warsaw, PAN, 1977.
5 See Chapter 7 for details of educational reforms being formulated at this time.
6 M. Sokołowska, 'Social Science and Health Policy in Eastern Europe: Poland as a Case Study', *International Journal of Health Services*, (1974), 441–50.
7 The reemergence of 'health policy' after 1971, and the need to identify the theoretical problems surrounding it are dealt with in J. Kaja, 'O potrzebie badań nad polityką zdrowotną polski ludowej', *Zdrowie Publiczne* 85 (1974), 779–86.
8 Space does not permit a detailed description of the health service and the background to the situation in 1970/71. Readers are referred to the following texts: A. Pacho, *Organizacja służby zdrowia w PRL*, Warsaw, PZWL, 1968 (3rd edn); E. R. Weinerman, *Social Medicine in Eastern Europe*, Cambridge, Mass., Harvard U.P., 1969; M. Kaser, *Health Care in the Soviet Union and Eastern Europe*,

London, Croom Helm, 1976, (Chapter 7: Poland); M. Roemer and R. Roemer, *Health Manpower in the Socialist Health Care System of Poland*, Washington, D.C., U.S. Department of Health, Education and Welfare, 1977.

9 'List otwarty do Ministra Zdrowia, profesora Jana Kostrzewskiego', *Polityka*, 18 December 1971.

10 'Whims' is in part an allusion to the bribery which frequently 'oils the wheels' at all levels of the health service; in the current wave of criticism it is discussed more openly, but in 1971 comments were still veiled.

11 One of the chief advocates for reform was Henryk Rafalski, now chairman of the Parliamentary Health Commission; many articles by him on the subject of rural reform in the health service are to be found in the Polish Peasant Party Journal, *Wieś współczesna*.

12 This 'norm' corresponds to the first stage of a three-part plan indicated by the Minister of Health in 1973; see M. Sliwiński, in *La Santé Publique*, 16 (1973), 403-6.

13 S. Marcinowski, 'The Main Areas of Activity of the Ministry of Health and Public Welfare in 1972 and Actions Planned for 1973', *La Santé Publique*, 17 (1974), 415-27.

14 J. Biernacik, 'O płacach bez emocji', *Służba Zdrowia*, 16 January 1981, pp. 1, 4.

15 J. Kamiński, 'The Programme of Development of Health Protection and Public Welfare in the Polish People's Republic', *La Sante Publique*, 17 (1974), 317-29.

16 'Nowe obiekty w służbie zdrowia', *Trybuna Ludu*, 10 March 1978.

17 Komitet Samoobrony Społecznej (KOR), *Stan szpitalnictwa*, Warsaw, May 1979, 22 pp. See also n. 26.

18 *Rocznik Statystyczny Ochrony Zdrowia 1979*, p. 166, Table 8.

19 The reorganization of the Health Service in 1973 coincided with, and was closely associated with the first stage of territorial/administrative reorganization. This, together with the subsequent change (in 1975) from a three-tier to two-tier system of administration (which also had important consequences for the health system) are discussed by Paul Lewis in Chapter 5.

20 *Health Service in Poland* (official booklet), Warsaw, P.A.N., 1974, pp. 50-1.

21 Private communication, March 1980.

22 For example, the ZOZ director in Łódź is responsible for over 4,000 health service staff (of whom between one and one-and-a-half thousand are medically qualified) his task is to co-ordinate medical services in 800 separate health facilities, serving 350,000 people. He is hard-pressed to meet each of the ward-chiefs (*ordynator*) of 'his' hospital (i.e. of which he is director) more than about twice per year, and almost certainly never meets any of the senior nursing staff. This ZOZ is unusually large, but the problem is not thought to be easier in 'small' ZOZy.

23 See for example M. Pruss, 'Torunska droga do integracji', *Zdrowie Publiczne*, 85 (1974), 453-63. Also J. Muniak, 'Ocena dostępnościa świadczeń działu opieki specjalistycznej ZOZ w Zakopanem', *Zdrowie Publiczne*, 76 (1975), 999-1004.

24 See G. Stasiak, 'Czas reformy', *Służba Zdrowia*, 23 January 1981, pp. 1, 4, 5; and 6 February 1981, pp. 1, 4, 5. Also, 'Dyskusja o ZOZach', *Służba Zdrowia*, 13 March 1981, pp. 1, 4.

25 Major reforms of the 1970s are dealt with in this chapter, but it should be added that a number of smaller-scale measures were taken throughout the decade in an attempt to make the health service function more efficiently; they were not instrumental in removing the problems of the health system, but many of them were of benefit in particular areas – for example, the introduction of new courses in administration/organization for doctors, piecemeal measures with regard to salary levels, etc. This chapter deals only with the reforms which directly resulted from Gierek's new strategy.

26 Komitet Samoobrony Społecznej (KOR), *Stan szpitalnictwa*. One might at first be tempted to think that the view presented in this rather 'picturesque' report is over-exaggerated, but in fact much of the material is taken from articles in establishment periodicals such as *Polityka* and *Zdrowie Publiczne*, while the figures are taken largely from the official statistical yearbooks.

27 An equally grim picture of hospital life (bribery, filth, overcrowding . . .) was given in Zanussi's film *Konstans* (The Constant Factor), 1980, Polish Films.

28 M. Kubasiewicz, 'Choroby zawodowe u pracowników służby zdrowia w 1977 roku', *Zdrowie Publiczne*, 90 (1979), 345–53.

29 How many deaths? I have heard different estimates from different people. It was as a result of pressure from the KOR, who threatened to ask the West to air-lift supplies of drugs, that the government backed down. This incident was the subject of a special report by the KOR in 1978.

30 Further investigation of the trends in mortality figures will be necessary before firm conclusions can be reached. Similar investigations have been carried out with regard to the Soviet Union, with interesting results; see, for example: C. Davis and M. Feshbach, *Rising Infant Mortality in the USSR in the 1970s*, Washington, D.C. U.S. Department of Commerce, Series P. 95, No. 74, 1980.

31 As in all East European countries, the Health Service is defined as preventive in orientation, but this merely means that the definition of preventive care is distorted to include aspects of care which would otherwise be regarded as purely curative. For example, a standard textbook on health service organization provides a diagram of 'three stages of prophylaxis', in which the third stage covers treatment of the illness in its more advanced stages – 'preventing' further deterioration. J. Indulski, *et al. Organizacja ochrony zdrowia*, Warsaw, PZWL, 1978, p. 39.

32 The idea of shared resources is very limited, however, and only applies to co-operation between the main health service and the Ministry of Communication's health service (serving transport workers); the 'elite' health service is left untouched by this.

33 Personal communication, March 1980.

34 J. Indulski, 'Kryzys . . . i co dalej?, *Służba Zdrowia*, 19 June 1981, pp. 1, 4; 3 July 1981, p. 3.; 10 July 1981, p. 3.

35 Raport Konwersatorium, 'Doświadczenie i Przszłość', 'Stan zdrowia i ochrony zdrowia ludności Polski', *Życie i Nowoczesność*, No. 559, 2 April 1981, 4pp.

36 S. Klonowicz, 'Wykorzystamy ten czas', *Służba Zdrowia*, 5 June 1981, pp. 1, 4.

37 Personal communication, July 1981.

Index